PLATO'S S

A PRIMER

And what, Socrates, is the food of the soul?
Surely, I said, knowledge is the food of the soul.

Plato, *Protagoras*

PLATO'S SHADOW
A PRIMER ON PLATO

Neel Burton
BSc, MBBS, MRCPsych, MA (Phil), AKC

Illustrated by Tom Stockmann

A

Acheron Press
Flectere si nequeo superos
Acheronta movebo

Reprinted in 2010 with minor changes and the addition of figure 4 and the four indexes.

Published by Acheron Press
2 Morrell Avenue
Oxford OX4 1NE
United Kingdom

A CIP catalogue record for this book is available from the British Library.

ISBN 978 0 9560353 2 5

Typeset by Phoenix Photosetting, Chatham, Kent, United Kingdom
Printed and bound in the United Kingdom

Contents

SECTION I – INTRODUCTION

SECTION II – PLATO'S DIALOGUES

A note on translations
All quotations from Plato are from the Jowett translation,
except where otherwise stated.

SECTION I –
INTRODUCTION

I. History of Athens up to the time of Plato

Athens, the eye of Greece, mother of arts
And eloquence

John Milton, *Paradise Regained*

The Minoans
At the beginning of the 20th century, digs led by the British archaeologist Sir Arthur Evans (1851-1941) on the island of Crete uncovered the existence of a complex civilisation whose people he named the *Minoans* after the legendary King Minos. The Minoans flourished from 2700 to about 1450BC, and their civilisation came to revolve around a series of palace complexes, the largest of which was at Knossos in the north of the island. The Minoan economy was based on trade, which enabled the Minoans to gain a hold on some of their neighbours, including perhaps the city of Athens. According to legend, King Minos used to exact an annual tribute of seven boys and seven girls from Athens. These children were fed to the half-man, half-bull Minotaur, who was the illegitimate son of Minos' wife Pasaphae, and who lived in the labyrinth beneath Minos' palace. In the third year of the tribute, the Athenian hero Theseus volunteered to go as one of the seven boys and put an end to this barbaric practice. Theseus killed the Minotaur

with the help of Minos' daughter Ariadne, who had given him a ball of red fleece thread with which to trace his way out of the labyrinth. Theseus escaped with Ariadne but then abandoned her on the island of Naxos, where she was discovered and wedded by the god Dionysos. The Minoan civilisation came to an abrupt end around 1400BC, possibly as a result of an important volcanic eruption on the island of Thera (modern-day Santorini), or an invasion by the Mycenaeans. The Thera eruption may have given rise to the myth of Atlantis, which features in Plato's *Timaeus* and *Critias*.

The Mycenaeans

The Mycenaeans flourished from about 1600 to 1100BC in mainland Greece, and had important centres in Mycenae, Pylos, Thebes, and Athens, amongst others. Rather than advancing by trade like the Minoans had, the Mycenaeans advanced by conquest, and their society was dominated by a warrior aristocracy. Their greatest achievement was the conquest of the wealthy city of Troy in around 1250BC. The legends surrounding this conquest are the subject of Homer's Iliad, to which Plato more than occasionally makes reference. Towards the close of the Bronze Age, in about 1100BC, the Mycenaeans came under attack from a northern people called the Dorians. According to legend, the Dorians descended from the exiled Heracleidae, who were the descendents of the Greek hero Heracles (Hercules). Zeus had originally intended Heracles to be ruler of Mycenae, Lacedaemon (Sparta), and Argos, and so the Dorian Invasion represented the return of the Heraclids to reclaim their ancestral right to rule.

The Dark Ages

Following the destruction of the Mycenaean civilisation, it took some three hundred years for the Greek and Eastern Mediterranean world to recover. During these Dark Ages, old trade links dissolved, the arts and crafts regressed, and famine set in. Many Greeks left mainland Greece and dispersed across the Mediterranean, from Italy and Sicily to Asia Minor (modern-day Turkey) and further beyond. The Greeks in the east came into close contact with the Phoenicians, and in around 750BC they first began to use the Phoenician system of language notation. This alphabetic system replaced the syllabic Linear B system, which was itself an adaptation of the Minoan Linear A system.

Rise of the City-State

By the eighth century BC, the communities remaining on mainland Greece were small and simple, and gradually became organised around a much larger centre under the rule of a small aristocratic elite. In Athens those born into certain leading aristocratic families could be elected by their aristocratic peers to join the ruling council of *archons*. These families called themselves the *Eupatridai* or 'sons of good fathers'. By the seventh century BC, a prominent middle class had come into being, and their exclusion from the ruling council of archons gave rise to social unrest. During the Festival of Zeus in 640BC, a former winner of the Olympic games called Cylon tried to seize power and set himself up as sole ruler or 'tyrant'. When his plan failed, he fled to the temple of Athena from which he was coaxed out and duly stoned to death. To deal with the increasing social unrest, the aristocrat Draco published a code of law which made it clear that the state would be responsible for administering justice, and thus that the aristocrats could no longer act as they saw fit. The code of law was 'written not in ink, but in blood,' with the death penalty meted out for even minor offenses. Despite this, Draco was popular with the people. The Suda tells of his death in the Aeginetan theatre. In a traditional ancient Greek show of approval, the people 'threw so many hats and shirts and cloaks on his head that he suffocated, and was buried in that selfsame theatre'.

In 594BC, Solon was appointed as archon, and gained such a reputation for wisdom that he was given *carte blanche* to reform the city. He broadened political participation by extending the right to be elected as archon to anyone who possessed agricultural wealth, and established a council of 400 citizens called the *boule* which was to be elected annually from a larger popular assembly called the *ecclesia*. The aristocracy resented Solon's reforms to such an extent that, in 589BC, no archons were elected for a period of two years – a period referred to as The Anarchy. Nevertheless, Solon had laid the foundations for Athenian democracy, and is listed in Plato's *Protagoras* as one of the 'seven sages of Greece' alongside Thales of Miletus, Pittacus of Mytilene, Bias of Priene, Cleobulus of Lindus, Myson of Chen, and Chilon of Sparta. In the *Protagoras*, Plato says that the seven sages 'met together and dedicated in the temple of Apollo at Delphi, as the first-fruits of their wisdom, the far-famed inscriptions, which are in all men's mouths – 'Know thyself,' and 'Nothing too much.'" Stobaeus in the *Florilegium* relates a story about a *symposium* (drinking party) at which Solon's nephew was singing one of Sappho's poems. When Solon wanted to be taught the poem, one of the guests asked him why he should waste his time on it. Solon replied, 'So that I may learn it and die'.

The tyranny of Peisistratos
In 561BC, a popular Athenian general called Peisistratos staged an attempt on his own life, and the resulting public outcry gave him the momentum to seize power. He ruled as tyrant for five years before being exiled by an aristocratic faction led by Megacles. Five years later Megacles recalled Peisistratos, who rode back into the city in a golden chariot. Peisistratos married Megacles' daughter, but then refused to recognise her as his wife so as not to weaken the position of his two sons, Hippias and Hipparkhos. As a result, Megacles betrayed Peisistratos to his enemies and Peisistratos was once again exiled.

Ten years later, Peisistratos returned at the head of a foreign army and reinstated himself as tyrant. For the next 13 years, he was the ideal of a classical tyrant, cutting taxes and promoting the arts. When he died his son Hippias took control, but Hippias did not have his father's charisma or ability, and came to be resented by the people. In 514BC, two aristocratic lovers, Harmodius and Aristogeiton, tried to end Hippias' rule by assassinating his brother Hipparkhos. The plot succeeded, but Harmodius was killed and Aristogeiton was captured and died under torture. Even though they were aristocrats, Harmodius and Aristogeiton became martyrs for democracy, and innumerable statues were erected to their memory. After the assassination of Hipparkhos, Hippias became increasingly ruthless. The several aristocrats that he exiled appealed to Sparta for help, and in 510BC king Kleomenes of Sparta entered the city, forcing Hippias to flee and restoring democracy.

The reforms of Kleisthenes
Following the restoration of democracy, an aristocrat called Kleisthenes attempted to get elected as archon, but was defeated by a fellow aristocrat called Isagoras. Kleisthenes turned to the disenfranchised peasantry for support, and proposed new laws to allow them to take part in government. Isagoras called on king Kleomenes for help, but Kleisthenes eventually got the upper hand and completed his reforms. Kleisthenes abolished Solon's wealth-based divisions and divided the Athenian population geographically into ten tribes or *phulai*, which were further divided into a number of *demoi* or *demes*, with each deme represented in the ecclesia. Whilst in theory any citizen could now be elected as archon, in practice most archons continued to be drawn from the ranks of the aristocracy.

The First Persian War
In 546BC the Persian emperor Cyrus the Great defeated king Croesus of Lydia, in Asia Minor. The Spartans sent an embassy to Cyrus ordering him to leave Greek settlements alone, to which Cyrus responded, 'Who are the Spartans?'

By 512BC, Cyrus' successor Darius had extended the Persian Empire as far as Thrace and Macedonia. Darius appointed one Aristagoras to rule over the Greek settlement of Miletus, in Asia Minor. With the help of Athens, Aristagoras revolted against the Persians. However, the revolt was put down, and Aristagoras fled to Thrace.

In 490BC, the Persian army landed at Marathon with the intention of invading Athens and mainland Greece. A runner called Pheidippides ran the 240km from Athens to Sparta to summon help, but the Spartans refused to budge. The Persians set camp in the bay of Marathon with a large marsh behind them, and detached a contingent by ship to Athens. The Athenians needed not only to defeat the Persians at Marathon, but also to rush back to Athens to defend their city – an almost impossible task. As the Persian army advanced, the Athenian general Miltiades ordered his vastly outnumbered troops to converge onto the centre of the Persian infantry line, which miraculously began to crumble. Instead of pursuing the fleeing Persians, the Athenians marched back to Athens, arriving just in time to put off an attack on their city. The Athenians had sent Pheidippides ahead of them to announce their victory at Marathon. Pheidippides ran the 40km from Marathon to Athens, breathed Νενικήκαμεν (nenikekamen, 'we have won'), and died on the very spot.

The Second Persian War
The discovery of silver in the mines at Laureion in 483BC brought immense wealth to Athens. The archon Thermistocles persuaded the Athenians to spend this wealth on building a naval fleet of almost 200 ships to defend Athens and Greece against Darius' son, Xerxes. The Persian threat became so palpable that Sparta, Athens, and 29 other Greek city-states consorted to form a joint army under the overall command of Sparta. Even so, when the Persians returned in 480BC, their troops vastly outnumbered those of the Greeks. The Greeks positioned themselves at the natural sulphur springs of

Thermopylae ('hot gates') in a small pass near the mountains and the sea, and sent their fleet to Artemision to prevent the Persian fleet from joining up with the Persian army. The Spartan king Leonidas and a band of 300 Spartan heroes succeeded in holding the pass for three days, fighting to the death of the last man, as according to Spartan customs. The poet Simonides composed the epigram for their epitaph at Thermopylae, 'Go tell the Spartans, passerby / That here, by Spartan law, we lie.'

As a consequence of the Spartan action at Thermopylae, Xerxes diverted his elite troops of immortals on an alternative route which had been indicated to him by a treacherous goatherd. Meanwhile at Artemision the Persian fleet lost many ships to the stormy weather and several others to the Greeks. What remained of the Persian fleet sailed south in an attempt to join up with the Persian army. By the time the Persian army reached Athens, the Athenians had fled to the island of Salamis, where they were joined by the Greek fleet. The Greeks sent a false message to Xerxes saying that the Greek fleet was about to sail north-east to the Isthmus of Corinth, and Xerxes dispatched the Egyptian section of the Persian fleet to block off the phantom move. At dawn the Greek fleet sailed north into the narrow channel between Salamis and the mainland, whilst a small number of Greek ships stayed behind, hiding away in the bay of Ambelaki. The Persian fleet pursued the Greek fleet, but once the Persian ships had sailed up the channel, the Greek ships suddenly turned around to face them. The Persian ships fled back down the channel, but were ambushed by the Greek ships that had stayed behind in the bay of Ambelaki. The Persians lost about 200 ships, as to the Greeks' 40.

Cut off from its navy, the Persian army retreated north for the winter. Xerxes returned to Asia Minor, leaving his general Mardonius in command. In the spring of 479BC the Persian army advanced south again. Pausanias, who was acting as regent for the young son of Leonidas, led the Greek army north near Plataea. The Persian army attacked the Greek army while it was manoeuvring, but the Greek troops regrouped and the Persians suffered a devastating defeat with even Mardonius killed. The Greek fleet pursued the fleeing Persian fleet, which the Persians beached at Mycale. The Greeks stormed the beach and burnt down every last ship.

The Delian League
Athens received much of the credit for the defeat of the Persians. In the winter of 478-77BC, ambassadors from a number of Greek states held an assembly on the sacred island of Delos and ratified the formation of an anti-Persian league of Greek city-states, the so-called 'Delian League'. Athens soon took control over the Delian League, and reduced its supposed allies to the condition of subjects and tributaries. Miltiades' son Cimon won a number of victories against Persian-held territories, adding more and more territory to Athens' empire. The immense wealth entering Athens from its subject states combined with the influence of the statesman Pericles led to a cultural efflorescence the likes of which had never been seen before. This 'golden age' lasted from approximately 448BC to 404BC, and in it moved an unparalleled number of great men: Pericles himself, of course, but also the artists Phidias and Polygnotus, the historians Herodotus and Thucydides, the dramatists Aeschylus, Sophocles, Euripides, and Aristophanes, and the philosophers Socrates, Anaxagoras, Democritus, Empedocles, Hippias, Parmenides, and Protagoras.

> *I have found power in the mysteries of thought,*
> *Exaltation in the changing of the Muses;*
> *I have been versed in the reasonings of men;*
> *But Fate is stronger than anything I have known.*

Euripides, *Alcestis* (438BC)

The First Peloponnesian War
In 464BC Sparta suffered a devastating earthquake after which
its disenfranchised peasantry, the helots, took their chance to
revolt. Sparta appealed to Athens for help, and the pro-Spartan
Cimon persuaded the ecclesia to send him at the head of an
expeditionary force. 'Let not Greece,' he said, 'be lamed, and
thus Athens herself be deprived of her yokefellow.' (Cimon
had such warmth of feeling towards Sparta that he called his
son 'Lacedaemonius'.) When the Athenians arrived in Sparta,
they began sympathising with the helots, and the Spartans felt
obliged to dismiss them. Following this diplomatic accident,
relationships between Athens and Sparta went from bad to
worse, and in 460BC war broke out. The First Peloponnesian
War lasted for 15 years during which Athens and Sparta
attacked each others' allies, but neither succeeded in getting
the upper hand. In 446BC Pericles began negotiations with the
Spartans, and both sides agreed to a peace of 30 years known
as the 'Peace of Pericles' or 'Thirty Years' Truce'. In effect,
Athens and Sparta agreed that Hellas would remain a house
divided, with Athens maintaining supremacy over the seas,
but giving up its ambition to establish a land empire to rival
that of Sparta.

The Second Peloponnesian War
In the event, the peace lasted for only 15 years before the
Second Peloponnesian War broke out, triggered by increasing
conflict between Athens and Sparta's allies. Pericles avoided
engaging the Spartan army but used the Athenian fleet
to damage Sparta's allies. Meanwhile, Sparta carried out a
series of attacks on the Athenian countryside, leading many
Athenian countrymen to seek refuge within the city's newly
rebuilt walls. These were connected by long walls to the walls
of the port of Piraeus, from which Athens was able to maintain vital access to the sea. In 430BC, overcrowding within
the city walls led to an outbreak of plague which killed some
30,000 people, including even Pericles and his sons. As Athens

weakened, some of its allies revolted. When in 428BC the town of Mytilene on the island of Lesbos revolted, the ecclesia, under the influence of the radical demagogue Cleon, voted to have all the men executed and all the women and children sold into slavery. Mercifully, the issue was revisited on the following day, and a messenger ship arrived in Mytilene just in time to avert a massacre. In the summer of that year, Sparta and its allies captured the city of Plataea, and showed no compunction in executing all the men, selling all the women and children into slavery, and turning the site of the city into pastureland.

Athens continued its naval raids on Sparta's allies and began fortifying posts around the Peloponnese. In 426BC Sparta attacked an Athenian post at Pylos on the coast of Messenia. The Athenian general Demosthenes succeeded in trapping Brasidas and four hundred Spartans on the small island of Sphacteria, but then the battle dragged on for weeks and weeks. Cleon boasted that he could do a better job than Demosthenes and, at the urging of the general Nicias, went on to win a great victory for Athens.

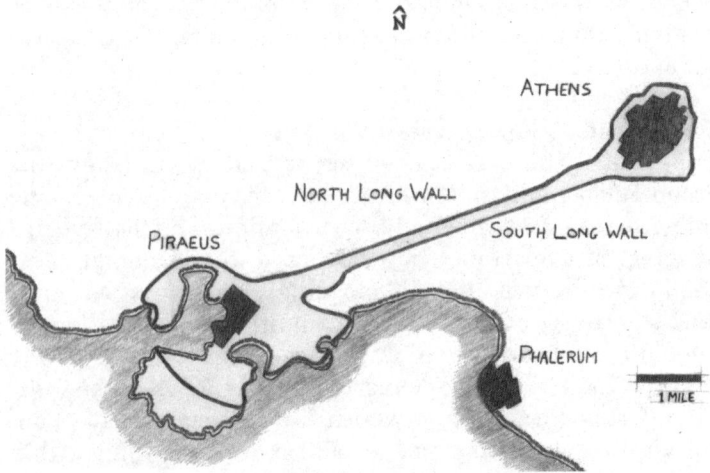

Figure 1: The Athenian city walls

I. History of Athens up to the time of Plato

In 424BC, some towns in north-east Greece that had previously been loyal to Athens decided to revolt. Sparta sent a large force to the area under the command of Brasidas who, by force or by guile, won over several of the towns. When Brasidas attacked the town of Amphipolis in the winter of 424-423BC, Athens dispatched a force under the command of Thucydides. The force arrived too late to prevent the capture of Amphipolis, and the Athenians punished Thucydides by exiling him. This enabled Thucydides to come into closer contact with the various warring factions and so to record the history of the war more objectively, 'not as an essay with which to win the applause of the moment, but as a possession for all time'. In Book V of his *History of the Peloponnesian War*, Thucydides drily observed, 'Right, as the world goes, is only in question between equals in power, while the strong do what they can and the weak suffer what they must'. In 422BC, Athenian troops led by Cleon attacked the Spartan force outside Amphipolis, but the Athenians were defeated and both Cleon and Brasidas were killed. In 421BC Nicias led peace negotiations with Sparta and both sides agreed to an exchange of hostages and captured territory and to a truce of fifty years, the so-called 'Peace of Nicias'.

Some of Sparta's allies felt hard done by the Peace of Nicias and made an alliance with the city of Argos instead. In 420BC, a handsome aristocrat by the name of Alcibiades argued in the ecclesia that Sparta's former allies were now Sparta's enemies, and by extension, Athens' allies. (According to Aristophanes, the misanthrope Timon of Athens disliked everyone except Alcibiades, whom he thought would bring ruin to the city.) As a result, Athens made an alliance with Argos and Argos' allies Mantinea and Elis. The allies attempted to seize the city of Tegea, near Sparta, which provoked the Battle of Mantinea. The Spartans emerged victorious from the Battle of Mantinea, leading to the disintegration of the Argive alliance and to the restoration of Spartan hegemony in the Peloponnese. Athens fell back on the time-tested strategy of attacking Sparta's allies and annexing them to its empire. In 416BC Athens attacked the island of Melos, and did to the Melians that which it had once threatened to do to the Mytilenes.

In 416BC, the city of Egesta in Sicily asked Athens for help against its neighbour Selinous, and Alcibiades persuaded the ecclesia to let him lead a force to Sicily. As the Athenian fleet was about to set sail, some *hermai* (small statues of the god of travel Hermes) were vandalised, and the ecclesia accused Alcibiades of mocking the sacred ritual of the Eleusinian Mysteries. Alcibiades was recalled to face prosecution on charges of sacrilege, but he feared that he would be unjustly convicted, and so defected to Sparta! Alcibiades told the Spartans of Athens' plans to conquer Sicily and Italy, and to use their tremendous resources to conquer the Peloponnese.

Under the command of Nicias the Athenian force prepared to invade Syracuse, but prevaricated and delayed. Meanwhile, a Spartan force arrived in Sicily, and its general Gylippus took command of the combined Spartan and Syracusan troops. When Gylippus prevailed over the Athenian force, Nicias called for reinforcements. Athens sent a second force under Demosthenes, but the Athenians once again suffered a defeat. Demosthenes argued for a retreat, but Nicias hesitated, and then a lunar eclipse was interpreted as a bad omen for a retreat. As a result, the Athenians were forced into a major battle in the harbour of Syracuse. The Athenians suffered a crushing defeat, with Nicias and Demosthenes executed and seven thousand Athenian prisoners taken.

The failure of the Sicilian expedition in 413BC weakened Athens to such an extent that its empire began to fragment and disintegrate. Meanwhile, Alcibiades left Sparta to become an advisor to the Persian satrap Tissaphernes. He used his newfound position to persuade some Athenian generals to stage a coup, install an oligarchy, and have him returned to Athens with Persian support. In 411BC the conspirators succeeded in installing the oligarchy of the Four Hundred, but abandoned any plans to return Alcibiades to Athens. Ever ready to turn his cloak, Alcibiades allied himself with the exiled democrats. Four months later, the democrats succeeded in installing the intermediate regime of the Five Thousand, and Alcibiades was given the command of the Athenian army. Athens rebuilt its fleet and carried on prosecuting the war, scoring victories at Cynossema and then, under the command of Alcibiades, at Cyzicus. After the Battle of Cyzicus, the Athenians intercepted a 'laconic' dispatch from the defeated Spartans: 'Ships lost; Mindarus dead; men starving; can't figure out what to do.' Sparta sued for peace, but Athens refused her.

Cyrus, the youngest son of Darius, entered into an alliance with Sparta and helped to finance the Spartan fleet. In 407BC, the Spartan fleet under the command of Lysander won an important victory at Notium which led to the downfall and exile of Alcibiades. Fortunes were reversed the following year at the Battle of Arginusae. However, a sudden storm prevented the Athenians from picking up their survivors and about three thousand men were left to drown. Despite the protests of Socrates, whose turn it was to chair the assembly meeting, the generals in charge of the campaign were tried, condemned, and executed. Once again Sparta sued for peace and, once again, Athens refused her, very foolishly as it later turned out. The following year, Lysander initiated a surprise attack on the Athenian fleet which had been beached at Aegospotami in the Hellespont. In the ensuing Battle of Aegospotami, the Spartans captured almost the entire Athenian fleet, and the 36-year-long Peloponnesian War was at an end. The ship carrying the news of the defeat arrived in Piraeus at night. According to the historian Xenophon, 'one man passed it on to another, and a sound of wailing arose and extended first from Piraeus, then along the Long Walls until it reached the city. That night no one slept. They mourned for the lost, but more still for their own fate.'

The Spartans resisted calls to turn the site of Athens into pastureland, but Athens had to agree to Sparta's terms of surrender and became a Spartan territory under Spartan control. The Spartans determined that Athens should be ruled by thirty individuals, mostly aristocrats such as Plato's relatives Critias and Charmides who had been exiled after the coup of 411BC. The regime of the Thirty Tyrants was so oppressive as to be unsustainable, and after less than a year the Spartans agreed to restore a limited form of democracy to the city. It is during this period, in 403BC, that Socrates was condemned to death. Plato was present at the trial of Socrates, which is the subject of the *Apology*.

II. The Pre-Socratics

...I, an immortal God, no longer mortal,
wander among you, honoured by all,
adorned with holy diadems and blooming garlands.

Empedocles, *Purifications*

Thales of Miletus (624-546BC) and the Milesian School
Along with Solon, Thales of Miletus in Asia Minor was regarded
by Plato as one of the seven sages of Greece. Thales sought to
explain the origin and nature of the world without resorting to
myths and gods, which is why he is often regarded as the first
genuine philosopher, as well as the first genuine scientist. He
held that all things are one, that water is the basic constituent
of the universe, and that the earth floats on water like a log
on a stream. Thales was a geometer who travelled to Egypt
to receive instruction from Egyptian priests. Whilst in Egypt
he measured the height of the pyramids by measuring their
shadows at the time of day when his own shadow was as long
as he was tall. He discovered that triangles with one equal
side and two equal angles are congruent, and applied this
knowledge to calculate the distances of ships at sea. He also
discovered the method for inscribing a right-angled triangle
into a circle, and celebrated by sacrificing an ox to the gods,
which he believed were in all things ('all things are full of
gods'). Thales was also an astronomer and a meteorologist who
determined the dates of the summer and winter solstices and

predicted the solar eclipse of 585BC which halted the battle of Halys between the Lydians and the Medes. One year he predicted a good harvest of olives, took a lease on all the olive presses in Miletus, and made a fortune, simply to prove to his fellow Milesians that philosophers could easily be rich, if only they did not have better things to do with their life. He was legendary for his absent-mindedness. In the *Theaetetus* Plato recounts that,

> *Thales was studying the stars and gazing into the sky, when he fell into a well, and a jolly and witty Thracian servant girl made fun of him, saying that he was crazy to know about what was up in the heavens while he could not see what was in front of him beneath his feet.*

Thales was succeeded at the head of the Milesian School by his pupil Anaximander (610-546BC). Like Thales, Anaximander was looking for the 'origin' or 'principle' of all things, which he identified with *apeiron* or 'the boundless,' from which everything else is generated 'in all the worlds'. A more obvious choice, such as, for example, water, could only be wet but never dry, and so could not embrace all the opposites found in nature. In his one surviving fragment, he wrote,

> *Whence things have their origin,*
> *Thence also their destruction happens,*
> *According to necessity;*
> *For they give to each other justice and recompense*
> *For their injustice*
> *In conformity with the ordinance of Time.*

According to Anaximander, the earth is an unsupported cylinder with a height equivalent to one third of its diameter. The earth does not need to be supported because it is in the middle of everything else and there is no reason for it to move one way rather than another. The sun, moon, and stars are gigantic wheels of fire that appear to us through holes or vents. Phases of the moon and eclipses of the sun occur as a result of blockages in the vents. As for mankind, it sprang from other species of animals, most likely aquatic animals. Anaximander travelled widely, and is said to have led a mission that founded a colony called Apollonia on the coast of the Black Sea. His other achievements include the first map of the world, the first star chart, and the first Greek sundial. Diogenes reports that he enjoyed singing: 'They say that when he sang, the children laughed; and that he, hearing of this, said, 'We must then sing better for the sake of the children."

Anaximander had a friend and pupil called Anaximenes (585-525BC) who was the last of the three Milesian cosmologists. Anaximenes held that air is the primary substance: when air undergoes rarefaction it becomes fire, and when it undergoes condensation it becomes wind, then cloud, then water, then earth, then stone. To defend his thesis, Anaximenes made appeal to a simple experiment involving blowing air onto the hand, first with the lips pursed, when the air feels cool, and then from an open mouth, when the air feels warm. Anaximenes conceived of the earth as a flat disc that floats on a cushion of air. The heavenly bodies are also flat, and rotate horizontally around the earth like a bonnet around a head, with their rising and setting accounted for by a tilting movement of the earth. The gods too consist of air, as does the human soul. Thus, everything shares in a single divine substance.

Pythagoras (c.570-500BC) and the Pythagoreans
Pythagoras held that there are three sorts of men, just as there are three classes of strangers who go to the Olympic Games. There are the lovers of gain who come to buy and sell, the lovers of honour who come to compete, and the lovers of wisdom who come simply to look on. Pythagoras was born on the island of Samos, not far from Miletus. On the advice of

Thales he travelled to Memphis in Egypt, where he came into contact with priests renowned for their wisdom. As the age of 40, he fled the tyranny of Polycrates to Croton in Southern Italy, where he established a philosophical and religious community. Those who entered the community's inner circle were governed by a strict set of ascetic and ethical rules, forsaking personal possessions, assuming a mainly vegetarian diet, and – since words are so often careless and misrepresentative – observing silence. Some of the community's more eccentric rules, such as 'do not break bread' or 'do not poke the fire with a sword,' may have been riddles or allegories that required interpreting. Pythagoras' community has been seen as a prototype for the monastic life and for later philosophical institutions such as Plato's Academy, Aristotle's Lyceum, and Epicurus' Garden. Music played an important role in Pythagoras' community. Pythagoreans recited poetry, sang hymns to Apollo, and played on the lyre to cure illnesses of both body and soul. It is said that one day Pythagoras passed by some blacksmiths at work, and found that their hammering on anvils produced especially harmonious sounds. He then found that the anvils were simple ratios of one another, one being half the size of the first, another two thirds of the size, and so on. This discovery of a relationship between numerical ratios and musical intervals led Pythagoras to believe that the study of mathematics is the key to understanding the structure and order of the universe. According to his 'harmony of the spheres,' the heavenly bodies move according to mathematical equations which correspond to musical notes and form part of a grand cosmic symphony. Pythagoras never separated religion from science and philosophy, which, even in his day, left him open to accusations of mysticism. He believed in the transmigration of the soul, that is, in the reincarnation of the soul over time into the bodies of human beings, animals, or plants ('metempsychosis'), until such a time as it became moral. He claimed to have lived four lives and to remember them in detail, and once recognised the cry of his dead friend in the yelping of a puppy. After his death, the Pythagoreans deified him, and attributed him with a golden thigh and the gift of bilocation. However, Pythagoras had always been a modest man, declining to be called a 'wise man' (*sophos*), and preferring instead to be called a 'lover of wisdom' (*philosophos*).

Xenophanes of Colophon (570-470BC)

Xenophanes lived for about a hundred years, and hailed from Colophon, not far from Miletus. After Colophon fell to the Medes, he erred through the Greek world for 67 years, reciting poems and philosophical verses. He criticised Hesiod and Homer for anthropomorphising the gods (conceiving of them in human form) and portraying them as immoral.

> *Yes, and if oxen and horses or lions had hands, and could paint with their hands, and produce works of art as men do, horses would paint the forms of the gods like horses, and oxen like oxen, and make their bodies in the image of their several kinds.*

Instead, Xenophanes suggested that there is one god that is 'greatest among gods and men' and 'not at all like mortals in body or in thought'. He assimilated this god to the cosmos, and thought of it as abstract, universal, and unchanging. For this reason, he is often thought of as an early monotheist, even though he probably allowed for of the existence of other gods. Xenophanes held that the primary substance was neither water nor air, but earth. 'All things are from earth and in earth all things end.' However, he also recognised the importance of water, and his early observation of the fossil record led him to suggest that the earth had at one time been covered by the sea. Xenophanes thought that earth stretched beneath us to infinity, for which reason he could not conceive of the sun going below the earth when it set in the evening. Instead, he suggested that a new sun came into existence every morning. To his credit, he recognised that if knowledge can only be gained through sense experience, then knowledge of the underlying nature of reality is unattainable. Even if sense experience is objective, which it is not, the underlying nature of reality cannot be observed through sense experience. Thus, the best that can be hoped for is not knowledge, but true belief.

Heraclitus of Ephesus (535-475BC)

Heraclitus hailed from the city of Ephesus, not far from Miletus and Colophon. He was an aristocrat with a claim to be king (*basileus*). However, he abdicated in favour of his brother, explaining that he preferred talking to children rather than to politicians. Although fragments of his writings have survived, they take the form of obscure and ambiguous aphorisms, for which reason he is sometimes known as 'Heraclitus the Obscure' or 'Heraclitus the Riddler'. As he suffered from melancholy, he is also sometimes known as 'the weeping philosopher,' in opposition to Democritus, 'the laughing philosopher'.

> *They say that Euripides gave Socrates a copy of Heraclitus' book and asked him what he thought of it. He replied: 'What I understand is splendid; and I think what I don't understand is so too – but it would take a Delian diver to get to the bottom of it.*
>
> Diogenes Laertes, *Lives of Philosophers*

Heraclitus was a misanthrope with no interest in the vast majority of people, whom he found to be singularly lacking in understanding, and whom he compared to cattle. He wished the citizens of his native Ephesus great wealth, as a punishment for their worthless lives. The Persian king Darius once invited him to his resplendent court, but he refused to go, replying, 'All men upon earth hold aloof from truth and justice, while, by reason of wicked folly, they devote themselves to avarice and thirst for popularity'. He eventually removed himself to the mountains, where he fed on grasses and other plants. He claimed that he 'inquired of himself' and learned everything from himself, since 'Nature loves to hide'. Heraclitus' big idea was that everything is in a constant state of flux or becoming, as epitomised by his saying that 'You cannot step into the same river twice, for fresh waters are ever flowing in upon you'. In his *Metaphysics* Aristotle reasoned that, if everything is in a constant state of flux, then nothing can be known, and it is likely that Heraclitus thought this too. Since fire is a symbol of perpetual change, Heraclitus pronounced it to be the primary substance. The underlying order of change is the product of God's reason or *Logos*, and fire is the expression of *Logos*, and thus of God. Accordingly, an enlightened man's soul is hot and dry, whereas a drunk 'is led by an unfledged boy, stumbling and not knowing where he goes, having his soul moist'. It is a testament to Heraclitus' enduring influence that the *Logos* entered the Bible at John 1:1, with the *Logos* translated from Greek into English as *the Word*: 'In the beginning was the Word, and the Word was with God, and the Word was God'. Heraclitus also taught about the 'unity of the opposites,' for instance, that hot and cold are the same, as are light and dark and day and night. These opposites appear to be in a constant state of strife, but the resulting cosmic tension is, in fact, an expression of essential harmony. He wrote, 'It is wise to agree that all things are one. In differing it agrees with itself, a backward-turning connection, like that of a bow and a lyre. The path up and down is one and the same.' His pronouncement that 'an unapparent harmony is stronger than an apparent one' seems to be just as applicable to his cosmology as it is to human psychology.

Parmenides (c.515BC-?) and the Eleatics

In stark contrast to Heraclitus, who believed that everything is in a state of flux, Parmenides believed that nothing ever changes. Parmenides was a nobleman from Elea in Southern Italy, where he was much admired for his excellent legislation and exemplary life. He was either a pupil of Xenophanes or very familiar with his teachings, and most probably came into contact with Pythagoreans. At the age of 65 he travelled with his pupil and *eromenos* (beloved) Zeno to Athens, where he met with the young Socrates. Their alleged conversation is recounted by Plato in the *Parmenides*. Parmenides wrote a philosophical poem, *On Nature*, in clumsy hexameter verse, but only 160 lines survive. The poem begins with a proem in which a young Parmenides ascends to the abode of a goddess who reveals to him 'the path of truth' and 'the path of mortal opinion'. There are two methods of inquiry into the path of truth, what is, and what is not. What is, is, and it is impossible for it not to be. And what is not is not, and it is impossible for it to be. One cannot conceive of what is not, because one cannot think or speak about nothing. Conversely, if one can think or speak about something, then it must be. 'For thought and being are the same.' As it is possible to think about Reality, Reality must be and, if it is, it cannot not be. Something cannot come into being nor pass out of being, because something cannot come into being from nothing. *Ex nihilo nihil fit*. Thus, if something comes into being, it does so not from nothing but from something – in other words, it does not really come into being at all. This line of reasoning leads to the conclusion that there can be no becoming and thus no real changes, even though our sense experience tells us that there are. While the world as it appears through sense experience is contingent, changing, and temporal, pure reason leads to the logical conclusion that it is in fact necessary, unchanging, and atemporal. Motion is impossible because it requires moving into 'the void', that is, moving into nothing, which does not exist. In this context, Parmenides' pupil Zeno produced a set of arguments, including the famous 'Achilles and the Tortoise,' to demonstrate that motion is impossible. From all this, Parmenides concluded that the universe consists of a single, undifferentiated, indivisible, unmoving, and unchanging unity which he called 'the One'. Parmenides is the first philosopher to enquire into being qua being, and so is often regarded as the first metaphysician and the first ontologist. His duality of appearance and reality exerted a strong influence on Plato and, through him, on much that came after.

Empedocles (c.490-430BC)

Empedocles was an aristocrat from Acragas, now Agrigento, in Southern Italy. He had a reputation as a mystic and a miracle-worker, and people flocked to him for advice and healing. He thought of himself as divine, claiming that he could cure old age and control the winds. When he was offered the kingship of Acragas, he turned it down, preferring instead to write poetry in the style of Parmenides, and to dedicate it to his eromenos, the physician Pausanias.

Empedocles synthesised the thought of the Ionian philosophers by holding that there are four primordial elements, air, earth, fire, and water. The four primordial elements are driven together and apart by the opposed cosmic principles of Love and Strife. Love causes the primordial elements to combine, and unopposed Love leads to 'The One,' a divine and resplendent sphere. Strife gradually causes the sphere to disintegrate back into the primordial elements, and this cosmic cycle repeats itself *ad infinitum*. If the phenomenal world, that is, the world of appearances, is full of contrasts and oppositions, this is because of the dual action of Love and Strife on the elements. Change can occur, but only in form of the combination and separation of the elements. The noumenal world, that is, underlying reality, is fundamentally changeless. Empedocles developed a crude theory of evolution by survival of the fittest, beginning with the haphazard combination of the elements to form various bits of misassembled anatomy. He shared in the Pythagorean doctrine of metempsychosis, and maintained that the souls of wise and virtuous people such as poets and seers can progress to the divine and thereby achieve liberation. According to legend, he killed himself by leaping into the flames of Mount Etna, either to prove that he was immortal, or to make people believe that he was. Matthew Arnold put the following last words into his mouth,

> *The heart will glow no more; thou art*
> *A living man no more, Empedocles!*
> *Nothing but a devouring flame of thought –*
> *But a naked, eternally restless mind!*
> *To the elements it came from*
> *Everything will return*
> *Our bodies to earth,*
> *Our blood to water,*
> *Heat to fire,*
> *Breath to air.*
> *They were well born, they will be well entomb'd –*
> *But mind?*

Matthew Arnold, *Empedocles on Etna*

Anaxagoras (c.500-428BC)

Anaxagoras was born in Clazomenae in Asia Minor, and may have been a pupil of Anaximenes. He gave up wealth and influence in favour of the search for knowledge, and went to Athens which was then the cultural centre of the Greek World. He remained for 30 years in Athens, where he was always talking about 'the nature of wisdom and folly,' and came to be admired by Euripides and Pericles. His assertion that the sun was a mass of blazing metal larger than the Peloponnese eventually led to his prosecution on the grounds of impiety, after which he fled to Lampsacus on the Hellespont. According to Diogenes, when someone lamented that he would die in a foreign land, Anaxagoras replied, 'The descent to Hades is much the same from whatever place we start'. The citizens of Lampsacus had great respect for him, and when the authorities asked him how he might be honoured, he replied that children should be given a school holiday in the month of his death. Anaxagoras agreed with Parmenides that something cannot come into being nor pass out of being, and with Empedocles that change occurs in the form of the combination and separation of the elements. He held that everything is infinitely divisible, and that everything contains a bit of everything, albeit in varying combinations. Thus, there are no indivisible particles, no atoms. Everything springs from 'the One' through a process of separation mediated by *nous* or mind, which is the supreme ordering force or principle. Anaxagoras held that the cosmos came into being as a result of the rotary motion of a spiral, with all mass initially united in its centre but then spreading out and differentiating. For this reason, he is sometimes regarded as the father of the Big Bang Theory.

Democritus of Abdera (c.460-370)

Leucippus of Miletus and Democritus of Abdera are often mentioned in the same breath as the founders of atomism, the culmination of early Greek thought. Leucippus was the teacher of Democritus, but little else is known about him. Democritus was born in Abdera, on the Thracian coast. His father was tremendously wealthy, and he fritted his inheritance away on books and learned travel, reputedly travelling as far as India and Ethiopia. In contrast to Heraclitus, who was referred to as 'the weeping philosopher,' Democritus was referred to as the 'laughing philosopher,' because he was ever ready to laugh at the foolishness of people. The term 'Abderitan laughter' – scoffing, incessant laughter – derives from him. Despite this, people held him in high esteem, not least because they thought that he could predict the future. Like all early Greek philosophers, he eschewed wealth and power for a good life and a prominent place in the history of human thought; he once said that he would prefer to discover one true scientific principle than to become king of Persia. Democritus wrote nearly 80 treatises on an eclectic range of topics ranging from tangencies and irrationals to farming, painting, and fighting in armour. Unfortunately, only fragments of his writings survive. He claimed that 'nothing exists except atoms and empty space;

everything else is opinion'. In stark contrast to Anaxagoras, he held that matter is not infinitely divisible, but consists of tiny, indivisible bodies which he termed 'atoms' (Greek for 'indivisible'). Atoms are infinite in number and in shape and variety, and do not pass in and out of existence. They are in random motion, like motes in a sunbeam when there is no wind. Their collision can lead them either to bounce off one another, or to build up into clusters that form the objects of our perception. Democritus' theory is purely mechanistic, as he does not give any account of the cause or purpose of atoms. Perhaps for this reason, Plato does not mention him at all – not even once.

The Sophists

The sophists were a group of itinerant speakers and teachers in Greece and particularly in Athens in the second half of the fifth century BC. They taught rhetoric and philosophy and a broad range of subjects besides, and charged fees to their students, who were often wealthy young men with ambitions of holding public office. The sophists typically boasted that, as skilled rhetoricians, they could 'make the weaker argument appear the stronger'. They are mostly known to us through Plato and his pupil Aristotle, who held them in slight regard and most likely presented them in an unfavourable light. The Sophists included Protagoras, Gorgias, Prodicus, Hippias, Thrasymachus, Callicles, and Euthydemus – all characters in Plato's dialogues. Only the first three are presented here.

According to Plato, Protagoras of Abdera (c.490-420BC) was the very first sophist, and charged extortionate fees for his services. It is said that Protagoras once took on a pupil, Euathlus, on the understanding that he would be paid once Euathlus had won his first court case. However, Euathlus never won a case, and Protagoras eventually sued him for non-payment. Protagoras argued that if he won the case he would be paid, and if Euathlus won the case, he would still be paid, because Euathlus would have won a case. Eualthus retorted that if he won the case he would not have to pay, and if Protagoras won the case, he still would not have to pay, because he still would not have won a case. Protagoras lived in Athens for a period, and in 444BC his friend Pericles invited him to write the constitution for the newly founded Athenian colony of Thurii. Protagoras was both a relativist and an agnostic, and thereby a controversial if not a heretical figure. He famously held that 'man is the measure of all things'. His lost work, *On the Gods*, opened with the memorable and oft quoted line,

> *About the gods, I cannot be sure whether they exist or not, or what they are like to see; for many things stand in the way of the knowledge of them, both the opacity of the subject and the shortness of human life.*

Protagoras represented a shift from the natural philosophy of his predecessors to human philosophy. His relativism, particularly in the moral sphere, may have prompted Plato's quest for a moral anchor, which culminated in the concept of permanent and transcendent forms.

Gorgias (487-376BC) was born in Leontini in Sicily, where he may have been a pupil of Empedocles. He moved to Athens at the relatively late age of 60, but then lived to be almost 110, thereby proving that the philosophical life is, if not the best, at least the longest. In *On Nature or the Non-Existent*, he used his rhetorical skills to argue that nothing exists, thereby both refuting and parodying the Eleatic thesis (see above). His sceptical argument is often summarised in the form of a trilemma:

1. Nothing exists;
2. Even if something exists, it cannot be known; and
3. Even if it could be known, this knowledge could not be communicated to others.

Thus, all that can be investigated is the *logos* itself, since it is the only thing that can be known. In the *Encomium of Helen*, Gorgias attempted to rehabilitate the reputation of Helen of Troy by making the weaker argument seem the stronger. He argued that Helen succumbed either to love, physical force (Paris' abduction), or verbal persuasion (*logos*); in either case, she could not be held responsible for her actions. Gorgias famously likened the effect of logos on the soul to the effect of drugs on the body. He wrote, 'Just as different drugs draw forth different humours from the body – some putting a stop to disease, others to life – so too with words: some cause pain, others joy, some strike fear, some stir the audience to boldness, some benumb and bewitch the soul with evil persuasion.'

Prodicus of Ceos (465-415BC) came to Athens as an ambassador of Ceos. Referred to as a 'babbling brook' by Aristophanes, he privileged linguistics over rhetoric, and insisted upon the correct use of names and the accurate discrimination between near synonyms. In Plato, he is often mocked by Socrates for his pedantry and love of gain.

> *Now if I had attended Prodicus's fifty drachma course of lectures, after which, as he himself says, a man has a complete education on this subject, there would be nothing to hinder your learning the truth about the correctness of names at once; but I have heard only the one drachma course, and so I do not know what the truth is about such matters.*

Plato, *Cratylus*

III. Socrates

*The usual picture of Socrates is of an ugly
little plebeian who inspired a handsome young
nobleman to write long dialogues on large topics.*

Richard Rorty

The 'real' Socrates is shrouded in mystery as he did not leave a written corpus of his own and there is no purely historical account of his life and thought. The three principal sources on Socrates are his pupils Plato and Xenophon and the comedian Aristophanes. These sources do not claim historical accuracy, and their portrayals of Socrates are undoubtedly influenced by their authors' biases and agenda. The richest source on Socrates is Plato, in whose writings it is always uncertain whether the character Socrates is the real Socrates or a ventriloquist's dummy. It is generally agreed that, as Plato's thought developed, the character Socrates became less and less of the real Socrates and more and more of a ventriloquist's dummy.

Socrates was born in Athens in 469BC, after the final defeat of the Persians at Plataea and Mycale, and before the start of the Peloponnesian Wars against Sparta and her allies. According to Plato, Socrates' father, Sophroniscus, was a stonemason, and his mother, Phaenarete, was a midwife. Socrates grew up under Pericles, in the heyday of Athen's imperial hegemony. He grew up to be ugly: short in stature, pot-bellied, snub-nosed, and pop-eyed. In the *Theaetetus*, Socrates asks the geometer Theodorus to tell him which of the young men of Athens are 'showing signs of turning out well'. Theodorus immediately singles out Theaetetus, the son of Euphronius of Sunium, whom he describes to Socrates as 'rather like you, snub-nosed, with eyes that stick out; though these features are not so pronounced in him'.

Socrates married Xanthippe, a shrew of a woman, but some forty years younger than him. According to Xenophon, Socrates married her because, 'If I can tolerate her spirit, I can with ease attach myself to every human being else'. According to Aelian, she once trampled underfoot a cake sent to Socrates by his eromenos Alcibiades, the famous or, rather, infamous Athenian statesman and general. 'Xanthippe' has entered the English language as a term for an ill-tempered woman, although Plato himself portrays her as nothing other than a devoted wife and the mother of Socrates' three sons, Lamprocles, Sophroniscus, and Menexenus. In the *Symposium*, Alcibiades says that Socrates is crazy about beautiful boys, constantly following them around 'in a perpetual daze'. Yet he also says that Socrates cares very little about whether a person is beautiful or rich or famous: 'He considers all these possessions beneath contempt, and that's exactly how he considers all of us as well'.

Socrates' friend Chaerephon once asked the oracle at Delphi if any man is wiser than Socrates, and the pythia (priestess) replied that no one is wiser. To discover the meaning of this divine utterance, Socrates questioned a number of wise men and in each case concluded, 'I am likely to be wiser than he to this small extent, that I do not think I know what I do not know'. From then on, Socrates dedicated himself to the service of the gods by seeking out anyone who might be wise and, 'if he is not, showing him that he is not'. In the *Apology*, he says that the gods attached him to Athens as upon a great and noble horse which 'needed to be stirred up by a kind of gadfly'. In the *Symposium*, Alcibiades says of Socrates that,

> *...he makes it seem that my life isn't worth living!*
> *...He always traps me, you see, and he makes me*
> *admit that my political career is a waste of time,*
> *while all that matters is just what I most neglect:*
> *my personal shortcomings, which cry out for the*
> *closest attention. So I refuse to listen to him; I stop*
> *my ears and tear myself away from him, for, like*
> *the Sirens, he could make me stay by his side till*
> *I die.*[1]

According to Plato, Socrates devoted himself entirely to discussing philosophy, for which he never accepted payment. It is unclear how he earned a living, but a combination of meagre needs and rich friends may have been enough to get him by. Socrates seldom claimed any real knowledge, and when he did it was always because he had learned it from somebody else or because he had been divinely inspired. For example, he claimed to have learned the art of love from the priestess Diotima of Mantinea, and the art of rhetoric from Aspasia, the mistress of Pericles. In the *Theaetetus*, Socrates famously compares himself to a midwife who attends not to the labour of the body but to the labour of the soul, helping others to 'discover within themselves a multitude of beautiful things, which they bring forth into the light'. When Socrates asks Theaetetus to define knowledge, Theaetetus says that he has never come up with an adequate answer to this question and cannot stop worrying about it. Socrates tells him, 'Yes; those are the pains of labour, dear Theaetetus. It is because you are not barren but pregnant.' Socrates' method, the celebrated 'elenchus' or Socratic method, consists in questioning one or more people about a certain concept, for example, courage or temperance, so as to expose a contradiction in their initial assumptions about the concept, and thereby to provoke a reappraisal of the concept. As the process is iterative, it leads to an increasingly

---

1   Translated by Alexander Nehamas and Paul Woodruff.

precise or refined definition of the concept or, more often than not, to the conclusion that the concept cannot be defined, and thus that we know nothing.

In the *Phaedrus*, Socrates says that there are two kinds of madness, one resulting from human illness, and the other resulting from a divinely inspired release from normally accepted behaviour. This divine form of madness has four parts: inspiration, mysticism, poetry, and love. Socrates probably believed that madness, like virtue, is a gift from the gods and that the two are intimately connected.[2] He frequently questioned the sophists' doctrine that virtue can be taught, and observed that virtuous men rarely, if ever, produced sons that matched them in quality. For Socrates, virtue and knowledge are one and the same, as no one who really knows the best course of action can fail to choose it, and all wrongdoing results from ignorance. Whilst Socrates seldom claimed any real knowledge, he did claim to have a *daimonion* or 'divine something,' an inner voice or instinct that prevented him from making grave mistakes such as getting involved in politics. In the *Phaedrus*, he says,

> *Madness, provided it comes as the gift of heaven, is the channel by which we receive the greatest blessings... the men of old who gave things their names saw no disgrace or reproach in madness; otherwise they would not have connected it with the name of the noblest of arts, the art of discerning the future, and called it the manic art... So, according to the evidence provided by our ancestors, madness is a nobler thing than sober sense... madness comes from God, whereas sober sense is merely human.*[3]

---

2   This subject is more fully explored in my book, *The Meaning of Madness*.
3   Translated by Walter Hamilton.

Several of Plato's dialogues refer to Socrates' military service. Socrates served in the Athenian army during the campaigns of Potidaea (432BC), Delium (424BC), and Amphipolis (422BC), which were more or less the only times he ever left Athens. In the *Laches*, Laches calls on Socrates for advice because of his courageous behaviour during the retreat from Delium. In the *Symposium*, Alcibiades says that Socrates singlehandedly saved his life at Potidaea, and that he took the hardships of the campaign 'much better than anyone in the whole army'.

In the *Apology*, Socrates says that 'a man who really fights for justice must lead a private, not a public, life if he is to survive for even a short time'. He cites the time in 406BC when he was chairing the assembly meeting and alone opposed the trial as a body of the generals who, after the Battle of Arginusae, failed to pick up the Athenian survivors because of a violent storm. At the time the orators had been ready to prosecute him and take him away, although later everyone realised that the prosecution would have been illegal. He also cites the time in 404BC when the Thirty Tyrants asked him and four others to bring the innocent Leon of Salamis to be executed, and he alone refused, even though his refusal may have cost him his life.

In 399BC, at the age of 70, Socrates was indicted by Meletus, Anytus, and Lycon for offending the Olympian gods and thereby breaking the law against impiety. He was accused of 'studying things in the sky and below the earth,' 'making the worse into the stronger argument,' and 'teaching these same things to others'. The real basis for Socrates' indictment may have been his anti-democratic leanings and his close association with aristocrats such as Critias and Charmides, who had been prominent in the oligarchic reign of terror. Yet his behaviour when faced with the demands of the Thirty Tyrants suggests that he placed his ethics far above his politics.

In the *Apology*, Socrates gives a defiant defence, intimating to the jurors that they should be ashamed of their eagerness to possess as much wealth, reputation, and honours as possible, whilst not caring for or giving thought to wisdom or truth, or the best possible state of their soul. In an aristocratic flourish, he insists that 'wealth does not bring about excellence, but excellence makes wealth and everything else good for men, both individually and collectively'[4]. After being convicted and sentenced to death, he tells the jurors that he was sentenced to death not because he lacked words, but because he lacked shamelessness and the willingness to say what they would most gladly have heard from him. 'It is not difficult to avoid death, gentlemen; it is much more difficult to avoid wickedness, for it runs faster than death.'

After being sentenced to death, Socrates had an opportunity to escape from the Athenian prison. In the *Crito*, one of the main reasons he gives for not escaping is that, by choosing to live in Athens, he tacitly agreed to abide by her laws. In the *Phaedo*, which was known to the ancients as *On the Soul*, Socrates prepares to die. He tells his friends that a philosopher disdains the body in favour of the soul, because the just or the beautiful or the reality of any one thing cannot be apprehended through the senses, but through thought alone. Socrates warns his friends not to become 'misologues,' as there is no greater evil than to shun rational conversation. Instead, he urges them to take courage and be eager to 'attain soundness'. After joking with his gaoler, Socrates drinks the poisonous hemlock. His famous last words are, 'Crito, I owe a cock to Asclepius; will you remember to pay the debt?'[5]

After his sentencing, Socrates told the jurors: 'You did this in the belief that you could avoid giving an account of your life, but I maintain that quite the opposite will happen to you. There will be more people to test you, whom I have now held back, but you did not notice it.'[6]

His pupil Plato was standing in the audience.

---

4   Translated by GMA Grube.

5   A cock was sacrificed by ill people hoping for a cure, and Socrates probably meant that death is a cure for the ills of life.

6   Translated by GMA Grube.

IV. Plato and his works

I throw the apple at you, and if you are willing to
love me, take it and share your girlhood with me;
but if your thoughts are what I pray they are not,
even then take it, and consider how short-lived
is beauty.

Plato, *Epigrams*

Plato was born in Athens or possibly Aegina in 428–7BC. His mother, Perictione, descended from Solon, and his father, Ariston, may have traced his descent from Codrus, the last king of Athens. Perictione was also sister to Charmides and niece to Critias, who were both prominent amongst the Thirty Tyrants. The ancients later claimed that Ariston was merely Plato's step-father, and that his real father was Apollo, the god of the arts, light, and truth – whence Plato's epithets of 'son of Apollo' and 'divine teacher'. Plato had two elder brothers, Adeimantus and Glaucon, and a sister, Potone. After Ariston's early death, Perictione married her maternal uncle Pyrilampes, who was friends with Pericles. Pyrilampes and Perictione had a son, Antiphon, who was the second son of Pyrilampes, and the half-brother of Plato. Plato had a tendency to use his distinguished relatives as characters in his dialogues. For instance, Charmides has a dialogue named after him, Critias appears in the *Charmides* and *Protagoras*, Adeimantus and Glaucon appear in the *Republic*, and Antiphon appears in the *Parmenides*.

According to legend, while the infant Plato was sleeping in a bower of myrtles on Mount Hymettus, bees settled upon his lips, auguring the honeyed words that would one day flow through his mouth. Plato was named Aristocles after his grandfather, but his wrestling coach, Ariston of Argos, dubbed him 'Platon' or 'broad' on account of the width of his shoulders. Alternatively, the name derived from the size of his forehead or the breadth of his eloquence. Both Critias and Charmides were friends with Socrates, so Plato was likely entrusted to Socrates at a young age. Prior to that, Plato had received instruction from Cratylus, who had once been a disciple of Heraclitus.

> *It is stated that Socrates in a dream saw a swan on his knees, which all at once put forth plumage, and flew away after uttering a loud sweet note. And the next day Plato was introduced as a pupil, and thereupon he recognized in him the swan of his dreams.*

Diogenes Laertes, *Lives of Philosophers*

Plato served in the Athenian army from 409 to 404BC, but had his eye on a political, rather than a military, career. In 404BC he was invited to join the administration of the Thirty Tyrants but held back, repelled by its oppression and violence and, in particular, by its attempt to implicate Socrates in the seizure of Leon of Salamis. At the Battle of Munychia in 404 or 403BC, the democratic Athenians in exile defeated the forces of the Thirty Tyrants and both Critias and Charmides were killed. Plato once again considered a political career, but the execution of Socrates in 399BC left him thoroughly disillusioned with Athenian politics.

Following Socrates' death, Plato left Athens and travelled to Egypt, Sicily, and Italy, where he came into contact with some Pythagoreans, and held on to their belief that the study of mathematics is the key to understanding the structure and order of the universe. In Sicily he made friends with the philosopher Dion, and was introduced to Dion's brother-in-law, Dionysius I of Syracuse. Upon his return to Athens in 387BC, Plato founded a school of science and philosophy on a site named 'Academia' after the legendary Athenian hero Akademos. The school became known as the Academy, and Plato remained its head or *scholarch* until his death some forty years later.

After the death of Dionysius I in 367BC, Dion invited Plato back to Syracuse to tutor Dionysius II and transform him into the sort of philosopher-king described in the Republic. Plato never had high hopes for the dissolute Dionysius II, but he felt bound to Dion, and did not want to be 'solely a mere man of words'. In 366BC Dionysius II charged Dion with conspiracy and expelled him, after which Plato was held in semi-captivity for some time. At the insistence of Dionysius II, and hoping to mediate for the restoration of Dion, Plato returned to Syracuse in 361BC, where he was no doubt once again reminded of Socrates, of his belief that virtue cannot be taught, and of his divinely-inspired reluctance to engage in politics.

When Plato died in 348–7BC, he was succeeded as scholarch of the Academy not by Aristotle, his pupil of 20 years, but by his sister's son Speusippus, who was himself succeeded by a long line of distinguished philosophers. The Academy survived in one form or another for some 900 years[7] until it was closed by the Christian emperor Justinian in 529AD, a date that is often cited for the end of classical antiquity.

Works

Plato has traditionally been ascribed 35 dialogues, although modern scholars doubt the authenticity of six (Second Alcibiades, Hipparchus, Rival Lovers, Theages, Minos, and Epinomis), and do not agree about the authenticity of three

---

7   Longer than, so far, the University of Oxford.

(First Alcibiades, Greater Hippias, and Clitophon). The 35 dialogues are arranged in tetralogies according to a scheme devised by Thrasyllus, a Plato scholar from Alexandria and court astrologer to the Roman Emperor Tiberius (42BC-37AD). The thirty-sixth entry, that is, the fourth entry of the ninth tetralogy, consists of thirteen 'Letters'.

I.   Euthypro, Apology, Crito, Phaedo
II.   Cratylus, Theaetetus, Sophist, Statesman
III.   Parmenides, Philebus, Symposium, Phaedrus
IV.   First Alcibiades, Second Alcibiades, Hipparchus, Rival Lovers
V.   Theages, Charmides, Laches, Lysis
VI.   Euthydemus, Protagoras, Gorgias, Meno
VII.   Greater Hippias, Lesser Hippias, Ion, Menexenus
VIII. Clitophon, Republic, Timaeus, Critias
IX.   Minos, Laws, Epinomis, Epistles

Thrasyllus did not include in his tetralogical arrangement those dialogues which were transmitted under Plato's name, but whose authenticity was doubted even in antiquity. Referred to as *Notheuomenoi* (spurious) or *Apocrypha*, they include Axiochus, Definitions, Demodocus, Epigrams, Eryxias, Halcyon, On Justice, On Virtue, and Sisyphus.

Thrasyllus' tetralogical arrangement is based on various factors, and does not claim to present the dialogues in their likely order of composition by Plato. Today the dialogues are often roughly classified into three groups, 'early,' 'middle,' and 'late,' based upon their presumed order of composition, and with the intention of tracing the likely development of Plato's thought. To determine the order of composition of the dialogues, scholars rely upon historical near certainties, internal references, and comparisons of format, content, and style. However, the order of the composition of the dialogues continues to arouse much debate and controversy.

Plato's authorship likely spanned some fifty years, from

the death of Socrates in 399BC to his own death in 348–7BC. The dialogues in the early group are relatively short in length. They are sometimes referred to as the Socratic dialogues because they set forth more of the 'real' Socrates, typically discussing ethical subjects with friends or with a supposed expert. Socrates uses elenchus to demonstrate to his interlocutors that they do not really understand the subject under discussion, and to stimulate the reader to participate in the reasoning process and perhaps to arrive at an independent conclusion. Examples of subjects under discussion are courage, as in the *Laches*, or temperance, as in the *Charmides*. The early group also includes several pieces surrounding the trial and execution of Socrates, namely, the *Euthyphro*, *Apology*, and *Crito*. The *Protagoras*, *Gorgias*, and *Meno* are considered either early transitional or middle period dialogues. Thus, the group of early dialogues may be held to comprise the *Euthyphro, Apology, Crito, Alcibiades, Laches, Charmides, Lysis, Ion, Greater Hippias, Lesser Hippias, Menexenus, Protagoras, Gorgias,* and *Meno*.

Starting from these beginnings, Plato gradually elaborated distinct philosophical ideas, such as his Theory of the Forms, which is developed in middle dialogues such as the *Symposium*, *Phaedo*, and *Republic*. In these dialogues the character Socrates is thought to be less of the real Socrates and more of a mouthpiece for Plato, and is accordingly more didactic, putting forth positive doctrines and no longer content merely to question and refute. The group of middle dialogues might be held to comprise the *Euthydemus, Cratylus, Phaedrus, Symposium, Phaedo, Republic, Parmenides,* and *Theaetetus*.

Compared to the early and middle dialogues, the late dialogues are longer and more philosophically challenging, but also lacking in dramatic power. The character Socrates stops taking an active part in the conversation, which is now more reminiscent of an *ex-cathedra* lecture than of a dialogue. Except in the *Timaeus*, the theory of the Forms is either absent or peripheral, suggesting that it had perhaps been abandoned by Plato. The group of late dialogues might be held to comprise the *Sophist, Statesman, Philebus, Timaeus, Critias,* and *Laws*. The *Laws* is the last and longest of Plato's dialogues and remained unpublished at the time of his death.

The Stephanus pagination
Modern editions and translations of Plato employ a system of referencing and organisation called the Stephanus pagination, after a 1578 edition of Plato by Henricus Stephanus (Henri Estienne). The text is divided into numbers which refer to the page numbers of the 1578 edition, and each number is further divided into equal sections a, b, c, d, and e. As the 1578 edition runs into multiple volumes, the page numbers repeat themselves, and must be used in conjunction with a title in order to refer uniquely. An example is 'Symposium 197a,' in which can be found the phrase, 'He whom Love touches not walks in darkness'.

Influence
After Plato's death, the Academy survived in one form or another for some 900 years until it was closed by the Christian emperor Justinian in 529AD. As part of his programme to enforce Christian orthodoxy, Justinian issued an edict declaring: 'Henceforth never again shall anyone lecture on philosophy or explain the laws in Athens'. By then Platonism had already exerted a profound influence on the development of Christian thought. In the first century AD, Philo of Alexandria harmonised Greek philosophy and Judaism to provide a philosophical foundation for the latter. Philo's example in turn inspired early Christian philosophers such as Origen and St Augustine, who considered Platonism and Neoplatonism to be the best available instruments with which to understand and defend the teachings of Scripture and Church tradition. 'Neoplatonism' is the modern term for a school of religious and mystical philosophy that took shape in the third century AD, founded by Plotinus and based on Platonism. In this context,

the specific importance of Neoplatonism is that its mystical dimension made it, and therefore Platonism, compatible with monotheism.

During mediaeval times, scholastic philosophers in the West did not have access to any of Plato's writings other than an incomplete Latin translation of the *Timaeus*. However, the study of Plato continued in the East, where Persian and Arab philosophers such as Al-Farabi, Avicenna, and Averroes wrote extensive commentaries on his writings. Plato's writings were re-introduced to the West by the Byzantine Platonist philosopher George Gemistos Plethon, whose lectures in Florence moved Cosimo de' Medici to found the *Accademia Platonica* in 1462. Cosimo de' Medici appointed Marsilio Ficino as head of the Academy, and commissioned him to translate all of Plato's writings into Latin. This Ficino translation rehabilitated Plato and exerted an important influence on the Renaissance movement, including on Cosimo's grandson, Lorenzo the Magnificent. In contrast to his pupil Aristotle, whose writings had never been lost, Plato was chiefly interested in moral philosophy, and held natural philosophy, that is, science, to be an inferior and unworthy type of knowledge. Raphael's Renaissance masterpiece, *The School of Athens* (c.1511), depicts Plato and Aristotle walking side by side, surrounded by a number of other philosophers and personalities of antiquity, including Socrates, Alcibiades, and several of the pre-Socratics. An elderly Plato is holding a copy of the *Timaeus* and pointing vertically to the lofty vault above their heads, whilst a younger Aristotle is holding a copy of his *Nichomachean Ethics* and gesturing horizontally towards the descending steps at their feet. As their gazes cross, one can imagine the Divine Teacher quoting from the *Timaeus*, 'As being is to becoming, so is truth to belief'. And The Philosopher perhaps quoting back from the *Nicomachean Ethics,* 'Plato is my friend, but truth is a greater friend still'.

In *Process and Reality* (1929), the philosopher Alfred North Whitehead wrote that 'the safest general characterisation of the European philosophical tradition is that it consists of a series of footnotes to Plato'. Plato thought that only philosophy can bring true understanding because it alone examines the presuppositions and assumptions that other subjects merely take for granted. He conceived of philosophy as a single discipline defined by a distinctive intellectual approach, and capable of carrying human thought far beyond the realms of common sense or everyday experience. He created and systematically elaborated upon all the principle branches of philosophy, including epistemology, metaphysics, philosophy of religion, aesthetics, ethics, and political philosophy. The unrivalled scope and incisiveness of his writings as well as their enduring aesthetic and emotional appeal have captured the hearts and minds of generation after generation of readers. Unlike the pre-Socratic philosophers who preceded him, Plato never spoke with his own voice. Instead, he presented readers with a variety of perspectives to engage with, leaving them free to reach their own, sometimes radically different, conclusions. 'No one', he said, 'ever teaches well who wants to teach, or governs well who wants to govern.'

SECTION II –
PLATO'S DIALOGUES

CHAPTER 1

Alcibiades

... your beauty, which is not you, is fading away,
just as your true self is beginning to bloom.

The Alcibiades features Socrates in a private conversation with a young Alcibiades who is about to enter into public life. Socrates says that, if Alcibiades intends to fulfil his ambition and advise the Athenians, then he must know more than they do, either because he has learned it from others or because he has discovered it for himself. However, he could only have been willing to do one or the other if there had once been a time when he thought that he did know what he now supposes to know.

Socrates asks what Alcibiades intends to advise the Athenians about. He notes that Alcibiades' entire schooling consisted in nothing more than writing, playing the lyre, and wrestling, and although Alcibiades is noble, rich, and good-looking, these qualities do not qualify him to advise the Athenians about anything. For example, there is no doubt that a builder could give the Athenians better advice about building than he could, regardless of whether the builder was great or little, rich or poor, fair or ugly. Thus, if a man is to give good advice about anything, it is not because he has riches, but because he has knowledge.

Alcibiades says that he intends to advise the Athenians 'about their own concerns,' which, he then specifies, means 'war and peace' and 'any other concerns of the state'. Socrates asks him to explain the meaning of 'better' in matters of making war and peace, and feigns surprise when he is unable to do so. Socrates then suggests that 'better' in matters of making war and peace means justice; since Alcibiades claims expertise in justice but has never had a teacher of justice, he must no doubt have discovered it for himself. However, he would only have been willing do so if there had once been a time when he thought that he did know what he now supposes to know. Was there ever such a time? Socrates recalls that, when Alcibiades was a boy, he used to play dice and charge his playmates with cheating; this suggests that, even then, he thought he knew what justice was.

Since Alcibiades never had a teacher of justice and never discovered it for himself, he cannot possibly know what justice is. When Alcibiades suggests that he learnt justice from the many, Socrates replies, 'Do you take refuge in them? I cannot say much for your teachers'. Socrates then argues that, since the many could hardly teach Alcibiades how to play draughts, it seems highly unlikely that they could teach him something as complex as justice. Alcibiades disagrees, and points out that it is from the many that he learnt Greek. Socrates replies that he was only able to learn Greek from the many because the many agreed with one another and with themselves about Greek words, and could thus be said to have knowledge of Greek. However, the many clearly do not agree with one another and with themselves about justice, and there is in fact no subject in which they could be at greater variance: whereas people do not go to war and kill one another over the principles of health and disease, it is an argument about the principles of justice and injustice that sparked the Trojan War, and many other wars besides. For this reason, Alcibiades could not have learnt justice from the many, and since he neither learned it from a teacher nor discovered it for himself, he cannot possibly know what justice is. 'For indeed, my dear fellow, the design which you meditate of teaching what you do not know, and have not taken any pains to learn, is downright insanity.'

Alcibiades rejoins that what the Athenians really want to know from him is not what course of action is the most just, but what course of action is the most *expedient*. Justice and expediency must be different things since many people who act unjustly profit from it and many people who act justly come to no good. Socrates replies that, even if this is so, Alcibiades cannot claim to know what is expedient, just as he cannot claim to know what is just. However, can Alcibiades even prove that the just is not always the expedient? When Alcibiades fails to come up with a proof, Socrates offers to prove just the opposite, so long as Alcibiades answers his questions. Alcibiades protests that it is Socrates who should be answering his questions, and the following exchange takes place:

S: *What, do you not wish to be persuaded?*
A: *Certainly I do.*
S: *And can you be persuaded better than out of your own mouth?*
A: *I think not.*

Socrates then argues through Alcibiades that if all that is just is honourable and all that is honourable is good, then all just things are also good. Alcibiades objects that some honourable things are evil and some dishonourable things are good; for example, a man who rescues a companion from the battlefield may be killed in the process, whereas a man who simply runs away may have his life spared. Socrates says that Alcibiades must mean that, whereas to rescue a companion from the battlefield is good in so much as it is honourable, it is evil in so much as it may result in death. But how can the same action be both good *and* evil? 'Nothing honourable, regarded as honourable, is evil; nor anything base, regarded

49

as base, good.' He who acts honourably acts well, and he who acts well is happy, and so the happy are those who obtain good by acting well and honourably. Whatever we find to be honourable, we also find to be good, and whatever we find to be good, we also find to be expedient. For, if all that is just is honourable, and all that is honourable is good, and all that is good is expedient, then all that is just is also expedient. To this, Alcibiades responds, 'I solemnly declare, Socrates, that I do not know what I am saying. Verily, I am in a strange state, for when you put questions to me I am of different minds in successive instants.'

Socrates says that Alcibiades is perplexed about justice because he is ignorant of justice *and* does not know that he is ignorant of justice. In contrast, he is not perplexed about how to ascend into heaven because, in this case, he knows that he is ignorant of how to ascend into heaven. Thus, a man need not be perplexed about that of which he is ignorant, so long as he knows that he is ignorant of it. On the other hand, if he thinks that he knows what he does not in fact know, then he will make mistakes, and his biggest mistakes will be concerned with the greatest matters, namely, matters of the just, the honourable, the good, and the expedient.

> *My good friend, you are wedded to ignorance of the most disgraceful kind, and of this you are convicted, not by me, but out of your own mouth and by your own argument; wherefore also you rush into politics before you are educated. Neither is your case to be deemed singular. For I might say the same of almost all our statesmen with the exception, perhaps, of your guardian, Pericles.*

Socrates argues that a man who is wise in anything should be able to impart his wisdom, and thereby give an excellent proof of it. However, Pericles never made anyone wise, not even his two sons, Xanthippus and Paralus, or his two wards,

Alcibiades and his brother Cleinias. Alcibiades promises that he will, with Socrates' help, take greater pains about himself, so that he might get the better of other politicians. Socrates points out that Alcibiades' true rivals are not other politicians but the Lacedaemonian and Persian kings, and that they can only ever be overcome by pains and skill, and by following the Delphian inscription to 'Know thyself'.

The purpose of making such great efforts is to achieve the virtue of good men, but what is this virtue? Perhaps a man is good in respect of that in which he is wise and evil in respect of that in which he is unwise. However, if this were so, a shoemaker who was wise with respect to making shoes and unwise with respect to making garments would be both good and evil, which is impossible. So perhaps a man is good insofar as he is able to rule the city, that is, rule over other men who have dealings with one another? Alcibiades is at great pains to explain the virtue of good men and variously suggests that it is 'the better order and preservation of the city,' 'friendship and agreement,' and 'when everyone does his own work'.

> A: *But, indeed, Socrates, I do not know what I am*
> *saying; and I have long been, unconsciously to*
> *myself, in a most disgraceful state.*
> S: *Nevertheless, cheer up; at fifty, if you had*
> *discovered your deficiency, you would have*
> *been too old, and the time for taking care of*
> *yourself would have passed away, but yours*
> *is just the age at which the discovery should*
> *be made.*

What, asks Socrates, is the meaning of a man taking care of himself? Clearly, the art is not one that makes any of our possessions better, but one that makes us ourselves better. Just as we could not know what art makes a shoe better if we did not know a shoe, so we cannot know what art makes us ourselves better if we do not know ourselves. However, self-knowledge is a difficult thing to which few attain to. Man is either one of three things: body, soul, or body and soul together. Man uses his body like a harper uses his harp, and just as a harper is not his harp, so man is not his body. If man is not his body and yet rules over it, then perhaps he is body and soul together. This seems impossible, for how could body and soul rule united when body is so evidently subject to soul? Thus, either man has no real existence or man is soul. 'And if the proof, although not perfect, be sufficient, we shall be satisfied...' When a man bids another to know himself, he would have him know his soul. Neither the physician, nor the trainer, nor any craftsman knows his soul, for which reason their arts are accounted vulgar, and are not such as a good man would practise. He who cherishes his body cherishes not himself but that which belongs to him, and he who cherishes money cherishes neither himself nor that which belongs to him, but that which is at one stage further removed from himself. He who loves the person of Alcibiades does not love Alcibiades but the belongings of Alcibiades, whereas he who loves Alcibiades' soul is the true lover. The lover of the body goes away when the flower of youth fades, but the lover of the soul does not go away, so long as the soul follows after virtue.

> S: *And I am the lover who goes not away, but*
> *remains with you, when you are no longer*
> *young and the rest are gone?*
> A: *Yes, Socrates; and therein you do well, and I*
> *hope that you will remain.*
> S: *Then you must try to look your best...*

> *...I loved you for your own sake, whereas other*
> *men love what belongs to you; and your*
> *beauty, which is not you, is fading away,*
> *just as your true self is beginning to bloom.*
> *And I will never desert you, if you are not*
> *spoiled and deformed by the Athenian people;*

*for the danger which I most fear is that you
will become a lover of the people and will be
spoiled by them. Many a noble Athenian has
been ruined in this way.*

To know ourselves, then, we must have a perfect knowledge of
the soul. But how are we to gain this knowledge? If one were
to say to the eye, 'See thyself,' the eye should look into a mirror
to see itself. Since the pupil of the eye is just like a mirror, an
eye can see itself by looking into an eye. Similarly, the soul
can see itself by looking into the soul and, particularly, into
that part of the soul which has most to do with wisdom, and
which is therefore most akin to the divine. Self-knowledge is,
in fact, no other than wisdom, and unless we find it, we can
never know our own good and evil, nor our belongings, nor the
belongings of our belongings, nor the belongings of others, and
nor the affairs of states. If he who had not found self-knowledge
were to become a statesman, he would fall into error and be
miserable, and would make everyone else miserable too. He
who is not wise cannot be happy, and it is better for such a
man to be commanded by a superior in wisdom. Since what
is better is also more becoming, slavery is more becoming for
such a man. And the condition of a slave is to be avoided, not
by the help of Pericles, not even by the help of Socrates, but by
the help of God.

CHAPTER 2

Laches

We make our decisions based on knowledge,
not on numbers.

The *Laches* opens with Lysimachus and Melesias asking Laches and Nicias for advice as to whether or not their sons should be trained to fight in armour. Lysimachus is the son of Aristides, who was one of the ten commanders under Miltiades at the Battle of Marathon. Melesias is the son of Thucydides, who had for many years been the leader of the Athenian conservative faction. The sons of Lysimachus and Melesias are named after their celebrated grandfathers, that is, Aristides and Thucydides. Unlike Aristides and Thucydides, Lysimachus and Melesias are not particularly distinguished; they are keen that their sons should avoid their fate, and live up to the honour attached to their names. Laches and Nicias are two distinguished Athenian generals. In 421BC Nicias led peace negotiations with Sparta which led to the so-called 'Peace of Nicias'. He was executed eight years later, following the total defeat of the Athenians at the Battle of Syracuse. In the *Laches*, Lysimachus and Melesias are asking Laches and Nicias for advice on the basis that they are distinguished generals, and on the basis that they have already raised children. Laches expresses surprise that Lysimachus and

54

Melesias have not consulted Socrates on the matter, since Socrates is not only a famed teacher of youth, but also a shining example of courage. Laches recalls Socrates' behaviour during the retreat from Delium, and says that Athens may have emerged victorious if only the other Athenians could have behaved like him. Lysimachus accordingly asks Socrates to join in the conversation.

Lysimachus asks Socrates whether he approves of training to fight in armour. Socrates replies that he himself is relatively young and inexperienced, and they should first listen to Laches and Nicias and learn from them. Nicias says that he approves of training to fight in armour since it is in any case a form of bodily exercise. Furthermore, it inspires boldness and braveness in battle; it is useful in battle, especially once the ranks are broken; and it leads to the study of the science of tactics and thence to the study of the 'art of the general'. Laches says that it is difficult to argue against training to fight in armour, since in theory it seems like a good idea to learn about everything. However, he suspects that fighting in armour may not be a real subject of knowledge or, at least, not a very important one. In fact, he has met several men who are skilled at fighting in armour, but who have never been distinguished in war. Stesilaus, for example, is a seemingly competent teacher of fighting in armour, but is so poor on the battlefield that he attracts laughter from the other men. Laches' considered opinion is thus that he disapproves of training to fight in armour.

Given that Nicias and Laches are in disagreement, Lysimachus asks Socrates to cast the deciding vote. Socrates replies that, 'We make our decisions based on knowledge, not on numbers,' meaning that decisions should be based on knowledge, rather than on popular sentiment. Thus, they must first find out whether anyone present is an expert in the subject under debate, in which case they should listen to his opinion and disregard that of everyone else. If no one present is an expert in the subject under debate, then they must look for someone who is. Socrates reminds the company that the subject under debate is ultimately a very important one, since it could determine whether the sons of Lysimachus and Melesias turn out to be worthwhile persons, rather than 'put their ancestors to shame by turning out to be worthless'.

But even before they can find an expert in the subject under debate, they must first find out what the subject is really about. Socrates gives the example of a man who takes counsel about whether or not he should use a certain medicine to anoint his eyes. Is he taking counsel about the medicine, or about his eyes? Socrates argues that whenever a man considers a thing for the sake of another thing, he is in fact taking counsel not about the former, but about the latter thing. In other words, one must focus more on the end than on the means. Thus, the subject under debate is in fact the souls of the young men. Socrates asks whether anyone present is an expert in the care of the soul, and has had good teachers in the subject.

Socrates discounts himself from being an expert in the care of the soul, saying that he has never been able to afford a teacher in the subject, even though he has always longed after one. However, Nicias and Laches are both wealthier and more experienced than he is, and thus stand a much better chance of being experts in the care of the soul. Socrates asks them whether they have been a discoverer of such things or whether they have been anyone's pupil in them. If they have been either one or the other, whom have they already made into fine men by their care? For no one, he says, would be so foolish as to 'begin pottery on a wine jar' (the wine jar being the largest pot).

Nicias is annoyed at Socrates' blatant sarcasm, and says that he realised some time ago that, if Socrates were present, the conversation would 'not be about the boys but about ourselves'. Laches says that he is both a lover and a hater of such discussions. He loves them when a man is worthy of the wise words that he utters, since there is then a harmony between the man and his words. 'And such a man,' he says, 'seems to me to be genuinely musical, producing the most beautiful harmony, not on the lyre or some other pleasurable instrument, but actually rendering his own life harmonious by fitting his deeds to his words in a truly Dorian mode... the only harmony that is genuinely Greek.' Despite the fact that Socrates has already discounted himself as an expert in the care of the soul, Laches invites him to teach them about the subject. This is purely on the basis that Laches has had firsthand experience of Socrates' deeds, and has invariably found them to be virtuous.

But what, asks Socrates, does virtue consist in? As he deems it too ambitious to investigate all of virtue, he instead chooses to investigate only one of its parts, namely, courage, since courage is the part of virtue that appears to be most closely related to fighting in armour. Socrates questions Laches about courage, asking him to state what courage is. Laches thinks that this is an easy question, and replies that courage is when a man is willing to remain at his post and defend himself against the enemy, like Socrates once did at Delium. Socrates objects that a man who flees from his post can also sometimes be considered to be courageous. He gives the examples of the Scythian cavalry, who fight both in pursuing and in retreating, and of the hero Aeneas who, according to Homer, was always fleeing on his horses. Homer praised Aeneas for his knowledge of fear, and called him the 'counsellor of fear'.

Laches objects that Aeneas and the Scythian cavalry are cases concerning horsemen and chariots, not hoplites (foot soldiers). For this reason, Socrates also gives the example of the Spartan hoplites at the Battle of Plataea, who fled from the enemy but turned back to fight once the enemy lines had broken. What Socrates really wants to know is what courage is in every instance, for the hoplite, for the horseman, and for every sort of warrior, and also for those who 'show courage in illness and poverty,' 'are brave in the face of pain and fear,' and so on. What is it that all these instances of courage share in common? For example, quickness can be found in running, in speaking, or in playing the lyre, and in each of these instances, 'quickness' can be defined as 'the quality that accomplishes much in a little time'. Is there a similar, single definition of 'courage' for every instance of courage?

Laches defines courage as a sort of endurance of the soul. Socrates says that this cannot be, since endurance can be accompanied by folly rather than by wisdom, in which case it is harmful. Courage, in contrast, is always a fine thing. Laches accordingly revises his definition, and says that courage is wise endurance. Who, asks Socrates, is the more courageous: the man who is willing to hold out in battle in the knowledge that he is in a stronger position, or the man in the opposite camp who is willing to hold out nonetheless? Laches admits that the second man is clearly the more courageous, even though his endurance is more foolish than that of the first man. Yet foolish endurance is both disgraceful and harmful, whereas courage is always a fine, noble thing.

Despite their obvious confusion, Socrates insists that they should persevere with their enquiry 'so that courage itself won't make fun of us for not searching for it courageously'. Laches still thinks he knows what courage is, but does not understand why he cannot express it in words. Nicias says that he once heard from Socrates' mouth that each of us is good with respect to that in which he is wise, and bad in respect to that in which he is ignorant. Thus, courage must be some sort of knowledge or wisdom. If courage is some sort of knowledge, what, asks Socrates, is it the knowledge of? Nicias replies that courage is the knowledge of the fearful and the hopeful in war and in every other sphere or situation.

Laches accuses Nicias of 'talking nonsense,' and holds that wisdom is a different thing from courage. Laches' argument, says Nicias, is motivated by nothing more than a desire to prove him wrong, because Laches was proven wrong just a moment ago, and cannot accept that Nicias might do better than him. To buttress his argument, Laches asks Nicias to consider the case of an illness, in which the doctor is the one who knows best what is to be feared, but the patient is the one who is courageous. Nicias retorts that a doctor's knowledge amounts to no more than an ability to describe health and disease, whereas the patient has knowledge of whether his illness is more to be feared than his recovery. In other words, the patient knows what is to be feared and what is to be hoped. Socrates says that if Nicias means that courage is knowledge of the grounds of fear and hope, then courage is very rare amongst men, and animals could never be called 'courageous,' but at most 'fearless'. Nicias agrees with this, and adds that the same is also true for children: 'Or do you really suppose I call all children courageous, who fear nothing because they have no sense?'

Socrates next proposes to investigate the grounds of fear and hope. Fear is produced by anticipated evil things, but not by evil things that have happened or that are happening. In contrast, hope is produced by anticipated good things or by anticipated non-evil things. Nicias agrees with Socrates that courage amounts to knowledge of just these things. Socrates argues further that for any science of knowledge, there is not one science of the past, one of the present, and one of the future: knowledge of the past, the present, and the future are not different types of knowledge, but the same type of knowledge. Thus, courage is not simply knowledge of fearful things and hopeful things, but knowledge of all things, including those that are in the present and in the past. A man who possessed such knowledge could not be described as lacking in courage, but nor could he be described as lacking in any of the other virtues such as justice, piety, or temperance. Thus, by trying to define courage, which is a part of virtue, they have succeeded in defining virtue itself. Virtue is knowledge.

Nicias and Laches are suitably impressed, and conclude that Socrates should take care of the education of the sons of Lysimachus and Melesias. Socrates replies that, whilst it would be 'a terrible thing to be unwilling to join in assisting any man to become as good as possible,' he still does not understand virtue. He suggests instead that they should continue seeking the best possible teacher for the boys, and also for themselves. 'And if anyone laughs at us because we think it worthwhile to spend our time in school at our age, then I think we should confront him with the saying of Homer, 'Modesty is not a good mate for a needy man."

CHAPTER 3

Charmides

*He said the soul was treated with certain charms,
my dear Charmides, and that these charms were
beautiful words.*

The cast of the *Charmides* consists of Socrates, Socrate's friend Critias, and Critias' youthful ward and nephew Charmides. Both Critias and Charmides were relatives of Plato, whose mother Perictione was sister to Charmides and niece to Critias. The dialogue takes place in 432BC, upon Socrates' return to Athens from service at the battle of Potidaea. Its subject is the virtue of *sophrosyne*, usually translated as 'temperance'. *Sophrosyne* derives from an 'ordered soul' and is the aristocrat's virtue *par excellence*. It translates into a sense of dignity and self-command and a consciousness of one's legitimate duties in relation to others and to oneself. The fact that both Charmides and Critias later became notorious for their involvement with the Thirty Tyrants should not be lost on readers. Both men died at the Battle of Munychia in 404 or 403BC, fighting against the forces of the democratic Athenians in exile.

The scene of the Charmides is the Taureas palaestra, one of Socrates' old haunts. Socrates has just returned to Athens from service at the battle of Potidaea and is greeted by a number of old friends and acquaintances, who ask him a litany of questions about the army and the battle. Socrates in turn asks them about the state of Athens, and whether there are any youths who are particularly wise or beautiful. Critias tells Socrates about Charmides, who then walks in with a crowd of admirers in train. Socrates is taken by Charmides' beauty, and convinces Critias to beckon him over. When Charmides sits down, Socrates catches a glimpse of the 'inwards of his garment' and is aroused by a 'wild-beast appetite'. Charmides has been suffering from headaches, and Socrates tells him about a charm for headaches which he has recently learned about from one of the mystical physicians to the king of Thrace. According to this physician, however, it is best to cure the soul before curing the body, since health and happiness ultimately depend on the state of the soul.

As temperance is the marker of the health of the soul, Socrates asks Charmides whether he thinks that he is sufficiently temperate. Charmides replies that to claim that he is sufficiently temperate would be boastful, whereas to claim that he is lacking in temperance would be an untoward self-accusation. Socrates agrees with him, and suggests instead that they inquire into the question together. If Charmides is temperate, he must surely have an opinion about what temperance is? After some hesitation, Charmides offers that temperance is doing everything quietly, 'a sort of quietness'. Socrates replies that temperance cannot be a sort of quietness because temperance is always a good thing, whereas there are many things – for example, running, reading, and remembering – in which quickness and sharpness are better than slowness and quietness. If these things were done 'slowly or quietly,' they would be done badly and thus not temperately. Charmides next offers that temperance is modesty, since it makes people ashamed and bashful. Socrates quotes Homer in saying that 'modesty is not a good mate for a needy man,' so as to demonstrate on authority that modesty can be both a good thing and a bad thing. In contrast, temperance can only ever be a good thing. Thus, temperance cannot be modesty. Charmides suddenly recalls something that he once heard from 'someone,' namely, that temperance is 'minding one's own business'. Socrates replies that if this is so, then the law of a city that is well governed and so temperately governed would command each man to 'weave and wash his own cloak, make his own shoes and oil flask and scraper, and perform everything else by this same principle...' As this would be absurd, temperance cannot amount to 'minding one's own business'.

Critias appears uncomfortable and Socrates suspects that he may be the 'someone' from whom Charmides once heard that temperance is 'minding one's own business'. Socrates asks Critias to defend his position against the charge that craftsmen who make and do things for themselves as well as for others can nonetheless be temperate. Critias quotes Hesiod in saying that 'work is no disgrace', and argues that *making* something for others is not the same as *doing* something for others. Insofar as it is useful and noble, a man's work is his own business, and so the man who works can nonetheless be temperate. Socrates objects to Critias' hairsplitting over the definitions of doing, making, and working, which he compares to the 'endless distinctions' of Prodicus, a pedantic sophist who insisted upon the correct use of names and the accurate discrimination between near synonyms. Perhaps Critias simply means that temperance is the doing of good things? Critias agrees that this is in fact what he means, but Socrates is not yet satisfied: temperance cannot be the doing of good things, since a man can act temperately and yet not be conscious of whether he acted for better or for worse. Critias next offers that temperance is self-knowledge, and argues that the Delphic oracle's commandment to 'Know thyself' is in fact a commandment to be temperate. Socrates argues that, if temperance is self-knowledge, then it is a kind of knowledge or science such as medicine or architecture. If the product of medicine is health and the product of architecture is houses, what is the product of temperance? Critias replies that not all the sciences need have similar sorts of products; the product of geometry, for example, is nothing like the product of medicine or the product of architecture. Socrates agrees with Critias on this point. However, with respect to sciences such as geometry or medicine or architecture, one can at least say what they are the science of. Critias advances that temperance is the science of itself and of the other sciences, and accuses Socrates of refuting him for the sake of refuting him and ignoring the real question at issue. Socrates says that he is trying to refute him because he is searching for the truth, primarily for his sake 'but perhaps also for the sake of my friends'.

Socrates continues that, if temperance is the science of itself and of the other sciences, then a man with temperance is able to know both what he knows and does not know, as well as what other people think they know and do not know. Socrates asks whether it is possible for a man to know what he knows and does not know. For example, could there be a form of hearing that 'hears no sound but hears itself and the other hearings and non-hearings?' He argues that it is in the nature of a science to be the science *of* something, since it seems that everything has a defining relation to something else, and never to itself. Socrates considers possible examples of something that has a defining relation to itself, such as 'the power of heat to burn' or 'the power of self-motion'. However, he remains unconvinced by these examples. Even if the science of itself exists, how might it lead one to self-knowledge, and how might this self-knowledge be useful? Self-knowledge may not enable one to differentiate between what one knows and does not know, since knowing about what one knows and does not know is not the same as knowing about the knowledge or ignorance of something specific, such as medicine or architecture. Thus, self-knowledge may enable one to know *that* one knows, but not *what* one knows. For instance, a man who is temperate, and thus wise, could not have knowledge of good or bad medicine unless he was himself a doctor. In an ideal, and therefore temperate, city, every person would know exactly what he did and did not know, as a result of which everything would proceed perfectly. The fact that such an ideal city does not exist suggests that neither does such knowledge. But perhaps this is asking too much of such knowledge, which perhaps does nothing more than assist and facilitate the study of specific things such as architecture or medicine. Socrates returns once more to the notion of the ideal city and doubts that its inhabitants would be truly happy. However, he does not explain why.

Socrates concludes that their inquiry into temperance has ended in *aporia* (a state of inconclusive non-knowledge), not only because too many concessions were made (such as, for example, that it is possible for a man to know what he does not know, or that there is such a thing as a science of science), but also because it did not seem that temperance or wisdom have any use. Socrates accuses himself of being a worthless inquirer and a 'babbler,' and encourages Charmides to go on believing that temperance is a great good. Charmides replies that he can hardly be expected to know whether or not he is sufficiently temperate, if Socrates and Critias cannot even define temperance. Despite this, he asks to become Socrates' pupil and to be 'charmed by him everyday'.

CHAPTER 4

Lysis

*Yea, by the dog of Egypt, I should greatly prefer
a real friend to all the gold of Darius, or even to
Darius himself.*

Socrates is going from the Academy straight to the Lyceum
when he comes across Hippothales and Ctesippus. Hippothales
accosts Socrates and asks him to join them in conversation
in the newly erected palaestra. Socrates asks whether there
is a teacher there, and Hippothales replies that Socrates' old
friend and admirer Miccus is there. Socrates asks who the
favourite amongst them is. Hippothales replies that there
is no clear favourite, so Socrates asks him who *his* favourite
is. When Hippothales blushes, Socrates says, '...I see that
you are not only in love, but already far gone in your love.
Simple and foolish as I am, the Gods have given me the
power of understanding affections of this kind'. Ctesippus
gently mocks Hippothales for being so coy, when he spends
all his time deafening his friends with praises of Lysis and
even with poems and songs dedicated to him. Socrates asks
to hear some of these poems and songs, but Hippothales flatly
denies their existence. So Socrates asks instead for an account
of Hippothales' general approach to Lysis. It turns out that
Hippothales has been praising Lysis' ancestors, and nothing

much else. Socrates says that such praises are directed not at Lysis, but at Hippothales himself as the eventual lover of Lysis. He also chides Hippothales for inflating Lysis with pride and vain-glory, and thus making him all the more difficult to seduce. Hippothales asks Socrates to advise him as to what he should be doing. Socrates offers to show Hippothales how to talk to Lysis, rather than sing his praises. With this in mind, the trio head for the palaestra to meet with Lysis.

They begin talking together and soon enough Lysis' friend Menexenus takes a seat beside them, followed by Lysis and a number of other youths. Hippothales stands in the crowd, out of sight of Lysis. Socrates asks Menexenus which of the two youths is the elder and which is the nobler, to which he replies that both are a matter of dispute. He then asks him which is the fairest, to which they simply laugh. He says that he cannot ask them which is the richest, since they are friends, and friends have all things in common. At this point, Menexenus is called away by the gym master. Socrates turns to Lysis and puts it to him that his parents keep him in the condition of a slave by forbidding him to do things such as drive the chariot or even the mule cart. Lysis says that the reason for this is that he is not yet of age. Socrates points out that they let him do many other similarly important things such as read and write for the family or tune the lyre. Lysis says that the reason for this is that he understands certain things but not yet others. Socrates this time agrees with him: 'the reason is not any deficiency of years, but a deficiency of knowledge'. He then asks Lysis whether his parents, the neighbours, the people of Athens, and even the king of Asia would not trust him to manage their affairs if they felt certain that he was wise enough to do so. Socrates concludes that 'in things which we know everyone will trust us'. Conversely, no one will trust us in things which we do not know, not even our parents or closest friends. In fact, if we had no wisdom at all, we would not even have any friends to speak of, since we would be of no use to anyone. Not even our parents would love us.

> *And therefore, my boy, if you are wise, all men will*
> *be your friends and kindred, for you will be useful*
> *and good; but if you are not wise, neither father,*
> *not mother, nor kindred, nor anyone else will be*
> *your friends.*

Socrates says that, on the basis that he still needs a teacher, Lysis is not yet wise, and therefore has nothing to be conceited about. Lysis agrees with him. Socrates almost makes the mistake of calling out to Hippothales, who is 'in great excitement and confusion about what has been said'. When Menexenus returns, Lysis begins whispering into Socrates' ear. He asks Socrates to debate with Menexenus, since Menexenus is very pugnacious, and needs to be brought down a peg or two.

Before continuing, Socrates tells the youth that, whereas some people desire horses, or dogs, or gold, or honour, he would rather have a good friend than the best cock or quail in the world: 'Yea, by the dog of Egypt, I should greatly prefer a real friend to all the gold of Darius, or even to Darius himself: I am such a lover of friends as that'. Lysis and Menexenus appear to possess this treasure in each other, so perhaps Menexenus can tell him: when one person loves another, which of the two becomes the friend of the other, the lover or the beloved? Menexenus replies that either may be the friend of the other, that is, that they both are friends. Socrates says that this cannot be the case, since one person may love another who does not love him back, or even hates him. Menexenus offers that, unless they both love, neither is a friend. Socrates argues that, if nothing which does not love in return is beloved by a lover, then there can be no lovers of things such as horses, dogs, wine, or wisdom. Thus, what is beloved, whether or not it loves in return, may be dear to the lover of it. This is the case, for example, with children who are too young to love, or who hate their parents for punishing them. This suggests that the beloved is the friend of the lover and the hated one is the enemy of the hater, but the implication is that many men are loved by their enemies and hated by their friends, which seems absurd. Thus, neither the lover not the beloved can always be said to be a friend to each other.

Socrates suggests to Menexenus that they may have been wrong in their conclusions. At this point, Lysis interjects that they must have been wrong. Lysis blushes, but Socrates is pleased at his interest in their conversation. Socrates turns for guidance to the poets and philosophers, who say that 'like loves like'. Socrates argues that this aphorism must only apply to good people, since bad people are in some way unlike themselves and are just as likely to hate other bad people as anyone else. This implies that good people are friends with other good people, whereas bad people do not have any friends at all. Socrates thinks that they can now answer 'Who are friends?' with 'The good are friends'. However, he remains unconvinced, because like cannot be of any use to like, and if two people cannot be of any use to each other, then they cannot love each other. It remains possible that they love each other in the sense that they are both like because they are both good, but the good is by definition self-sufficient, and so has no desire for friendship.

> *What place then is there for friendship, if, when absent, good men have no need of one another (for even when alone they are sufficient for themselves), and when present have no use of one another? How can such persons ever be induced to value one another?*

Socrates suggests that they may once again have been wrong. He quotes Hesiod in saying that 'the most like are most full of envy, strife, and hatred of one another, and the most unlike, of friendship.' Menexenus thinks that Hesiod is right in saying that friendship is born not in likeness but in unlikeness, but Socrates remains unconvinced. He argues that Hesiod implies not only that the enemy is the friend of the friend and the friend the friend of the enemy, but also that the just man is the friend of the unjust, the good man the friend of the bad, and so on. This, he says, is simply monstrous. Thus, neither like and like nor unlike and unlike can be friends.

Socrates next suggests that that which is the friend of the good is neither the good nor the bad, but that which is neither good nor bad. Furthermore, the good is also the beautiful, that 'soft, smooth, slippery thing' that 'easily slips in and permeates our souls'. As like and like cannot be friends, the neither good nor bad cannot be friends with the neither good nor bad and, as no one can be friends with the bad, they cannot be friends with the bad either. Thus, the neither good nor bad must be friends with the good and the beautiful. And whilst the good and the beautiful cannot be friends with the good and beautiful or with the bad, there is nothing to stop them from being friends with the neither good nor bad. For example, the body is neither good nor bad, but if it is corrupted by sickness, which is bad, then it becomes the friend of the physician. The fact that the body is corrupted by something bad does not make it bad, just as covering Menexenus' auburn locks with white lead does not make them white, inasmuch as they are still really auburn. Socrates concludes that they have discovered the nature of friendship: 'it is the love which by reason of the presence of evil the neither good nor evil has of the good, either in the soul, or in the body, or anywhere'. However, an 'unaccountable suspicion' comes over him, and he feels that this conclusion is untrue.

In essence, Socrates argues that, if that which is neither good nor bad is the friend of the good because of the bad, and for the sake of the good and the friend, then the friend is a friend for the sake of the friend, and because of the enemy. Thus, medicine is a friend for the sake of health, and health is also dear and, if dear, then dear for the sake of something, something that must also be dear, and so on. Is there then not a first principle of friendship or dearness for the sake of which all other things are dear? For example, if a father values his son above all things, he also values other things for the sake of his son. If, for instance, his son had drunk hemlock, and he thought that wine would save him, then he would value the wine and even the vessel which contains it. However, it is not really the wine or the vessel that he is valuing, but his son. 'That which is only dear to us for the sake of something else is improperly said to be dear, but the truly dear is that in which all these so called dear friendships terminate.' Socrates infers that the truly dear is the good, but points out that the good appears to be loved not for its own sake but for the sake of the bad. However, if the bad were eradicated, love and friendship would still exist, suggesting that there must be some other cause of friendship. Socrates suggests that desire is the cause of friendship, and that he who desires, desires that of which he is in want, and therefore that which is dear to him. Thus, desire, love, and friendship appear to be of the congenial, whether in soul, character, manners, or form. Socrates says that if love is of the congenial, then the true lover must necessarily have his love returned, at which Hippothales changes 'into all manner of colours'. However, he points out that this theory fails if the congenial is only the like, since they have already demonstrated that the like cannot be friends with the like.

> *Then what is to be done? Or rather is there anything to be done? I can only, like the wisemen who argue in courts, sum up the arguments: If neither the beloved, nor the lover, nor the like, nor the unlike, nor the good, nor the congenial, nor any other of whom we spoke – for there were such a number of them that I cannot remember all – if none of these are friends, I know not what remains to be said... O Menexenus and Lysis, how ridiculous that you two boys, and I, an old boy, who would fain be one of you, should imagine ourselves to be friends – this is what*

the bystanders will go away and say – and as yet we have not been able to discover what is a friend!

CHAPTER 5

Greater Hippias (Hippias Major)

*...when people who are trying to make laws fail
to make them good, they have failed to make
them lawful – indeed, to make them law.
What do you say?*

Hippias is a sophist and an ambassador from Elis who makes a lot of money by giving private tutorials and public displays of wisdom wherever he goes. In this dialogue, Socrates tests Hippias' claims to wisdom. Hippias tells Socrates that he has been sent from Elis on a diplomatic mission to Athens. Socrates asks him why most people who were famous for their wisdom kept themselves away from affairs of state. Hippias replies that this is because they were too weak to be successful in both the private and the public spheres. Socrates suggests that it is just as with early craftsmen, who were worthless compared to modern ones: the wisdom of thinkers such as Hippias, Gorgias, and Protagoras is so great that they are able to conduct both private business and public business, whereas earlier thinkers were so dull that they did not even see fit to charge fees. Perhaps they simply did not realise the great value of money. Hippias tells Socrates that he has made a fortune from travelling from place to place and giving private tutorials and public displays of wisdom – more money, in fact, than any other two sophists put together. Socrates says that the amount of money that one makes is a mark of one's wisdom, and that Hippias is proof enough of the superiority of modern thinkers over ancient ones. Witness Anaxagoras, who inherited a large sum of money and lost it all through neglect – the very opposite of Hippias.

Despite his financial acumen, Hippias has been unable to make any money in Sparta. Socrates says that this is surprising, given that Sparta is a law-abiding city, and that what is most highly prized in a law-abiding city is virtue. How can it be that a teacher of virtue such as Hippias is unable to make any money in Sparta? Hippias explains that there is an ancestral tradition in Sparta that forbids the Spartans from changing the laws of their city and from giving their sons any education that is contrary to established customs. Socrates argues that lawmakers make laws such that they are to the greatest good of the city; if they are not, then they are not lawful, and therefore not laws. Hippias agrees with Socrates, and deplores the fact that ordinary people do not use words as precisely as he does. If what is more beneficial is more lawful, then surely Hippias' education is more lawful than the Lacedaemonian education. Thus, the Spartans are breaking the law by not giving Hippias their money. Socrates asks what it is that the Spartans like hearing from him. Hippias replies that they do not like hearing about subjects such as astronomy or arithmetic, but only about ancient history. In fact, he will be giving a speech on ancient history in two days' time. The speech begins with Neoptolemus, son of Achilles, asking the wise and elderly Nestor to tell him what sort of activities are fine (see the *Lesser Hippias*).

Socrates says that he has just been criticising the speech of 'an acquaintance'. This man asked him how he knew what sorts of things are fine (*kalon* – beautiful, excellent, noble) and what sorts of things are foul. Unfortunately, he could not give the man an answer, and so had to leave. Perhaps Hippias, in all his wisdom, could give him an answer to take to the man? Hippias says that the question is an easy one, but Socrates insists on playing the part of the man and taking the other side of the argument. Socrates says that, just as it is by wisdom that wise people are wise, and by justice that just things are just, so it is by the fine that fine things are fine. But what sort of thing is the fine? Hippias cannot see any difference between a fine thing and the fine, and thinks that there is none. So he offers that a fine girl is a fine thing. Still playing the part of the man, Socrates asks whether a fine Elean mare, a fine lyre, or a fine pot, are not also fine things. Hippias concedes that they are, even though a fine pot is not worth judging compared to a fine horse or a fine girl. Socrates asks whether not even the finest girl is foul when compared to a goddess. If so, how can a fine thing be a fine girl? In any case, there are an infinite number of fine things besides fine girls. What is it that makes each of these things fine? Hippias offers that the fine is gold, since anything can be made fine by the simple addition of gold. Socrates argues that the fine cannot be gold, since Phidias' great statue of Athena at the Parthenon is mostly made out of ivory and precious stones. Did Phidias choose these materials out of ignorance? Also, a spoon made out of fig wood is better for stirring soup than a spoon made out of gold, so who is to say that the spoon made out of fig wood is not the finer? Hippias next offers that the fine is to be rich and respected:

> *I say, then, that it is always finest, both for every man and in every place, to be rich, healthy, and honoured by the Greeks, to arrive at old age, to make a fine memorial to his parents when they die, and to have a fine, grand burial from his own children.*

Socrates says that if he gave the man that answer, the man would probably beat him with a stick. What of Achilles or Heracles, who were buried before their parents? Is that which is fine for men not also fine for heroes and gods?

Tiring of Hippias' efforts, Socrates suggests that that which is the fine is that which is appropriate. However, he is unsure about this definition, since the appropriate may merely make things appear to be fine, rather than be fine. Perhaps the fine is that which is useful? If the useful is that which is able to accomplish a particular thing, then ability is fine, and inability is foul. However, people are able to accomplish both good things *and* bad things, so the fine cannot be that which is useful. Hippias suggests that the fine can be that which is useful, *if it is useful for doing good things*. If this is so, says Socrates, then the fine is the beneficial, that is, the maker of the good. The implication is that the fine cannot also be the good, since (according to logic) a cause must be different from its effect if it is not be the cause of itself. Both Socrates and Hippias think that this is preposterous, and so the definition is dropped.

Socrates next offers that the fine is that which is pleasant through hearing and sight. However, he is quick to point out that this definition excludes the higher fine things such as laws and activities, as well as that which is pleasant through the other senses. In what way is that which is pleasant through hearing and sight different from that which is pleasant through the other senses? Put differently, what is it that makes fine that which is pleasant through hearing and sight? Whatever it is, it must belong to both hearing and sight in common, and also to each one alone, or else they would not both and each be fine. In most cases, what applies to A and B also applies to A alone and to B alone, but there are some rare cases in which what applies to A and B does *not* apply to A alone and to B alone. For example, the sum of A and B is even-numbered, whereas A alone and B alone are odd-numbered. Luckily, the fine does not appear to be one of those rare cases, for which reason it also applies to A alone and to B alone. However, if the fine belongs to A alone and to B alone, then that which is pleasant through A and B is no longer fine, since 'through A and B' implies that only both can be fine, and not each one alone.

Hippias berates Socrates for his 'babbling nonsense,' and says that he should give up what he does to practice the art of the orator, which, in contrast, consists in making fine and convincing speeches. Socrates says that wise men such as Hippias berate him for spending time on things that are silly and small and worthless, whereas the man with whom he lives berates him for talking of the fine when he cannot even say what it is. All he really knows is that which the Greek proverb says,

'What's fine is hard'.

CHAPTER 6

Lesser Hippias (Hippias Minor)

It is, then, in the nature of the good man to do injustice voluntarily, and of the bad man to do it involuntarily.

Hippias has just exhibited his talents by giving a speech on Homer. Socrates is reluctant to praise or criticise the speech, no doubt because he has recently discovered that he has no knowledge of the fine (see the *Greater Hippias*). Socrates says that Homer's Iliad has been deemed to be a finer poem than his Odyssey, to the extent that Achilles, whom the Iliad is about, is a better man than Odysseus, whom the Odyssey is about. He asks Hippias which of these two men he thinks is the better. Hippias responds that he can answer any question put to him, and that he has never met anyone superior to him in anything. He says that Homer made Achilles the best and bravest man of those who went to Troy and Odysseus the wiliest. Socrates says that he does not understand what Hippias means, since Homer also made Achilles wily. Hippias quotes Achilles' words to Odysseus so as to demonstrate that Achilles is simple and truthful, whereas Odysseus is wily and a liar.

> *Son of Laertes, sprung from Zeus, resourceful*
>   *Odysseus,*
> *I must speak the word bluntly,*
> *How I will act and how I think it shall be*
>   *accomplished,*
> *For as hateful to me as the gates of Hades*
> *Is he who hides one thing in his mind, and says*
>   *another.*
> *As for me, I will speak as it shall also be*
>   *accomplished.*

Socrates now sees that Hippias means that the wily man is a liar, and asks Hippias whether Homer thought that the truthful man is one kind of person and the liar another, and not the same. Hippias replies that it would be strange if Homer had thought otherwise. Socrates gets Hippias to agree that the more a man knows about a subject, the more powerful he is, and the more power he has to lie about the subject. Anyone who can do what he wishes when he wishes is powerful. If someone were to ask the product of three and seven hundred, Hippias could, if he so wishes, tell him the truth best and quickest of all. Yet, the fact that Hippias has the most power to tell the truth about calculations also means that he has the most power to lie about calculations. In contrast, a person who did not have much power to tell the truth about calculations may involuntarily tell the truth. Thus, if Odysseus was a liar, he was also truthful, and if Achilles was truthful, he was also a liar.

As Hippias disagrees, Socrates quotes some lines spoken by Achilles in which Achilles clearly does not speak the truth. Hippias argues that, in contrast to Odysseus, Achilles did not lie voluntarily, but involuntarily. Socrates replies that it is impossible to believe that Achilles, who was the son of the goddess Thetis, and who was taught by the most wise centaur Chiron, was such a scatterbrain that he forgot that he had said that he was going to sail away to Odysseus, and that he was going to stay to Ajax. According to Hippias, it was because of his guilelessness that Achilles was led to say one thing to Odysseus and another to Ajax. In contrast when Odysseus tells the truth, it is always with a purpose, and when he tells a lie, as well. Socrates says that if this is the case, then Odysseus is better than Achilles, since men who lie voluntarily are better than men who lie involuntarily. Hippias disagrees with Socrates, and argues that there is more lenience for those who commit injustice involuntarily than for those who do it voluntarily. Socrates maintains that those who commit injustice voluntarily are better than those who do it involuntarily, although he confesses that he sometimes thinks the opposite, and sometimes goes back and forth, because he does not know.

> *My present state of mind is due to our previous argument, which inclines me to believe that in general those who do wrong involuntarily are worse than those who do wrong voluntarily, and therefore I hope that you will be good to me, and not refuse to heal me; for you will do me a much greater benefit if you cure my soul of ignorance, than you would if you were to cure my body of disease.*

Hippias accuses Socrates of arguing unfairly, but Socrates replies that if he is arguing unfairly, he is not doing so voluntarily, but involuntarily, and calls for leniency![8] Goaded on by his host Eudicos, Hippias agrees to carry on the conversation. Socrates says that one who runs well is a good runner, and one who runs quickly runs well. Thus, in a race, and in running, quickness is good and slowness is bad. It follows that the runner who runs slowly voluntarily is a better runner than

---

8   This is not only Socratic irony at its finest, but also an early example of the liar paradox.

the one who runs slowly involuntarily. And the same principle applies not only to running, but to everything. For this reason, it is better to do bad things voluntarily than to do them involuntarily.

Socrates next argues that justice is either some sort of power or some sort of knowledge, or both. If justice is power, the more powerful soul is the more just. And if justice is knowledge, the wiser soul is the more just. The more powerful and wiser soul is better able to accomplish both fine things and shameful things, and when it accomplishes shameful things, it does so voluntarily. For this reason, a man who voluntarily does shameful things can be no other than a good man. Both Hippias and Socrates feel unable to agree with this conclusion. And yet the argument appears to stand.

CHAPTER 7

Protagoras

And what, Socrates is the food of the soul?
Surely, I said, knowledge is the food of the soul.

The *Protagoras* takes place at the height of the Athenian
golden age, when Socrates was still a young man. Its subject
is the nature of virtue, and it sets forth a large number of
familiars including the sophists Protagoras, Hippias, and
Prodicus; the sons of Pericles Paralus and Xanthippus; Plato's
relatives Critias and Charmides; and most of the cast of the
Symposium. The dialogue begins with an unnamed friend
gently mocking Socrates for chasing Alcibiades. Socrates tells
his friend that he has put Alcibiades at the back of his mind
because he has discovered 'a much fairer love' in the elderly
Protagoras, who is currently on a visit to Athens.

> F: *And is this stranger really in your opinion a*
> *fairer love than the son of Cleinias?*
> S: *And is not the wiser always the fairer, sweet*
> *friend?*

Socrates relates his meeting with Protagoras earlier on that
same day. Whilst it was still night, his friend Hippocrates came
to his house and roused him from his sleep. Hippocrates had

discovered that Protagoras was staying at Callias' house, and was excited at the prospect of asking Protagoras to become his teacher. Socrates agreed to accompany Hippocrates to Callias' house and to speak to Protagoras on his behalf, but questioned Hippocrates' desire to become Protagoras' student. If Hippocrates was to give his money to Hippocrates of Cos, he would say that he had given his money to a physician in order to be made into a physician. But what is Protagoras and what can Protagoras make someone into? If a painter can be said to know wise things about painting, so a sophist can be said to know wise things about talking eloquently, but, whereas the painter can make one talk eloquently about painting, there appears to be nothing about which a sophist might make one talk eloquently about.

> *I proceeded: Is not a Sophist, Hippocrates, one*
> *who deals wholesale or retail in the food of the*
> *soul? To me that appears to be his nature.*
> *And what, Socrates is the food of the soul?*
> *Surely, I said, knowledge is the food of the soul;*
> *and we must take care, my friend, that the*
> *Sophist does not deceive us when he praises*
> *what he sells...*

When the pair reach Callias' house, the eunuch at the door mistakes them for sophists and refuses to let them in! Once inside, they find Protagoras taking a walk in the cloister surrounded by a sizeable retinue of Athenians and foreigners. Socrates tells Protagoras that his friend Hippocrates is unclear about the benefits of becoming his student. Protagoras replies that the sophist's art is an ancient one, although the ancients often disguised it under various forms such as the poetry of Homer, Hesiod, and Simonides, or the mysticism and prophecy of Orpheus and Musaeus. In contrast, Protagoras is open about calling himself a sophist and is happy to talk to them publicly about his art: if Hippocrates associates with him, he will become a better man day by day. Socrates asks Protagoras to be more specific, and to say in what way Hippocrates will become a better man. Protagoras replies that Hippocrates will learn the art of politics and become a good citizen. Socrates doubts that this sort of knowledge can be taught: when the Athenians meet together in assembly, they listen to experts on matters pertaining to the arts and crafts, but they listen to anyone on matters pertaining to politics; and whereas they may reproach a non-expert for advising on matters pertaining to the arts and crafts, they would never reproach anyone for advising on matters pertaining to politics. This is surely because they assume that this sort of knowledge cannot be taught. Furthermore, even the best and wisest citizens are unable to teach their virtue to others. For example, Pericles gave his sons excellent instruction in everything that could be learned from teachers, but when it came to virtue he simply left them to 'wander at their own free will in a sort of hope that they would light upon virtue of their own accord'.

Protagoras replies to Socrates with a genesis story. Once upon a time, the gods moulded the animals in the earth by blending together earth and fire. They then asked Prometheus and Epimetheus to equip them each with their proper qualities. Taking care to prevent the extinction of any of the animals, Epimetheus assigned strength to some, quickness to others, wings, claws, hoofs, pelts and hides. By the time he got round to human beings, he had nothing left to give them. Finding human beings naked and unarmed, Prometheus gave them fire and the mechanical arts, which he stole for them from Athena and Hephaestus. Unfortunately, Prometheus did not give them political wisdom, for which reason they lived in scattered isolation and at the mercy of wild animals. They tried to come together for safety, but treated each other so badly that they once again dispersed. As they shared in the divine, they gave worship to the gods, and Zeus took pity on them and asked Hermes to send them reverence and justice. Hermes asked Zeus how he should distribute these virtues:

should he give them, as for the arts, to a favoured few only, or
should he give them to all?

> *'To all,' said Zeus; I should like them all to have a
> share; for cities cannot exist, if a few only share in
> the virtues, as in the arts. And further, make a law
> by my order, that he who has no part in reverence
> and justice shall be put to death, for he is a plague
> of the state.*

Protagoras agrees with Socrates that all men regard every
man as having a share of political virtue: whereas a man
who says that he is not a good flute-player is thought to be
perfectly sensible, a man who says that he is dishonest is
thought to be quite mad. However, he disagrees with Socrates
that men do not regard political virtue as something that can
be taught: no one would punish a man for being ugly or short,
but everyone would punish him for being impious or unjust.
This is surely because they assume that piety and justice and
virtue in general do not come by nature or by chance, but
by study and exercise. What is more, they would not punish
this man for the sake of the wrong that he had done, but for
the sake of deterring him from doing wrong again, thereby
clearly implying that virtue can be taught. Socrates is equally
incorrect in claiming that good men do not teach their sons
virtue, since education and admonition begin in the first years
of childhood and continue throughout life: 'And if he obeys, well
and good; if not, he is straightened by threats and blows, like
a piece of bent or warped wood'. Just as everyone is a teacher
of the Greek language, so everyone is a teacher of virtue, and
virtue, like language, is learnt by living in a community. That
having been said, some people are better teachers of virtue
than others, and he, Protagoras, is a particularly good teacher
of virtue.

Still reeling from Protagoras' long and beautiful speech,
Socrates asks a series of short questions about the nature of

virtue. Protagoras replies that justice, temperance, and piety are not the names of one and the same thing, but are different parts of virtue. Thus, a man may have one part of virtue but not another, such that he might be courageous but not just, or just but not wise. Socrates disagrees with Protagoras and affirms that the parts of virtue share much in common. For example, whereas justice is certainly just, and piety is certainly pious, justice is also pious, and piety also just. Using examples such as strength/weakness and good/evil, Socrates argues that every opposite has one opposite and no more. Since the opposite of wisdom is folly and the opposite of temperance is also folly, temperance and wisdom must be one and the same. Protagoras is discomfited by Socrates' line of argument and returns to the relative safety of long and obfuscating speeches. Socrates complains that his memory is not good enough to engage with such speeches, but Protagoras refuses to return to simple dialogue. Socrates makes to leave but is held back by Callias. Hippias grandiloquently urges Socrates and Protagoras to compromise and suggests appointing an impartial arbiter to regulate the debate. In the end, Socrates agrees to stay, and appoints their audience as arbiter.

Protagoras proposes to discuss virtue with reference to a poem by Simonides. Protagoras thinks that Simonides is inconsistent when he says both 'Hardly on the one hand can a man become truly good' and 'I do not agree with the word of Pittacus, albeit the utterance of a wise man: Hardly can a man be good'. Socrates thinks that Simonides is perfectly consistent if one realises that 'being' is not the same as 'becoming'. Protagoras says that, if Socrates is correct, then Simonides is implying that it is easy to be good. Socrates says that Simonides is in fact implying that it is impossible (and not merely hard) to be good. Whereas it is hard for a man to *become* good, it is impossible for him to *be* (as in, to *remain*) good because he is constantly overcome by circumstances. Since a man is good insofar as he has knowledge of what is good, for him to be overcome by circumstances is for him to be made lacking in this knowledge. No man ever knowingly does evil, and all evil acts result from a lack of knowledge.

Socrates prefers to talk philosophy rather than poetry, and returns a recalcitrant Protagoras to where they left off. Protagoras had argued that the five aspects of virtue (courage, wisdom, justice, piety, temperance) are not different names for virtue, but different parts of virtue. Protagoras changes tack by claiming that four of the aspects of virtue are reasonably close to one another, but that courage is completely different. Indeed, some people can be extremely ignorant, unjust, impious, and intemperate, and yet extremely courageous. Socrates establishes that by 'courageous' Protagoras means 'confident,' and argues that people who are too confident are thought to be foolish or mad, in which case their confidence is hardly virtuous. Protagoras replies that, whereas all instances of courage are instances of confidence, not all instances of confidence are instances of courage. By analogy, if all the strong are powerful, this does not imply that all the powerful are strong, since strength and power are not the same things. Like confidence, power might derive from strength, just as it might derive from knowledge or madness.

Socrates next argues that everything that is pleasant is good, and everything that is painful is evil. Pleasant things such as food, drink, or sex may bring pleasure in the short-term, but disease and poverty and other evil things in the long-term. Conversely, unpleasant things such as athletics and doctors' treatments may bring pain in the short-term, but pleasure and relief and avoidance of pain in the long-term. Thus, there is no criterion other than pleasure and pain according to which things can be classified as either good or evil. Since it is impossible to live pleasurably whilst doing evil deeds, no one wants to do evil deeds. If people do evil deeds, it is because they are unable to measure and compare pleasures, not – as most people think – because their ethics are overwhelmed by a desire for pleasure. In other words, people only do evil deeds out of ignorance, and it is precisely this sort of ignorance that

Protagoras is claiming to cure. Returning to the subject of courage, that which people call courage is knowledge of what is and is not to be feared, and that which they call cowardice is ignorance of the same. If cowardice is ignorance and courage is the opposite of cowardice, then courage is none other than wisdom. This being so, how can Protagoras possibly argue that courage is different from the other aspects of virtue?

In conclusion, Socrates remarks that he began by arguing that virtue cannot be taught, but ended by arguing that virtue is no other than knowledge, and therefore that it can be taught. In contrast, Protagoras began by arguing that virtue can be taught, but ended by arguing that some forms of virtue are not knowledge, and therefore that they cannot be taught!

CHAPTER 8

Gorgias

> *...I hope I'll never be so busy that I'd forego discussions such as this, conducted in the way this one is, because I find it more practical to do something else.*

Gorgias was a famous teacher of oratory and author of oratical display pieces. Callicles invites Socrates and his friend Chaerephon to his house to meet Gorgias, who claims that he can accurately and convincingly answer any question asked of him. Socrates is keen to find out from Gorgias 'what his craft can accomplish,' and asks him to say what oratory is the knowledge of. Gorgias replies that oratory is the knowledge of speeches. Socrates argues that other crafts also involve the knowledge of speeches, with each craft concerned with those speeches that are about its object. For example, medicine is concerned with those speeches that are about health and disease. Should crafts such as medicine not also be called oratory? Gorgias replies that, in contrast to these other crafts, oratory exercises its influence entirely through the medium of speech. Socrates points out that crafts such as arithmetic or geometry also mostly exercise their influence through the medium of speech. In the case of arithmetic or geometry, it is possible to say what these crafts are about. But what is oratory about?

Gorgias says that oratory is about the greatest and noblest of human affairs, namely, the ability to persuade by speeches judges, councillors, and 'men in any other political gathering'. Thus, oratory is for each person the source of rule over others. Socrates re-defines oratory as a 'producer of persuasion,' and Gorgias agrees to this definition. Socrates says that other crafts, for example, arithmetic or teaching, also produce persuasion. So if oratory is a 'producer of persuasion,' what kind of persuasion does it produce? Gorgias replies that oratory produces the kind of persuasion that is found in courtrooms, that is, persuasion about right and wrong.

Socrates contrasts 'to be convinced' (belief) and 'to have learned' (knowledge). Whilst both people who have been convinced and people who have learned have come to be persuaded, the former have conviction without knowledge, whereas the latter have knowledge itself. In other words, whereas there can be both true belief and false belief, there can only be true knowledge, and never false knowledge. Is oratory the type of persuasion that results in belief and conviction, or is it the type of persuasion that results in knowledge and learning? Gorgias concedes that oratory is the type of persuasion that results in belief and conviction.

At this point Socrates says:

> *For my part, I'd be pleased to continue questioning you if you're the same kind of man I am, otherwise I would drop it. And what kind of man am I? One of those who would be pleased to be refuted if I say anything untrue, and who would be pleased to refute anyone who says anything untrue; one who, however, wouldn't be any less pleased to be refuted than to refute. For I count being refuted a greater good, insofar as it is a greater good for oneself to*

> *be delivered from the worst thing there is than to*
> *deliver someone else from it.*

Gorgias replies that, although he is this kind of man, they should put an end to their conversation because some of the people listening in may want to go off and do something else. However, Chaerephon goads him on by saying,

> *...I hope I'll never be so busy that I'd forego disc-*
> *ussions such as this, conducted in the way this one*
> *is, because I find it more practical to do something*
> *else.*

And so the conversation continues. Socrates asks Gorgias whether he can make anyone into an orator. Gorgias says that he can indeed make anyone into an orator, one that can, in a gathering, be even more persuasive about a given subject than a specialist in that subject. Socrates points out that 'in a gathering' simply means 'amongst those who do not have knowledge,' for surely an orator would not be even more persuasive than a doctor in an audience that consisted entirely of doctors. Socrates emphasises that whenever an orator is more persuasive about a subject than a specialist in that subject, a non-knower is more persuasive than a knower amongst non-knowers. If an orator lacks knowledge about medicine or any other subject, does he not also lack knowledge of what is just and unjust? A man who has learned music is a musician, and a man who has learned carpentry is a carpenter. Similarly, a man who has learned what is just is a just man. As a just man is one who does just things, an orator (whom one assumes is a just man) would never want to do unjust things. Gorgias is especially embarrassed by this line of reasoning, since he had previously let slip that an orator may at times act unjustly.

Polus, one of Gorgias' pupils, jumps in and asks Socrates what *he* thinks oratory is the knowledge of. Socrates says that he does not think that oratory is a craft, but a knack, and a part of flattery. A man who uses oratory lacks knowledge of what is good and bad, and so may do what he sees fit rather than what he wants, because he supposes that what he sees fit is better for him, when it is in fact worse, whereas what he wants is (by definition) always good for him. Contrary to what Polus thinks, such a man cannot be said to have any real power. Polus asks Socrates whether he would not be envious of someone who, when he saw fit, could put someone else to death, or bound him, or confiscate his property. Socrates replies that he would not at all be envious if these things were done unjustly, because '...you're not supposed to envy the unenviable or the miserable. You're supposed to pity them'. Polus next asks Socrates whether it is not rather the person who is put to death unjustly who should be miserable and be pitied. Socrates argues that the person who is put to death unjustly is in fact less miserable and less to be pitied than the person who put him to death or the person who is justly put to death, since doing what is unjust is the worst thing there is. Although Socrates would neither wish to put someone to death unjustly nor himself be put to death unjustly, he would prefer the latter over the former because those who do what is unjust are necessarily unhappy, and particularly so if they do not get their due punishment. In contrast to Socrates, Polus clearly believes that it is possible for a man to be unjust and happy, so long as he escapes from getting his due punishment. He cites the example of Archelaus, the tyrant of Macedonia, and asks whether a man such as Archelaus who unjustly but successfully plots to set himself up as a tyrant is not happier than the man who unjustly plots to set himself up as a tyrant but gets caught and tortured to death. Socrates replies that neither is happier, 'for of two miserable people one could not be happier than the other'. However, he thinks that the man who succeeds in setting himself up as a tyrant is the more miserable of the two. When Polus bursts out in laughter, he says,

> *What's this, Polus? You're laughing? Is this now
> some further style of refutation, to laugh when
> someone makes a point, instead of refuting him?*

Polus says that Socrates has already been sufficiently refuted,
since no one would share his point of view. Socrates replies
that he does not discuss things with the majority, and that
he can only ever call to witness the man with whom he is
having a discussion. He argues that doing what is unjust is
more shameful than suffering it, and therefore that it is worse.
When Polus disagrees with him, he says that Polus evidently
does not understand that 'admirable' and 'good' mean the same
thing, as do 'bad' and 'shameful'. So he demonstrates to Polus
that one would not call anything admirable that was not also
good, or anything shameful that was not also bad. Therefore,
if doing what is unjust is more shameful than suffering it,
it is also worse. Polus is obliged to concede on this point.
Socrates next argues that paying what is due and being justly
punished for wrongdoing are the same thing. In whatever way
a thing which acts upon another thing acts upon it, so the
thing which is acted upon is acted upon by the thing which
acts upon it. For example, if a hitter hits hard and quickly, the
thing being hit is hit hard and quickly. Paying what is due is
a case of being acted upon by someone who acts justly. As just
things are admirable, the person who pays what is due has
something admirable, and thus something good, done to him.
Of one's finances, one's body, and one's soul, there are three
states of corruption, namely, poverty, disease, and injustice.
Of these, injustice is the most shameful, and so the worst. The
remedy for poverty is financial management, the remedy for
disease is medicine, and the remedy for injustice is justice.
Of the three, justice is by far the most admirable. Taking
medicine for the body is unpleasant yet beneficial, and this is
also true of taking punishment for the soul. The man who has
badness in his soul and pays his due is happy, whereas the
man who has badness in his soul but escapes punishment is

so miserable that he goes to any lengths to secure funds and friends, and ways to speak as persuasively as possible. The logical conclusion is that the wrongdoer who hands himself in for punishment is in fact acting in his best interests.

Socrates tells Callicles that philosophy says astounding things and that one must engage with these things and live by them. He says,

> *...I think it's better to have my lyre or a chorus that I might lead out of tune and dissonant, and have the vast majority of men disagree with me and contradict me, than to be out of harmony with myself, to contradict myself, though I'm only one person.*

Callicles gets angry with Socrates and accuses him of playing with words. Callicles says that when he sees philosophy in a young boy, he finds it admirable, but when he sees it in someone older, he thinks that the man needs a good flogging. Socrates says that he is lucky to have run into Callicles, since Callicles has each of the three qualities required to put his soul to the test: knowledge, good will, and frankness. Whilst many people have one or other of these three qualities, few have them all. For example, Gorgias and Polus have both knowledge and good will, but not frankness. Socrates says that since both he and Callicles have all three qualities, whatever they agree between them must be the truth.

The topic of the discussion falls upon the nature of justice. Callicles argues that justice is natural justice, according to which the noble and the strong rule over the base and the weak. Socrates questions whether the noble and the strong can even rule over themselves, that is, exercise temperance and self-control. Callicles says that temperance is a sign of weakness, and that power and happiness accrue from allowing one's desires to grow without limitation. Socrates compares the soul of a man who allows his desires to grow without limitation to a leaky jar which is ever in need of more. Unless such a man exercises temperance and self-control, he cannot be said to be truly happy. Callicles denies this by equating what is pleasurable and thus desirable with what is good. Socrates demonstrates that what is pleasurable cannot be equated with what is good. He argues that a bodily appetite such as hunger is painful, whereas eating to alleviate this hunger is pleasurable. Thus, when one eats to alleviate hunger, one is experiencing both pleasure and pain at the same time. In contrast, one cannot both be faring well and faring badly at the same time. Therefore, what is pleasurable cannot be equated with what is good, and what is painful cannot be equated with what is bad. Callicles surrenders the argument to Socrates.

Socrates argues further that foolish men feel pleasure and pain to the same degree or to a greater degree than wise men, even though foolish men are bad and wise men are good. For this reason also, what is pleasurable cannot be equated to what is good, and what is painful cannot be equated to what is bad. If one is to have a proper existence, one should do things, including pleasant things, for the sake of good things, and not good things for the sake of pleasant things. A routine or knack such as pastry baking, which is concerned with that which is pleasant, must be differentiated from a craft or art such as medicine, which is concerned with that which is good. Since oratory is a knack and philosophy is an art, oratory is to philosophy as pastry baking is to medicine, or as beautification is to gymnastics. Craftsmen and artists provide order and discipline. For example, doctors and physical trainers provide order and discipline to the body. A properly ordered body is one that is healthy and strong, and a properly ordered soul is one that is just and temperate.

Callicles is reluctant to carry on the debate, and invites Socrates to carry on alone, asking questions and answering them himself. Socrates delivers a lengthy monologue, thereby demonstrating that the best kind of oratory is the kind that is used against one's own self. He says that the presence of justice and temperance is necessarily accompanied by that of courage and piety, and thus that one whose soul is just and temperate is one who is perfectly good and also perfectly happy. One should take better care of the soul than of the body, because the soul contains our most complex and most pure aspects, and because the soul survives the death of the body. And one should extend this pursuance of virtue to one's city and fellow citizens, in the hope that they too may become as good and as happy as possible. Socrates remarks that he would not be surprised if he were to be put to death, since he is one of the few Athenians – if not the only one – to practice true politics, that is, to make speeches that do not aim at gratification, but at what is best. Since he is unwilling to engage in oratory, his defence will be poor and he will be judged 'the way a doctor is judged by a jury of children if a pastry chef were to bring accusations against him'. Be this as it may, a man with courage and reason is far more afraid of doing what is unjust than he is of dying.

At the end of the *Gorgias*, Socrates relates an eschatological myth (or myth of death). After Zeus, Poseidon, and Pluto took over from their father Cronos, they divided the world amongst them. In the time of their father, a man who had lived a just and pious life went to the Isles of the Blessed, but a man who had lived an unjust and godless life went to Tartarus, where he suffered what was appropriate for him to suffer. Men were judged by living judges on the day that they were going to die. As their cases were poorly decided, Zeus found it beneficial to make three changes: first, that they should not know when they are going to die; second, that they should be judged only once they are dead and stripped naked of their dissimulating clothes and bodies; and third, that the judges themselves should be dead, so that they may judge only with their souls, 'instead of having eyes and ears and their whole bodies up as screens in front of their souls'. Zeus appointed three of his own sons, Minos, Rhadbamanthus, and Aeacus to act as judges at the three-way crossing from which the two roads go, one to the

Isles of the Blessed and the other to Tartarus. Those whom they punish most severely are from the ranks of tyrants, kings, potentates, and those active in politics, since they are in a position to commit the most grievous and impious errors. For this reason, those whom Homer depicts as undergoing eternal punishment in Hades are not simple people, but kings and potentates such as Sisyphus, Tantalus, or Tityus.

Socrates tells Callicles that, although those who are extremely wicked come from the ranks of the powerful, there is nothing to stop good men from turning up amongst them. Such men deserve much praise, because it is very difficult to live one's live justly when one has been given ample freedom to do what is unjust. Yet, as he has demonstrated all along, nothing truly bad can ever happen to a good man.

> *For it's a shameful thing for us, being in the condition we appear to be at present – when we never think the same about the same subjects, the most important ones at that – to sound off as though we're somebodies. That's how far behind in education we've fallen. So let's use the account that has now been disclosed to us as our guide, one that indicates to us that this way of life is best, to practice justice and the rest of excellence both in life and in death. Let us follow it, then, and call on others to do so, too, and let's not follow the one that you believe in and call on me to follow. For that one is worthless, Callicles.*

CHAPTER 9

Clitophon

Whither haste ye, O men?

Socrates has recently discovered that Clitophon has been criticising him to the orator Lysias, whilst praising the rhetorician Thrasymachus. Clitophon offers to tell Socrates what he said to Lysias.

Clitophon says that he was very impressed by Socrates' magnificent speeches, and particularly by his famous exhortation to virtue:

> *Whither haste ye, O men? Yea, verily ye know not that ye are doing none of the things ye ought, seeing that ye spend your whole energy on wealth and the acquiring of it; while as to your sons to whom ye will bequeath it, ye neglect to ensure that they shall understand how to use it justly... Yet truly it is because of this... that brother with brother and city with city clash together without measure or harmony and are at strife, and in their warring perpetrate and suffer the uttermost horrors. But ye assert that the unjust are unjust not because of their lack of education and lack of knowledge but voluntarily, while on the other hand ye have the*

> *face to affirm that injustice is a foul thing, and*
> *hateful to Heaven. Then how, pray, could any man*
> *voluntarily choose an evil of such a kind? Any*
> *man, you reply, who is mastered by his pleasures.*
> *But is not this condition also involuntary, if the act*
> *of mastering be voluntary? Thus in every way the*
> *argument proves that unjust action is involuntary,*
> *and that every man privately and all the cities*
> *publicly ought to pay more attention than they do*
> *now to this matter.*

Clitophon praises Socrates' fine conclusion: just as someone who does not know how to use a lyre should not use one, someone who does not know how to use his soul had best put his soul to rest and not live, or at least, live as a slave and hand over the rudder of his mind. After being roused by this and other similar speeches, Clitophon wanted to know what would come next, and put the question to Socrates' friends and followers:

> *I ask you, my very good Sirs, in what sense do we*
> *now accept the exhortation to virtue which Socrates*
> *has given us. Are we to regard it as all there is,*
> *and suppose it to be impossible to pursue the object*
> *further and grasp it fully; and is this to be our*
> *lifelong task, just to exhort those who have not as*
> *yet been exhorted, and that they in turn should*
> *exhort others? Or, when we have agreed that this*
> *is exactly what a man should do, ought we to ask*
> *Socrates, and one another, the further question –*
> *'What is the next step?' What do we say is the way*
> *in which we ought to begin the study of justice?*

The most formidable of Socrates' friends and followers replied that the skill which concerns the virtue of the soul is justice itself. Clitophon then asked him not only to name the skill, but also to describe its product. If the product of medicine is health and the product of carpentry is a house, what is the product of justice? The man replied that this product was 'the beneficial,' someone else said, 'the appropriate,' someone else, 'the useful,' and someone else, 'the advantageous'. Clitophon argued that all these words are to be found in the other skills as well, but what is it, in the case of justice, that they all aim at? What, in short, is the peculiar product of justice? Someone answered that the peculiar product of justice was 'friendship within cities'. However, he would not allow that the friendships of children or animals are really friendships, since friendship is always good and never bad, whereas the friendships of children or animals are more often harmful than good. In contrast, true friendship consists not in association but in *agreement*. Clitophon asked whether such agreement consisted in belief or knowledge, to which he replied that it consisted in knowledge, since man's shared beliefs are often harmful, whereas friendship is always good and never bad. Some bystanders pointed out that the argument had gone round in a circle, since medicine is also a sort of agreement. However, in the case of medicine, it is easy to say what this agreement is about. So what is justice an agreement about?

Finally, Clitophon put the question to Socrates himself, who replied that the aim of justice is to hurt one's enemies and help one's friends. However, it later turned out that the just man never harms anyone, since everything he does is for the benefit of all. Clitophon eventually came to the conclusion that, whilst Socrates is better than anyone at turning someone towards the pursuit of virtue, either he does not know anything about it, or he is keeping what he knows to himself. For this reason, he went to Thrasymachus instead.

> *For I shall maintain, Socrates, that while you are of untold value to a man who has not been exhorted, to him who has been exhorted you are almost an actual hindrance in the way of his attaining the goal of virtue and becoming a happy man.*

CHAPTER 10

Euthyphro

Is that which is holy loved by the gods because it is holy, or is it holy because it is loved by the gods?

Socrates is on his way to answer a charge of impiety pressed against him by a certain Meletus for corrupting young men and for creating new gods and not believing in the old ones. He runs into Euthyphro in the *agora* or central market place. Euthyphro is an orthodox and dogmatically religious man who, following the death of a servant, has just pressed a murder charge against his own father. Euthyphro tells Socrates that he is prosecuting his father for inadvertently killing the servant who, in drunken anger, had murdered one of the household slaves. After binding the servant and throwing him into a ditch, Euthyphro's father sent a messenger to a priest to enquire what should be done. Unfortunately, the servant died of hunger and cold before the messenger could return.

Socrates flatters Euthyphro, suggesting that he must be far advanced in wisdom if he is willing to prosecute his own father on so questionable a charge. Euthyphro says that his relatives are angry at him for prosecuting his father for murder on behalf of a murderer whom he had not deliberately killed. Whereas his relatives think that he is behaving impiously, he himself thinks that he is behaving piously, and that he has accurate knowledge of piety and impiety. Posing as ignorant, Socrates asks Euthyphro to define the pious and the impious. Euthyphro replies that the pious is to prosecute a wrongdoer regardless of one's relationship to him, and the impious is not to prosecute him. He gives the example of Zeus, 'the best and most just of gods,' who bound his father Cronus because he unjustly swallowed his sons. Socrates says that many actions can be pious, but what is it that makes all pious actions pious, and all impious actions impious? What, in short, is the essence of piousness? Euthyphro offers that the pious is that which is dear to the gods. Thus, an action or a man dear to the gods is pious, whereas an action or a man hated by the gods is impious. Socrates argues that the gods may be at odds with one another, and thus that what is pious to one god may not be so to another. Euthyphro replies that none of the gods would be at odds with one another on a matter such as the one at hand. Socrates argues that whilst both men and gods may agree that whoever has killed anyone unjustly should pay a penalty, they may yet disagree about who the wrongdoer is, what he did, and so on. Can Euthyphro be sure that all the gods are in agreement in this particular case? Even assuming that they are, this merely signifies that the action is hated by the gods. It does not signify that what is hated by the gods is impious, what is loved by the gods is pious, and what is hated by some gods but loved by other gods is neither or both. Even assuming that it does, is that which is pious loved by the gods because it is pious, or is it pious because it is loved by the gods?[9] If the gods love something because it is pious, then it cannot be their love that makes it pious. Whereas if something is pious because the gods love it, we still don't know for what reason they love it. Euthyphro complains that Socrates makes his arguments go around in circles, but Socrates points out that all he is doing is asking questions; it is Euthphro's answers and Euthyphro's arguments that are going round in circles.

---

9   This is the famous 'Euthyphro dilemma'.

Socrates next argues that all that is pious is necessarily just. Whereas all that is pious is necessarily just, not all that is just is necessarily pious: some of it is, and some of it is not. Thus, where there is piety there is also justice, but where there is justice there is not necessarily piety, because piety is a part of justice. So what part of justice is piety? Euthyphro replies that piety is the part of justice that is concerned with the care of the gods, and the remaining part of justice is the justice that is concerned with the care of men. Socrates asks Euthyphro what he means by 'care'. In most instances, 'to care' means 'to aim at the good of that which is cared for'. So does piety, which is concerned with the care of the gods, aim to make them better? Euthyphro suggests that piety, the care of the gods, is the sort of care that slaves have for their masters, and thus that it is a kind of service. If piety is a kind of service to the gods, asks Socrates, what is the goal of this service? The goal of service to doctors is health, and the goal of service to shipbuilders is the building of a ship. So what is the goal of service to the gods? Euthyphro replies that service to the gods is the knowledge of how to say and do what is pleasing to the gods at prayer and sacrifice, so as to preserve both private households and public affairs of state.

Socrates says that, if the pious is the knowledge of how to pray and sacrifice, it is the knowledge of how to beg and give to the gods. To beg correctly would be to ask from them the things that we need, whereas to give correctly would be to give them the things that they need, and piety would amount to a sort of trading skill between gods and men. Euthyphro says, 'Trading yes, if you prefer to call it that,' to which Socrates replies, 'I prefer nothing, unless it is true'. Socrates questions what benefit the gods derive from the gifts that they receive from us. Or do we have such a trading advantage over them that we receive all our blessings from them and they receive nothing from us? Euthyphro says that we give gifts to the gods so as to honour and please them. Socrates asks whether the pious is then pleasing to the gods, but not beneficial or dear to them, to which Euthyphro replies 'I think it is of all things most dear to them'. Socrates points out that they have returned to Euthyphro's original definition of piety, that piety is that which is dear to the gods. Socrates says that Euthyphro is more skilful than Daedalus, in that Daedalus could only make arguments move, whereas Euthyphro can make them go round in a circle. Socrates suggests that they begin their inquiry afresh, but Euthyphro says that he is in a hurry and leaves!

CHAPTER 11

Apology

*...the life which is unexamined is not worth
living...*

Socrates has been indicted by Meletus, Anytus, and Lycon for
breaking the law against impiety and offending the Olympian
gods, and delivers his 'apology' or defense speech before 501
jurymen. He begins by affirming that he could not recognise
himself in the speeches of his accusers. His accusers warned
the jurymen not to be deceived by his eloquence, but unless
by 'eloquence' they meant 'true-speaking,' he is anything but
eloquent. In contrast to his accusers, he is not going to deliver
a set oration that is full of study and artifice, but is simply
going to improvise as is his habit. Despite being advanced in
age, this is his first time in court, and he is not accustomed
to its language. The jurymen should forgive any slips into his
usual conversational style, and simply consider whether what
he says is true or not.

Before replying to his accusers, Socrates proposes to reply to
his 'older accusers,' who have been telling all and sundry that
he is an evil-doer who 'searches into things under the earth
and in heaven,' 'makes the worse appear the better cause,' and
'teaches these aforesaid doctrines to others'. His older accusers
are more dangerous than Meletus and his acolytes because

they have been machinating against him for many years, and are likely to have prejudiced the jurymen. With the exception of the comedian Aristophanes, who portrayed him as floating about in mid-air and talking nonsense about divine matters, he does not know who his old accusers are, and so is unable to challenge them. However, the jurymen can attest to the fact that he has never spoken out about divine matters. Unlike sophists such as Gorgias, Hippias, or Prodicus, he has never pretended to understand virtue, nor taken any money for his services. So what is it that has led to all these accusations against him?

Socrates explains that he developed a reputation for wisdom; not the superhuman wisdom of the sophists, but the sort of wisdom that can be attained to by men. Several years ago, his impetuous friend Chaerephon asked the Delphic oracle whether there was anyone wiser than Socrates, and the Pythian priestess replied that there was no one wiser. Knowing that he had only very little wisdom, he assumed that this reply was some kind of riddle, and sought out a particular politician who was 'thought wise by many and wiser still by himself'. However, the conversation that they had revealed that he was not wise at all.

> *...and I went and tried to explain to him that he thought himself wise, but was not really wise; and the consequence was that he hated me, and his enmity was shared by several who were present and heard me.*

Whereas both he and the politician knew nothing, he was wiser than the politician in that he at least knew that he knew nothing. He then went to one man after another, first politicians, then poets, then craftsmen, and found that those amongst them with the greatest reputation for wisdom were the most foolish of all. Thus, the god Apollo's meaning had been that the wisdom of men is little or nothing, and that the men who know this are as wise as any man can be. In obedience to Apollo, he made it his business to go around inquiring into the wisdom of anyone who laid claim to it. This took up so much of his time that he had none left to devote to either public or private affairs. He made many friends amongst the young men of the leisured classes, who began imitating his behaviour. However, he also made many enemies, since the people who were found to be wanting in wisdom did not get angry at themselves, but at him. As they could not say why they were angry, they came up with the sorts of charges that are levied against all philosophers, about 'searching into things under the earth and in heaven,' 'making the worse appear the better cause,' and so on.

Having said enough about his older accusers, Socrates turns to Meletus and accuses him of being all too ready to bring other men to trial for matters in which he has no interest. To demonstrate that Meletus has no interest in the improvement of youth, Socrates asks him to name the improver of youth. After some hesitation, Meletus replies that the improver of youth is the laws.

> S: *Who, in the first place, knows the laws?*
> M: *The judges, Socrates, who are present in court.*
> S: *What do you mean to say, Meletus, that they*
>   *are able to instruct and improve youth?*
> M: *Certainly they are.*
> S: *What, all of them, or some only and not others?*
> M: *All of them.*

Under pressure from Socrates' questioning, Meletus says that councillors and members of the Assembly also improve youth, and, by implication, that all Athenian citizens with the one exception of Socrates improve youth. Socrates asks Meletus whether it can also be said of horses that everyone does them good but one man only does them harm. Is it not rather that everyone does them harm except one man, the horse trainer, who alone does them good? Having thereby demonstrated that Meletus has never given any thought to the improvement of youth, Socrates sets out to demonstrate that he could not intentionally have corrupted the youth.

> S: *Do not the good do their neighbours good, and*
> *the bad do them evil?*
> M: *Certainly.*
> S: *And is there anyone who would rather be*
> *injured than benefited by those who live with*
> *him?*
> M: *Certainly not.*
> S: *And when you accuse me of corrupting and*
> *deteriorating the youth, do you allege that I*
> *corrupt them intentionally or unintentionally?*
> M: *Intentionally, I say.*

Socrates argues that he would not have corrupted the youth intentionally, because he would have known that doing so would have been tantamount to injuring himself. Thus, if he did corrupt the youth, he did so unintentionally, and deserves not to be tried and punished, but to be reproached and educated.

Socrates next asks what Meletus meant when he accused him of teaching the youth to acknowledge gods other than those acknowledged by the state: did Meletus mean (1) that he believes in some gods, although not in those acknowledged by the state, or (2) that he is an atheist and does not believe in any gods at all? Meletus affirms that Socrates is an atheist, since he believes that the sun is stone, and the moon earth. Socrates points out that this is not in fact his opinion, but that of the philosopher Anaxagoras. He then argues that, just as it is impossible to believe in the existence of human affairs but not of human beings, or to believe in the existence of horsemanship but not of horses, so it is impossible to believe in the existence of divine things but not of gods. Thus, by accusing him of teaching the youth to acknowledge gods other than those acknowledged by the state, Meletus has implied that he does believe in the existence of gods.

Having said enough about Meletus, Socrates explains that he chose to lead the life of the philosopher despite the dangers involved because one ought not to calculate the chance of living or dying, but only to consider whether what one does is good or bad. The great hero Achilles did not fear death, but feared to live in dishonour and fail to avenge the death of his lover Patroclus. 'Let me die at once,' he said, '... rather than remain here, a laughingstock by the curved ships, a burden upon the earth.' Socrates says that, just as he did not abandon his post at the battles of Potidaea, Amphipolis, and Delium, so he will not abandon the life of the philosopher. If he were to do so for fear of dying, he would be fancying that he was wise when he was not, since no one can know whether death is the greatest evil or the greatest good.

> *Men of Athens, I am grateful and I am your friend, but I will obey the god rather than you, and as long as I draw breath and am able, I shall not cease to practice philosophy, to exhort you and in my usual way to point out to any one of you whom I happen to meet: Good Sir, you are an Athenian, a citizen of the greatest city with the greatest reputation for both wisdom and power; are you not ashamed of your eagerness to possess as much wealth, reputation and honours as possible, while you do not care for nor give thought to wisdom or truth, or the best possible state of your soul?[10]*

No greater good has ever happened to the state than his service to the god, for all he does is go around persuading men not to care so much about wealth, reputation, and honours, but to care first and foremost for excellence and virtue. 'Wealth,' he

---

10 Translated by GMA Grube.

says, 'does not bring about excellence, but excellence makes wealth and everything else good for men, both individually and collectively.' This is the essence of his teaching; if it corrupts the youth, then so be it. By condemning him to death, the jury would be doing themselves far more harm than they would be doing him, since putting an innocent man to death is far worse than dying oneself. They would find it difficult to find another man like him, who was to the state as a gadfly is to a noble but listless horse, relentlessly goading and irritating it. He made himself into the gadfly of Athens in obedience to God, and his poverty is proof enough that he never took any money for it. He did consider entering the public arena, but his *daemonion* forbade him from doing so on the grounds that, if he became a politician, he would soon be killed and of no good to anyone.

> *For I am certain, O men of Athens, that if I had engaged in politics, I should have perished long ago and done no good either to you or to myself. And don't be offended at my telling you the truth: for the truth is that no man who goes to war with you or any other multitude, honestly struggling against the commission of unrighteousness and wrong in the state, will save his life; he who will really fight for the right, if he would live even for a little while, must have a private station and not a public one.*

He cites the time in 406BC when it was his turn to chair the assembly, and he alone opposed the prosecution as a body of the generals who, after the Battle of Arginusae, failed to pick up the Athenian survivors because of a violent storm. At the time, the orators had been ready to remove him, although later everyone realised that the prosecution would have been illegal. He also cites the time in 404BC when the Thirty Tyrants asked him and four others to bring the innocent Leon of Salamis to be executed, and he alone refused, even though doing so may have cost him his life. As he behaved in the public sphere, so he behaved in the private sphere. He never had regular disciples, but spoke freely to all those who came to ask questions, whether young or old, rich or poor. As he never taught them anything, he cannot take the credit or blame for their subsequent actions. However, if he did corrupt them, then why are their fathers and brothers not coming forth to accuse him? Several of them are here in the audience, including Crito and his son Critobulus, Lysanias of Sphettus and his son Aeschines, Adeimantus and his brother Plato, and several others. Why did Meletus not call on any of them as a witness?

This is all the defence that he has to offer. Some of the jurymen may take offence that he did not make recourse to prayers or supplications, shed tears, or produce his young children together with a posse of relatives and friends. Such pitiful scenes would not have been worthy of his years and reputation, nor of the jurymen, nor indeed of Athens herself.

> *I have seen men of reputation, when they have been condemned, behaving in the strangest mann-er: they seemed to fancy that they were going to suffer something dreadful if they died, and that they could be immortal if you only allowed them to live; and I think that they were a dishonour to the state, and that any stranger coming in would say of them that the most eminent men of Athens, to whom the Athenians themselves give honour and command, are no better than women.*

The jurymen should base their verdict not on their good pleasure, but on the relevant facts.

[The jury finds Socrates guilty and Meletus asks for the penalty of death.]

Socrates responds to the jury's verdict. He fully expected to be found guilty, and is surprised that the votes are so nearly equal. He asks to be given no more and no less than what he deserves, which is not death, but free meals in the Prytaneum[11], just like winners at the Olympic Games. After all, Olympic winners merely give the Athenians the appearance of happiness, whereas he gives them the reality. He has never wronged anyone, and will not start now by asking for a penalty that he does not deserve. He considers the options: a fine, which he could ill afford; imprisonment, which would turn him into a slave; or exile, which would turn him into an outcast and a pariah. Exile could be tolerable if he held his tongue, but he is not willing to do this.

> *For if I tell you this would be a disobedience to a divine command, and therefore that I cannot hold my tongue, you will not believe that I am serious; and if I say again that the greatest good of man is daily to converse about virtue, and all that concerning which you hear me examining myself and others, and that the life which is unexamined is not worth living – that you are still less likely to believe.*

In the end he proposes a fine of one minae[12], but then raises it to thirty minae on the advice of Plato, Crito, Critobulus, and Apollodorus.

[The jury condemns Socrates to death.]

Socrates comments on his sentence. The jurymen have not gained much time by condemning him to death, since he is more than seventy years old and not far from death. On the other hand, they have given the city's detractors the opportunity to say that the Athenians killed a wise man. If

---

11 A public hall in Athens in which official hospitality was extended to distinguished citizens and foreigners.

12 One hundred drachmae, where one drachma is the standard daily wage of a labourer.

they condemned him, this was not for a lack of words, but for an unwillingness to say and do whatever it takes. However, it is easier to outrun death than to outrun unrighteousness, and he had rather die than compromise his principles. He is old and sluggish and has been overtaken by death, whereas his accusers are keen and quick and have been overtaken by unrighteousness. He may have been condemned by them, but they have been condemned by Truth, and their punishment will be far worse than his. Once he is dead, other critics will come forth, and will ask them to give an account of their lives. It is not by killing men that they will escape from giving an account of their lives, but by improving themselves.

Socrates then addresses those who voted to acquit him. His daemonion has stayed silent throughout the proceedings, which is great proof that death is in fact a good thing. Either death is a state of nothingness and utter unconsciousness, or it is a journey to another place. If the former, it is like a deep and peaceful sleep, and eternity is but a single night. If the latter, it is a pilgrimage to a land populated by great men such as Orpheus and Musaeus, Odysseus and Sisyphus, and Hesiod and Homer.

> *Nay, if this be true, let me die again and again...*
> *What infinite delight would there be in conversing*
> *with them and asking them questions! For in that*
> *world they do not put a man to death for this;*
> *certainly not... Wherefore, O judges, be of good*
> *cheer about death, and know this of a truth – that*
> *no evil can happen to a good man, either in life or*
> *after death.*

Thus, he has come to the conclusion that it is better for him to die than to live, and he is not at all angry at those who accused and condemned him. Even though they did not mean to do him any good, they have not done him any harm. Finally, he asks his friends to take good care of his three sons.

When my sons are grown up, I would ask you, O my friends, to punish them; and I would have you trouble them, as I have troubled you, if they seem to care about riches, or anything, more than about virtue; or if they pretend to be something when they are really nothing...

The hour of departure has arrived, and we go our ways – I to die, and you to live. Which is better God only knows.

CHAPTER 12

Crito

> *Then, my friend, we must not regard what the*
> *many say of us: but what he, the one man who*
> *has understanding of just and unjust, will say,*
> *and what the truth will say.*

Socrates did not die until one month after his trial because no executions were permitted until the return of the Athenian state galley, which was out on its annual pilgrimage to Delos in honour of Theseus' victory over the Minotaur. It is still night when Crito bribes the guard and gains entry into the prison cell. Socrates looks so peaceful in his sleep that Crito does not wake him, but watches over him until daybreak, when he first stirs. Crito explains that he has come because the state galley has been spotted at Sunium and is likely to be in Piraeus later today, in which case Socrates will be executed tomorrow. Socrates says that he has just had a dream in which a beautiful woman in white raiment called to him and said, 'O Socrates– The third day hence, to Phthia shalt though go'.[13] This must surely mean that the state galley is going to be delayed by one more day.

Crito once more renews his pleas for Socrates to escape. If Socrates dies, people will think that Crito did not bribe the

---

13 Phthia was the homeland of the hero Achilles.

guards, and thus that he values money more than the life of a friend. Socrates tells Crito not to bother about the opinion of the many, but Crito points out that it is the opinion of the many that has condemned Socrates to death. Socrates says that, if the many could do the greatest evil, they could also do the greatest good. However, they can do neither, since they cannot make a man wise or foolish; whatever they do is the result of chance alone. Crito asks whether Socrates is unwilling to escape out of consideration for his friends, who would have to pay bribes and run the risk of being apprehended and punished. Crito reassures Socrates that his friends are of ample means and willing to run any risk. There are many places where he would be welcomed, such as Thessaly, where Crito has some friends. In any case, to remain would be unjust, since it would play into the hands of his enemies and leave his children without a father to educate them. People would think that he was a coward, and they would think the same of Crito and his other friends. Tonight is his last chance to escape; he must make up his mind, there is no more time for deliberation.

Socrates responds that they cannot cast away lifelong principles because death is suddenly at hand. Were they not right in holding that only the opinions of wise and good men are to be regarded? The student of gymnastics ought only to attend to the praise and blame of his physician or trainer if his body is not to deteriorate. What goes for gymnastics also goes for justice, and what goes for the body also goes for the higher part of man, except that the latter is far more important than the former. Crito is correct in saying that the opinion of the many may condemn a man to death. However, it is not life that is to be valued, but the good life, that is, the just and honourable life. Thus, he will only escape if they can show that doing so is just and honourable. Money, public opinion, or the bringing up of children are 'only the doctrines of the multitude, who would be as ready to call people to life, if they were able, as they are to put them to death – and with as little reason'. Crito concedes that Socrates is right.

If to do wrong is always evil and dishonourable, then they should do no wrong. In particular, they should do no wrong to those who wronged them. In escaping, he would be wronging the city by breaking his agreement to abide by her laws. [For the rest of the dialogue Socrates impersonates the city and has 'her' tell him the following.] It was through the city that his mother married his father and begat him, through the city that he was nurtured, and through the city that he was educated in the arts and in gymnastics. He owes more to the city than to his parents, and is like a son or a slave to her. When he came of age, the city gave him the opportunity to leave her. Not only did he remain, but he remained more consistently than anyone else, only ever leaving on a handful of occasions, mostly on military service. At his trial, he even asked for death over exile. In choosing to remain, he made a tacit agreement with the city that he would abide by her laws. The city is nothing if not her laws, and breaking them would be tantamount to destroying her. A son or a slave should not retaliate against the father or the master who punishes him, nor should a soldier flee the battlefield to save himself. If Socrates is to escape punishment, it is not by breaking the city's laws that he must do so, but by persuading the city that she condemns him unjustly.

Furthermore, if he were to break the city's laws and escape, his friends would most probably lose their property or be driven into exile. In any case, where would he go? What well-governed city would welcome a man who had broken the laws of the city in which he had remained for seventy years? The jurymen who condemned him would think that a man who breaks the city's laws is just as likely to corrupt its youth, and thus that they were justified in condemning him. What sort of life would he lead, fleeing from well-governed cities and no longer able to talk about justice and virtue? If he wished to live for the sake of his children, he would either have to take them into exile and deprive them of Athenian citizenship, or leave them behind to be cared for by friends who would care for them just the same whether he was alive or dead. As things stand, he will depart this life innocent, a victim of the people rather than of the laws, and he will fare well before the judges of the underworld. In contrast, if he were to break the city's laws and escape, he would no longer be a sufferer, but a doer, of evil, and suffer both in the dregs of this life and in the eternity of the next.

> S: *This is the voice which I seem to hear murmuring in my ears, like the sound of the flute in the ears of the mystic; that voice, I say, is humming in my ears, and prevents me from hearing any other. And I know that anything more which you will say will be in vain. Yet speak, if you have anything to say.*
> C: *I have nothing to say, Socrates.*
> S: *Then let me follow the intimations of the will of God.*

CHAPTER 13

Meno

*And how will you enquire, Socrates, into that
which you do not know?*

Meno is the scion of one of Thessaly's leading aristocratic
families and a sometime pupil of the sophist Gorgias. He
meets with Socrates of whom he asks whether virtue can
be acquired by teaching. Socrates begins by praising the
Thessalians for their fabled riches and horses, as well as for
their freshly acquired reputation for wisdom. If Meno were to
put his question to a Thessalian, he would surely receive his
answer in the grand and bold style of Gorgias. In contrast, an
Athenian would simply laugh in his face, saying that he did not
even know what virtue was, let alone whether it could or could
not be acquired by teaching. To Meno's surprise, Socrates says
that he himself does not know what virtue is. Not only that,
but he has never known of anyone who did. Perhaps Meno
could define it for him?

Meno thinks that this is an easy question, and offers that
there are different virtues for men, women, children, slaves,
and so on. For example, the virtue of a man is to manage
public affairs, help his friends, harm his enemies, and protect
himself, whereas the virtue of a woman is to manage the home,
preserve its possessions, and be submissive to her husband.

Socrates is delighted to be presented with so many different virtues, which he compares to a swarm of bees. If bees are many and varied, this is not insofar as they are bees, but in some other respect such as beauty or size. However, what is it that makes every bee a bee? Just as the nature of health or strength is the same in a man as it is in a woman, so the nature of virtue is the same in all its instances. Socrates gets Meno to agree that every instance of virtue involves temperance and justice, and thus that temperance and justice are the sorts of things that are common to every case of virtue.

Failing somewhat to grasp Socrates' point, Meno next offers that virtue is the ability to rule over people. However, if this is the case, how could a child or a slave ever be held to possess virtue? Surely, if virtue is the ability to rule over people, it is not the ability to rule over people *unjustly*, but the ability to rule over people *justly*. Meno agrees, and says that 'justice is virtue'. Socrates asks whether he means that justice is virtue or that justice is *a* virtue. Meno replies that justice is *a* virtue, and that there are also other virtues such as courage, temperance, and wisdom. Socrates points out that they are once again facing the same problem: in searching for one virtue they have found many, but they have been unable to find the common virtue that runs through them all. A round figure is 'a figure' and not 'figure,' just as white is 'a colour' and not 'colour'. Socrates sets out to define 'figure' and 'colour' as examples for Meno. He defines 'figure' in his manner as 'that which limits a solid' and defines 'colour' in the manner of Gorgias and Empedocles as 'an effluence of form, commensurate with sight, and palpable to sense'.

> M: *That, Socrates, appears to me to be an*
> *admirable answer.*
> S: *Why, yes, because it happens to be one which*
> *you have been in the habit of hearing.*

Meno offers another definition of virtue, this time in the form of a quote from a poet: 'Virtue is the desire of things honourable and the power of attaining them'. Socrates argues that one who desires honourable things desires good things, and that all people desire good things, since evil things are hurtful, and no one desires to be hurt. No one desires evil things, unless he is ignorant of their evilness, 'for what is misery but the desire and possession of evil?' If everyone desires good things and virtue is the desire of attaining good things, then one man is no better than another in that respect. Perhaps virtue is simply the power of attaining good things? Socrates says that, if by 'good things' Meno means things such as health, wealth, and honours, then virtue would only consist in the power of attaining them justly and piously, and not in the power of attaining them unjustly or impiously, which would amount to wickedness. However, justice and piety are parts of virtue, and Meno cannot simply define virtue in terms of itself. Meno confesses that he is unable to define virtue, even though he has delivered 'an infinite variety' of speeches on the subject. He compares Socrates to the flat torpedo fish, which torpifies or numbs all those who come near it. 'And I think that you are very wise in not [leaving Athens], for if you did in other places as you do in Athens, you would be cast into prison as a magician.'

Meno asks Socrates how he will look for virtue if he does not know what it is.

> *And how will you enquire, Socrates, into that which you do not know? What will you put forth as the subject of enquiry? And if you find what you want, how will you ever know that this is the thing which you did not know?*

Socrates understands Meno's meaning: one cannot enquire either about what he knows, or about what he does not know; for if he knows, he has no need to enquire; and if not, he does not know the very subject about which he is to enquire. Socrates has heard from certain wise men and women 'who spoke of things divine' that the soul is immortal, has been born often, and has seen all things on earth and below. Since the soul already knows everything, 'learning' simply means recollecting that which is already known. Meno asks Socrates to prove that this is true.

Socrates draws a square in the dirt and asks one of Meno's slave boys what the area of the square would be if the length of its sides was two feet. The boy correctly replies four feet. Socrates then asks him what the length of the square's sides would be if it had twice the area, that is, an area of eight feet. The boy incorrectly replies that the length of the square's sides would be double, that is, four feet. By extending the sides of the square and asking questions, Socrates gets the boy to recognise that the area of a square with sides of four feet would not be eight feet but sixteen feet, that is, four times the area of the original square of four feet. Given that the area of a square with sides of two feet is four and that the area of a square with sides of four feet is sixteen, what is the length of the sides of a square with an area of eight? The boy replies three feet, but Socrates gets him to recognise that the area of a square with sides of three feet would be nine feet, which is one more than the required eight feet. In an aside to Meno, Socrates points out that, despite being torpified, the boy is already better off than when he started the exercise, as he now knows what he does not know, and will wish to remedy his ignorance. Socrates continues with the boy, reminding Meno that he is not teaching the boy, but merely asking questions of him. Socrates divides the square of sixteen feet into four squares of four feet, and draws four diagonal lines that link the centres of each side of the square of sixteen feet (Figure 3). He then lets the boy see that the square contained within the four diagonal lines is in fact eight feet and therefore (1) that the length that he is looking for is the length of the diagonal, and (2) that double the area of a square is the square of its diagonal. Socrates claims to have proven that the boy found knowledge not through teaching, but through recollection.

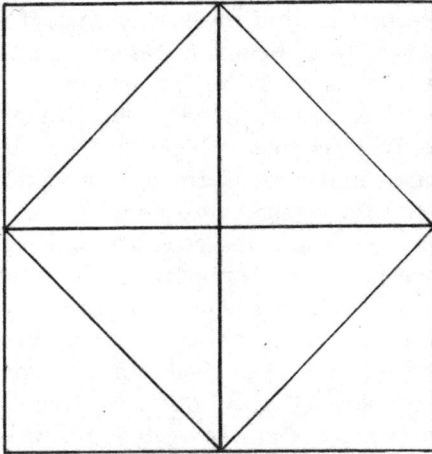

Figure 2: The slave boy's 'lesson' in geometry.

This knowledge was already in him, waiting to be stirred up as in a dream. If this is true, then one must confidently seek for the things that one does not 'know,' rather than believe – as Meno suggested – that this is impossible.

Since one must confidently seek for the things that one does not 'know,' Socrates suggests returning to the subject of the nature of virtue. Meno says that he would rather return to his original question, which was whether virtue can be acquired by teaching. Socrates replies,

> *Had I the command of you as well as of myself,*
> *Meno, I would not have enquired whether virtue*
> *is given by instruction or not, until we had first*
> *ascertained what it is. But as you think only of*
> *controlling me who am your slave, and never of*
> *controlling yourself, – such being your notion*
> *of freedom, I must yield to you, for you are*
> *irresistible.*

Socrates proceeds with the hypothesis that, if virtue was a kind of knowledge, then it could be taught just as other kinds of knowledge (such as geometry) can be taught. If everything good is knowledge, and if virtue is good, then virtue must be knowledge. What is good is beneficial and things such as beauty, strength, and wealth are also good and beneficial. However, these things might also be harmful, depending on how they are used. The same goes for qualities of the soul such as courage, justice, and temperance; for example, courage might be harmful if it amounts to recklessness. Thus, qualities of the soul are only beneficial if they are accompanied by wisdom. Given that virtue is good and beneficial, and given that what is beneficial is only so if accompanied by wisdom, virtue is either wholly or partly wisdom. If this is correct, the implication is that virtuous men are not so by nature, and if not by nature, then by teaching. Socrates is suspicious of this line of reasoning: if virtue is knowledge, and if virtue can be taught, why are there no teachers of virtue?

At this point, Socrates asks Anytus to join into the conversation. Anytus is a wealthy, powerful, and well-respected man, and is more likely than most to be able to answer this question. Socrates says that, if one wants to become a physician, he should seek instruction from a physician, and if he wants to become a cobbler, he should seek instruction from a cobbler; similarly, if he wants to become wise and virtuous, he should seek instruction from a sophist. Anytus is shocked by this suggestion, and affirms that sophists have a strong corrupting influence on all those who are entrusted to them. Socrates feigns disbelief: how could a reputed sophist such as Protagoras spend forty years practising his craft, and yet remain undetected as a fraud? Anytus affirms that all those who give their money to the sophists are out of their mind, and that if Meno wants to become wise and virtuous, he should seek instruction not from a sophist but from any one Athenian gentleman. Socrates asks how Athenian gentlemen are able to teach others that which they have never learned themselves.

Anytus replies that they learned of the previous generation of Athenian gentlemen. Socrates argues that men of wisdom and virtue seem to be very poor at imparting these qualities. For example, Thermistocles was able to teach his son Cleophantus skills such as standing upright on horseback and shooting javelins, but no one ever said of Cleophantus that he was wise and virtuous – and the same could be said for Lysimachus and his son Aristides, Pericles and his sons Paralus and Xanthippus, and Thucydides and his sons Melesias and Stephanus. Anytus gets angry at Socrates for defaming such eminent men, and warns him to be careful.

> *O Meno, think that Anytus is in a rage. And he may well be in a rage, for he thinks, in the first place, that I am defaming these gentlemen; and in the second place, he is of opinion that he is one of them himself. But some day he will know what is the meaning of defamation, and if he ever does, he will forgive me. Meanwhile I will return to you, Meno; for I suppose that there are gentlemen in your region too?*

Meno says that people in Thessaly are not agreed about whether or not virtue can be taught. He himself is unsure about whether even the sophists are able to teach virtue: when Gorgias hears other sophists promising that they can teach virtue he only laughs at them. Socrates says that even the poet Theognis had doubts about whether or not virtue could be taught, in some verses implying that it could, and in others that it could not. If even those who are supposed to be the teachers of virtue are confused about whether or not virtue can be taught, one can only assume that there are no teachers (and hence no students) of virtue, and that virtue cannot be taught. If virtue cannot be taught, then it is not a kind of knowledge.

If virtue cannot be taught, how, asks Meno, did good men

come into existence? Socrates says that they have so far overlooked that right action is possible under guidance other than that of knowledge. A man who has knowledge about the way to Larisa might be a good guide, but a man who has only correct opinion about the way, but has never been and does know, might be an equally good guide. Just as the man who thinks the truth is just as good a guide to Larisa as the man who knows the truth, so correct opinion is as good a guide to right action as knowledge. In that case, asks Meno, how does knowledge differ from correct opinion, and why should one prefer the one to the other? Socrates replies that correct opinions are like the statues of Daedalus, which run away unless they are tied down. Similarly, correct opinions do not remain long unless they can be tied down with an account of the reason why, whereupon they become knowledge. Since there are no teachers of virtue, virtue cannot be taught, and since virtue cannot be taught, it cannot be knowledge. All that remains is for virtue to be correct opinion, which explains why virtuous men such as Thermistocles, Lysimachus, and Pericles are unable to impart their virtue to others. These men are no different from soothsayers, prophets, and poets, who say many true things when they are divinely inspired, but have no knowledge of what they are saying. In conclusion, then, virtue is not taught, nor is it given by nature, nor does it occur by chance. Rather, it is a gift of the gods, and if ever there was a virtuous man who could teach his virtue to another, he would be said to be amongst the living as Homer says Tiresias was amongst the dead, 'he alone has understanding; but the rest are flitting shades'.

CHAPTER 14

Euthydemus

Is not this the result – that other things are
indifferent, and that wisdom is the only good,
and ignorance the only evil?

Crito asks an elderly Socrates whom he was speaking to at
the Lyceum yesterday. Socrates replies that he was speaking
to Euthydemus and Dionysodorus, a pair of brothers and
sophists with a reputation for teaching rhetoric and the art
of fighting in armour: such is their skill and wisdom that he
is thinking of becoming their student. Socrates relates their
encounter at the Lyceum to Crito.

Socrates is sitting with the young Cleinias, the grandson
of Alcibiades, when he is accosted by the brothers and a crowd
of their followers. The brothers declare that their principal
occupation is now the teaching of virtue, and that they are
able to teach virtue better and quicker than anyone. Socrates
replies that he is keen to learn from them, as are Cleinias and
his lover Ctesippus. Socrates asks the brothers whether they
are also able to teach virtue to someone who does not want to
learn it from them, either because he thinks that virtue cannot
be taught, or because he thinks that they are not the teachers
of it. If so, perhaps the brothers could do him a great favour

and persuade Cleinias that he ought to be a philosopher and study virtue.

Euthydemus asks Cleinias, 'Are those who learn the wise or the ignorant?' Cleinias blushes and hesitantly replies, 'The wise'. 'And yet when you learned you did not know and were not wise.' Dionysodorus takes over from Euthydemus, 'Who learns the dictation from the grammar master, the wise or the ignorant boys?' 'The wise.' 'Then the wise learn after all.' The crowd of followers bursts into laughter and Euthydemus starts again, 'Do those who learn, learn what they know or what they do not know?' 'What they do not know.' 'But dictation is of letters?' 'Yes.' 'And you already know letters?' 'Yes.' 'So you learn what you know.' Dionysodorus picks up the argument like a ball, 'Is not learning the acquiring of knowledge?' 'Yes.' 'In that case, you learn what you do not know.'

Socrates intervenes to rescue Cleinias from a third fall. No doubt the brothers are initiating him into their mysteries in the manner of the Corybantes, with 'dancing and sport'. By all this they are merely trying to make Cleinias understand that 'to learn' can mean both 'to learn' and 'to know'. He reassures Cleinias that,

> ...if a man had all that sort of knowledge that ever was, he would not be at all the wiser; he would only be able to play with men, tripping them up... with distinctions of words. He would be like a person who pulls away a stool from someone when he is about to sit down, and then laughs and makes merry at the sight of his friend overturned and laid on his back.

Socrates tells the brothers that it is time for them to begin their exhortation to virtue. So as to point the way, Socrates delivers his own 'clumsy and tedious' version of an exhortation to virtue. All men, he says, desire happiness. If all men desire happiness, then all men desire good things, since it is by good things that men are made happy. Thus, all men desire things such as beauty, health, wealth, power, and honours, but also courage, justice, temperance, wisdom, and, the greatest of all good things, fortune. However, a man with wisdom would be in no need of fortune, since by wisdom he would never err, but always act rightly and successfully. Good things, he continues, profit men not in their having, but in their using. However, the wrong use of a good thing is far worse than its non-use, for the one is an evil, whereas the other is neither a good nor an evil. What determines whether a good thing is used rightly or wrongly is wisdom, so it is by wisdom that a man has good fortune, success, and happiness. A man would be better off having a few things with wisdom than many without, for he would then make fewer mistakes, suffer fewer misfortunes, and be less miserable. Wisdom is the only good, and ignorance the only evil, and it follows that a man should make himself as wise as possible, and that nothing that he undertakes to this end can ever be dishonourable. This is, of course, assuming that wisdom can be taught. As Cleinias affirms that wisdom can be taught, Socrates sees no need to open that particular can of worms. Socrates turns to the brothers and suggests that they take up the enquiry where he left off and proceed to show Cleinias whether he should have all knowledge, or only the sort of knowledge that will make him good and happy.

Dionysodorus asks Socrates whether he really wishes Cleinias to become wise. 'And is he not wise yet?' 'No.' 'Then you wish him to be what he is not, that is, you wish him to perish!' An angry Ctesippus tries to take on the brothers but soon gets entangled in their sophistry. Socrates breaks their exchange by offering himself up to Dionysodorus' teaching: 'he may put me into the pot, like Medea the Colchian, kill me, boil me, if he will only make me good'. Ctessipus adds that the brothers may skin him alive, 'if only my skin is made at last, not like that of Marsyas, into a leathern bottle, but into a piece of virtue'. He affirms that he was not reviling the brothers, but merely contradicting them. Dionysodorus replies that there is no such thing as contradiction because words express things which are, and it is therefore impossible to speak of things which are not. Socrates asks Dionysodorus to explain this theory, which he has also heard from Protagoras and his followers; can there really be no such thing as ignorance, error, or falsehood? Dionysodorus says that there can be no such thing and invites Socrates to refute him. Socrates points out that he cannot possibly refute him if there is no such thing as ignorance, error, or falsehood. In which case, how can the brothers possibly claim to teach virtue? The sophists sidestep this question and carry on in the same vein. Things that have sense are alive, but words are not alive so they do not have any sense. Therefore, there is no point in asking them about the sense of their words. Ctessipus once again gets angry, but Socrates calms his temper and reassures him that the full beauty of the brothers will, no doubt, soon become apparent.

Socrates once again offers to point the way to the brothers. A man, he says, should seek to acquire knowledge, but only the sort of knowledge that will make him good and happy. However, what sort of knowledge might that be? Socrates suggests that it is the knowledge of the general, but Cleinias disagrees on the basis that the general does not know how to make use of captured cities, for which reason he hands them over to the statesman. In that case, perhaps it is the knowledge of the statesman, the so-called political art? If so, the political art ought to make one wise, since it is by wisdom that all things are made good use of. But in what does the political art make one wise? Socrates puts this question to the brothers.

Instead of answering the question, the brothers offer to prove that Socrates already knows its answer. If Socrates knows something, then he is knowing, and since he cannot be both knowing and not knowing, he must know all things. Socrates says that this implies that everyone knows every-thing, and Ctessipus pushes the envelope by asking each brother to say how many teeth the other has. The brothers once again sidestep the question and carry on in the same vein, playing with words and coming up with one logical fallacy after another. Ctessipus eventually picks up their weapons, but the conversation is brought to an end with an eruption of laughter and applause from the brothers' followers. Socrates delivers a panegyric in which he praises the brothers for their wit and wisdom, their magnanimous disregard of opinion, their kind and public-spirited denial of all differences, and, above all, their ability to teach their art in such a short space of time. He advises the brothers not to give any further public displays so that people might not profit so cheaply and so easily from their wisdom. Finally, he reverently asks the brothers to receive him and Cleinias amongst their students and followers.

Socrates asks Crito to join him in becoming a student of the brothers. Crito replies that, although he is ready to learn, he would prefer to be refuted by arguments rather than to use arguments in the refutation of others. In any case, his principal concern is not with his education but with that of his elder son, Critobulus. Given that the teachers of philosophy appear to be such outrageous beings, how can he possibly ask Critobulus to study philosophy? Socrates tells him that, in every profession, the bad are many and useless, whereas the good are few and beyond all price. Therefore, Crito need not mind whether the teachers of philosophy are good or bad, but think only of philosophy herself.

CHAPTER 15

Cratylus

*...the knowledge of names is a great part of
knowledge.*

The principal concern of the *Cratylus* is the 'correctness of
names': if a given name (or word or phrase) is the correct
one for denoting a given thing, what is it that makes it so?
Socrates discusses the correctness of names with Cratylus, a
former pupil of Heraclitus, and Hermogenes, the impecunious
brother of Callias, at whose house the *Protagoras* takes place.

Cratylus has been telling Hermogenes that a thing's
name is not whatever people agree to call it, but that there
is a 'natural correctness' of names such that a thing's name
belongs to it by nature and is the same for everyone, Greek or
foreigner. Cratylus says that his name is 'Cratylus,' and that
Socrates' name is 'Socrates,' but that Hermogenes' name is
not 'Hermogenes,' even though everyone agrees to call him so.
Hermogenes is baffled by this, and asks Socrates to 'interpret'
what Cratylus is saying. Socrates suggests that Cratylus is
simply making fun of Hermogenes, who is unable to make
any money despite being named after the god of profit[14].

---

14 'Hermogenes' means 'son of Hermes'.

Hermogenes argues that the correctness of names is simply determined by convention and agreement. For example, he says, when a new name is given to a domestic slave, the new name is just as correct as any of the old ones. It follows that a person or object can have more than one name, and also different names to different people: '...whatever each person says is the name of something, for him, that is the name'.

Socrates asks Hermogenes whether he agrees with Protagoras when he says that 'man is the measure of all things'. In other words, are things merely as they appear to a given person, or do they have some fixed being of their own? Hermogenes confesses that he has at times been so perplexed as to 'take refuge' in Protagoras' doctrine. Socrates is astonished: at such times, did Hermogenes actually believe that there was no such thing as a bad man? Hermogenes replies that, on the contrary, he has often thought that there were very bad men, and plenty of them. Socrates asks whether Hermogenes believed that there was no such thing as a *good* man, to which he replies 'some, but not many'. They agree that what distinguishes bad men from good men is that good men are wise whereas bad men are foolish. But how, asks Socrates, can one man be wise and another foolish if 'man is the measure of all things,' and whatever each man believes to be true is true for him? Furthermore, if one man can be wise and another can be foolish, then Euthydemus' doctrine that 'all things equally and always belong to all men' must also be false. Therefore, people and things must have some fixed being of their own. If people and things have some fixed being of their own, it follows that this is also true of the actions performed in relation to them. So if, for example, we want to cut something, we can only be successful in cutting it if we cut it in accordance with the nature of cutting and being cut and with the natural tool for cutting. Speaking is also an action performed in relation to people and things, and so is saying names. Thus, if we are to speak correctly or achieve anything, we cannot simply name things as we choose.

If we want to cut something, we must cut it with the natural tool for cutting, and if we want to name something, we must name it with the natural tool for naming, which is a name. If a name is a sort of tool, who, asks Socrates, makes this tool? In other words, who or what provides us with the names that we use? Socrates replies that the names that we use are provided by a legislator – a very rare kind of craftsman indeed. Just as a carpenter embodies in wood the type of shuttle naturally suited to each type of weaving, so the legislator embodies in sounds and syllables the name naturally suited to each type of thing. And just as different blacksmiths who are making the same tool do not necessarily need to make it out of the same iron, so different legislators who are naming the same thing do not necessarily need to use the same syllables, so long as the name that they give to the thing is naturally suited to it. This explains why the same thing can have different names in different languages. Thus, Cratylus is correct in saying that there is a 'natural correctness of names'.

But what is the best way to name things? Socrates suggests that the best way to find out is to ask a sophist, but since neither of them can afford to pay a sophist's fee, they should look instead to Homer and to the other poets.[15] For example, Homer says that the river god who fought with Hephaestus is called *Xanthos* by the gods and *Skamandros* by men. Socrates argues that the river god is more correctly called *Xanthos* than *Skamandros*, since the gods are bound to call things by their naturally correct names. Homer also ascribes two names to Hector's son, *Skamandrios* and *Astyanax*. Socrates argues that Hector's son is more correctly named *Astyanax* than *Skamandrios*, since the Trojan men call him *Astyanax* whereas the Trojan women call him *Skamandrios*, and Homer

---

15 Earlier in the dialogue, Socrates had said that if he had not been poor, he might have heard the fifty-drachma course of 'the great Prodicus,' which Prodicus himself billed as a complete education in grammar and language. However, Socrates only ever heard Prodicus' one-drachma course, and so does not know the truth about such matters.

thought that the Trojan men were wiser than their women. Socrates quotes Homer in saying, of Hector, that 'He alone defended their city and long walls'. Thus, it seems correct to call the son of the city's defender *Astyanax* or 'lord of the city'. Furthermore, *Hector* itself means 'holder,' which is very similar to 'lord of the city'. If it seems right to call a lion's whelp a lion, or a horse's foal a horse, then it also seems right to call the son of a king a king. Thus, those born according to nature should be given the same name as their fathers, even though the names of father and son may, as in the case of Hector and Astyanax, vary in their syllables.

Socrates now races through a long list of words to show how they have been correctly named, speaking like an oracle because inspired by Euthyphro. For example, *truth* or *alētheia* is a compression of the phrase 'a wandering that is divine' (*alētheia*). The god of the underworld is called *Hades* because he knows (*eidenai*) everything fine and beautiful, and *Pluto* because he is the source of wealth (*ploutos*). Most people prefer to call him *Pluto* rather than *Hades* because they are afraid of what they cannot see (*aeides*), and assume that *Hades* refers to that. Socrates says that many people are terrified of Hades because, after we die, our souls remain with him forever. However, the reason our souls do not escape from him is because they are bound to him by the strongest of desires, namely, the desire to associate with someone who can make us a better person. Socrates adds that Hades must be a philosopher, since he has realised that a person only becomes interested in virtue once he is detached from his body.

Some names, says Socrates, cannot be explained in this way, either because they have a foreign origin, or because they are so old and 'basic' that they cannot be recovered. Such 'primary' names are based on syllables and letters, and are used to make other 'derivative' names. Socrates argues that one must know about the correctness of primary names if one is to know about the correctness of derivative names. So, for example, the letter 'r' seemed to the legislator to be an appropriate tool for copying motion, for which reason he used it in words such as *rhoē* (flow), *trechein* (running), *tromos* (trembling), *thruptein* (breaking), and *rhumbein* (whirling). As the tongue glides most of all in pronouncing the letter 'l,' the legislator used this letter in *olisthanein* (glide), *leion* (smooth), *liparon* (sleek), and *kollōdes* (viscous). However, as the gliding of the tongue is stopped most completely in pronouncing the letter 'g,' he preferred to use this letter to imitate something cloying, as in *gloiodes* (clammy), *glischron* (gluey), and *gluku* (sweet). And so on.

Hermogenes turns to Cratylus and asks him whether he agrees with what Socrates has just been saying about names. Cratylus replies by quoting Achilles' words to Ajax,

> *Ajax, son of Telamon, seed of Zeus, lord of the*
> *people,*
> *All you have said to me seems spoken after my*
> *own mind.*

Socrates says that he has long been surprised at his own wisdom, and also doubtful of it. He insists on the importance of re-investigating whatever he says, since 'self-deception is the worst thing of all'.

Cratylus agrees with Socrates' statement that 'the correctness of a name consists in displaying the nature of the thing it names'. However, he thinks that all names have been correctly given, whereas Socrates argues that, just like paintings, some names are finely made and others are badly made. Just as there are good craftsmen and bad craftsmen, so there are good legislators and bad legislators. In particular, Socrates insists that a name cannot resemble the thing that it names in every respect, since it would then be a duplicate of that thing, and no one would be able to tell the difference between them. As a name cannot perfectly resemble the thing that it names, there is scope for a name to be well given or less well given.

Socrates says that there are times when we understand

a name that does not resemble the thing that it names, in which case our understanding of the name is a matter of usage and convention. Usage, it seems, enables both like and unlike names to denote things. Thus, whilst it may be possible to know things through their names, it is far better to know them in themselves. Socrates concludes that the matter calls for further investigation.

> *This may be true, Cratylus, but is also very likely to be untrue; and therefore I would not have you be too easily persuaded of it. Reflect well and like a man, and do not easily accept such a doctrine; for you are young and of an age to learn. And when you have found the truth, come and tell me.*

CHAPTER 16

Ion

Then, Ion, I shall assume the nobler alternative;
and attribute to you in your praises of Homer
inspiration, and not art.

Ion is a rhapsode from Ephesus, who just won the first prize in
a contest for rhapsodes held in the honour of the god Asclepius,
the god of medicine and healing. He runs into Socrates who
tells him that he envies rhapsodes their profession, not only
because they must learn the verses that they recite, but also
because they must understand the mind of the poets who
wrote them. Ion claims to speak more beautifully than anyone
on Homer, saying that 'neither Metrodorus of Lampsacus,
nor Stesimbrotus of Thasos, nor Glaucon, nor anyone else
who ever was, had as good ideas about Homer as I have, or
as many'. When Socrates asks him whether his art extends
to other great poets such as Hesiod or Archilochus, he replies
that Homer is in himself quite enough.

Socrates argues that, if Ion is an adequate judge of Homer,
he must also be an adequate judge of the other great poets.
Ion responds that whenever someone discusses a poet other
than Homer, he is unable to speak at all, and simply goes to
sleep. Socrates says that this is because Ion has not mastered
his subject, but is moved to speak on Homer by a divine power.

Socrates compares this divine power to a magnetic stone that can not only move iron rings, but also put power into the rings, so that they in turn can do just what the magnetic stone does, and so on. This creates a long chain of iron rings whose individual power depends on nothing other than the original magnetic stone. Similarly, the Muse inspires some people herself, and these people go on to inspire other people, and so on. Thus, if an epic poet or a lyric poet is any good, this is not because he has mastered his subject, but because he is divinely inspired, divinely possessed.

Socrates says that the Corybantes[16] are not in their right mind when they dance, nor are the Bacchic maidens when they draw honey and milk from rivers. 'For the poet is a light and winged and holy thing, and there is no invention in him until he has been inspired and is out of his senses, and the mind is no longer in him: when he has not attained to this state, he is powerless and is unable to utter his oracles.' Socrates asks Ion whether, when he recites Homer, he does not get beside himself, whether his soul does not believe that it is present at the actions which he tells of, wherever and whenever they may have taken place. Ion replies that, when he tells of something sad, his eyes are full of tears, and when he tells of something frightening, his hair stands on end and his heart jumps, such that he is no longer in his right mind. Socrates tells Ion that this is precisely the effect that a rhapsode has on his audiences. Thus, the Muse inspires the poet, the poet inspires the rhapsode, and the rhapsode inspires his audience, who are the last of the iron rings in the divine chain.

---

16 The Corybantes were male crested dancers who worshiped the Phrygian goddess Cybele with drumming and dancing.

CHAPTER 17

Phaedrus

*...madness comes from God, whereas sober sense
is merely human.*

Socrates runs into Phaedrus who is going for a walk outside
the city wall. Phaedrus has just been listening to a speech on
love by Lysias, 'the greatest rhetorician of the age,' in which
Lysias has advanced that a youth who is being courted both
by a lover and a non-lover should give his favour to the latter
rather than to the former. Socrates suspects that Phaedrus is
hiding Lysias' speech under his cloak, and persuades him to
pull it out and read it to him. Together they walk along the
banks of the Ilissus, looking for a quiet spot to settle down
with the speech. Phaedrus points to a tall plane-tree in the
distance, under which, he says, there are shade and gentle
breezes. As neither is wearing any sandals, they wade in the
water to cool off their feet. Phaedrus asks Socrates whether
they are not passing by the exact spot where Boreas is said
to have carried off Orithyia from the banks of the Ilissus.
Socrates replies that, while he is still in ignorance of his own
self, he sees no point in being curious about myths or, indeed,
about anything else which is not his concern. Upon reaching
the plane-tree, Socrates praises the beauty of the spot: the
summer sounds and scents, the chaste tree in the fullest

blossom, the cold stream beneath the plane-tree, and, above all, the soft green grass that is 'like a pillow gently sloping to the head'. He confesses that he rarely ventures outside the city gates, since he is a lover of knowledge, and the men who dwell in the city are his teachers. They lie down on the grass and Phaedrus reads out Lysias' speech, which begins thus:

> *Listen. You know how matters stand with me; and how, as I conceive, this affair may be arranged for the advantage of both of us. And I maintain that I ought not to fail in my suit, because I am not your lover...*

Lysias proceeds to catalogue the various reasons for which a youth should give his favour to the non-lover rather than to the lover. In essence, it is preferable for a youth to give his favour to he who can best return it rather than to he who needs it most because 'he is afflicted with a malady and is not in his right mind'. Since the non-lover is, amongst others, less jealous, less flattering, and less fickle, friendship with him is likely to be more rewarding and to last for longer.

Socrates mocks Phaedrus' apparent enthusiasm for Lysias' speech and proposes to deliver another speech that is both less repetitive and less ostentatious. He says that he has been filled, like an empty jar, by the words of other people flowing in through his ears. For this reason, none of the ideas in his speech are actually his. He covers his head, calls upon the Muses, and begins his speech. Everyone, he says, is ruled by two principles, namely, a desire for pleasure and 'an acquired opinion which aspires after the best'. These two principles can be in harmony, but, when they are not, one must conquer over the other. When the first principle conquers, this is called excess, and when the second principle conquers, this is called temperance. There are several forms of excess, for instance, gluttony, which is the desire to take pleasure in food, or love, which is the desire to take pleasure in the beauty of the beloved. Thus, the lover seeks not to make his beloved into a better person, but merely to make him as personally agreeable as possible. To this end, he may deprive his beloved from family, friends, and estate; debar him from improving company; and, worst of all, banish him from philosophy. In time, however, the lover's madness is replaced by 'right-minded reason,' and he breaks off all the oaths and promises that he once made to his beloved.

> *Consider this, fair youth, and know that in the friendship of the lover there is no real kindness; he has an appetite and wants to feed upon you: as wolves love lambs so lovers love their loves.*

Phaedrus bids Socrates to deliver a similar speech about all the advantages of accepting the non-lover, but Socrates insists that he has been overtaken by the Nymphs and cannot carry on speech-making. As he makes to leave, his *daimonion* tells him that he has been guilty of impiety and must make atonement to Love (*Eros*), who is a god and therefore cannot, as Socrates has implied, be evil. To make atonement to Eros, Socrates delivers a second speech in praise of the lover. He begins by criticising his first speech for overlooking that madness, as well as being an illness, can also be the source of man's greatest blessings.

> *Madness, provided it comes as the gift of heaven, is the channel by which we receive the greatest blessings... the men of old who gave things their names saw no disgrace or reproach in madness; otherwise they would not have connected it with the name of the noblest of arts, the art of discerning the future, and called it the manic art... So, according to the evidence provided by our ancestors, madness is a nobler thing than sober sense... madness comes from God, whereas sober sense is merely human.[17]*

---

17 Translated by Walter Hamilton.

He explains that there are four types of divine madness: prophecy, from Apollo; holy prayers and mystic rites, from Dionysus; poetry, from the Muses; and love, from Aphrodite and Eros. He then sets out to prove the divine origin of love, a proof, he says, that is more easily received by the wise than by the merely clever. In order to do this, he must first prove the immortality of the soul. The soul, he says, is not only self-moving, but also 'the beginning of motion' for things that are not self-moving. As the beginning is begotten out of nothing, the beginning is unbegotten, and, by the same token, unceasing, '...else the whole heavens and all creation would collapse and stand still, and never again have motion or birth'. Having thereby proved the immortality of the soul, Socrates compares the soul to a chariot with a charioteer and a pair of winged horses. Whereas the chariot of a god has two good horses, that of a human being has one good horse and one bad, unruly horse that is the cause of much hardship for the charioteer. The soul, he says,

> *...has the care of inanimate being everywhere, and traverses the whole heaven in divers forms appearing – when perfect and fully winged she soars upward, and orders the whole world; whereas the imperfect soul, losing her wings and drooping in her flight at last settles on the solid ground – there, finding a home, she receives an earthly frame which appears to be self-moved, but is really moved by her power; and this composition of soul and body is called a living and mortal creature.*

The chariot of a god is able to soar to the top of the vault of heaven, such that the god is able to step outside the rim of heaven and contemplate the colourless, formless, intangible essence of reality. The revolution of the spheres carries the god round and back again to the same place, and in the space of this circle he feasts his mind upon justice, temperance, and knowledge, not in the form of generation or relation, which men call existence, but in their absolute, universal form. Despite their bad, unruly horse, the chariots of the imperfect souls that are most alike to the gods are able to ascend high enough for their charioteers to lift their heads above the rim of heaven and catch a fleeting glimpse of the universals. However, the rest are not strong enough to ascend so high, and are left to feed their mind on nothing more than opinion. In time, all imperfect souls fall back to earth, but only those that have seen something of the universals can take on a human form; human beings are by their nature able to recollect universals, and so must once have seen them. The imperfect souls that have gazed longest upon the universals are incarnated as philosophers, artists, and true lovers. As they are still able to remember the universals, they are completely absorbed in ideas about them and forget all about earthly interests. Common people think that they are mad, but the truth is that they are divinely inspired and in love with goodness and beauty.

Socrates says that he has so far been speaking about the madness of love, which is the fourth and highest kind of madness. The madness of love arises from seeing the beauty of the earth and being reminded of true, universal beauty. When this happens, the soul is struck with such amazement that it begins to grow wings and to flutter them. Tragically, most earthly souls become so corrupt by the body, 'that living tomb which we carry about,' that they lose all memory for the universals. When they cast their eyes on the beauty of the earth, they are merely given over to pleasure, 'and like a brutish beast' rush on to enjoy and beget. In contrast, the earthly soul that is able to feel true love gazes upon the face of his beloved and reverences it as an expression of the divine: of justice, of temperance, and of knowledge absolute. As he looks into the eyes of his beloved, a shudder passes into an unusual heat and perspiration. The parts of the soul out of which the wings grew, and which had hitherto been closed and rigid, begin to melt open, and small wings begin to swell and grow from the root upwards.

> *Like a child whose teeth are just starting to grow in, and its gums are all aching and itching – that is exactly how the soul feels when it begins to grow wings. It swells up and aches and tingles as it grows them.*[18]

The lover feels the utmost joy when he is with his beloved and the most intense longing when they are separated. When they are separated, the parts out of which the lover's wings are growing begin to dry out and close up, and the pain is such that he prizes his beloved above all else, utterly unable to think a bad thought about him, let alone to betray or forsake him.

The lover whose soul was once the follower of Zeus amongst all the other gods seeks out a beloved who shares in his god's philosophical and imperial nature, and then does all he can to confirm this nature in him. Thus, the desire of the divinely inspired lover can only be fair and blissful to the beloved. In time, the beloved, who is no common fool, comes to realise that his divinely inspired lover is worth more to him than all his other friends and kinsmen put together, and that neither human discipline nor divine inspiration could have offered him any greater blessing.

> *Thus great are the heavenly blessings which the friendship of a lover will confer upon you, my youth. Whereas the attachment of the non-lover, which is alloyed with a worldly prudence and has worldly and niggardly ways of doling out benefits, will breed in your soul those vulgar*

---

18 Translated by Alexander Nehamas and Paul Woodruff.

> *qualities which the populace applaud, will send*
> *you bowling round the earth during a period of*
> *nine thousand years, and leave you a fool in the*
> *world below.*

Socrates concludes that he has paid his recantation to Eros with this 'tolerably credible and possibly true though partly erring myth'. Phaedrus doubts that Lysias can write a better speech, and the conversation turns to the subject of writing. Socrates suggests that there is no disgrace in writing, but only in bad writing. They decide to talk about the differences between good and bad writing, lest the cicadas laugh at them for avoiding conversation at midday, and mistake them for a pair of slaves who have come to their resting place as cattle do to a waterhole. On the other hand, if the cicadas see that they are not lulled by their chirruping, they may, out of respect, offer them their god-given gifts. For once upon a time, before the birth of the Muses, the cicadas used to be human beings. Then the Muses were born and song was created, and they were so overwhelmed with the pleasure of singing that they forgot to eat or drink, and died without even realising it. As a gift from the Muses, they were reborn as cicadas, singing from the moment they are born to the moment they die without ever feeling hunger or thirst. After dying, the cicadas report back to the Muses in heaven about who is honouring them on earth, and win the love of Terpsichore for the dancers, of Erato for the lovers, and of Calliope, the eldest Muse, for the philosophers.

Phaedrus has heard that a good orator has nothing to do with that which is truly good or truly honourable, but only with opinion about them, which comes from persuasion, and not from truth. Socrates suggests that, whilst there can be no genuine art of persuasion without knowledge of the truth, knowledge of the truth may be insufficient to produce conviction unless accompanied by the art of persuasion. However, knowledge of the truth and the art of persuasion are not different things but one and the same, since 'he who would deceive others, and not be deceived, must exactly know the real likenesses and differences of things... or he will never know either how to make the gradual departure from the truth into the opposite of truth which is effected by the help of resemblances, or how to avoid it'. For example, at the beginning of his speech Lysias failed to define love, and thereby failed to distinguish between things like 'iron' and 'silver' which suggest the same to all listeners, and things like 'justice' or 'love' which suggest different things to different listeners and even different things to the same listener, and in which rhetoric has the greatest power. Socrates compares the rest of Lysias' poorly ordered speech to the inscription on Midas' grave, in which the order of the lines makes no difference at all:

> *I am a maiden of bronze and lie on the tomb of*
> *   Midas;*
> *So long as water flows and tall trees grow,*
> *So long here on this spot by his sad tomb abiding,*
> *I shall declare to passers-by that Midas sleeps*
> *   below.*

Socrates says that a speaker should divide his speech according to its natural formation, 'where the joint is, not breaking any part as a bad carver might,' but points out that this art pertains to dialectic rather than to rhetoric. To find out more about rhetoric specifically, they go through the various tools of speechmaking, listing everything from pithy sayings to pathetic appeals. This leads them to conclude that an orator is like a doctor who knows all manner of cures, but does not know how, when, or to whom they should be applied: 'a madman or pedant who fancies that he is a physician because he has read something in a book, or has stumbled on a prescription or two, although he has no real understanding of the art of medicine'. Just as the art of medicine should define the nature of the body, so the art of rhetoric – insofar as there is an art of rhetoric – should define the nature of the soul, in which it seeks to produce conviction. Thus, the rhetorician should be able to give an exact description of the nature of the soul, how many different types there are, and when and how they might be acted upon. In the courts of law, men care only about conviction, which is based on probability rather than on truth. For this reason, improbable truths should be withheld in favour of probable untruths. For example, when a weak but courageous man attacks a strong but cowardly one, the weak man should say that he could never have assaulted such a strong man, and the strong man should say that he was assaulted by several men. However, a true rhetorician who knows the nature of the soul does not lie, because he is a philosopher who has discovered the art of rhetoric *through his pursuit of a much higher goal*.

The conversation shifts to what is good and bad in writing, and Socrates makes up a story about the origins of writing:

> *At the Egyptian city of Naucratis, there was a famous old god, whose name was Theuth; the bird which is called the Ibis is sacred to him, and he was the inventor of many arts, such as arithmetic and calculation and geometry and astronomy and draughts and dice, but his great discovery was the use of letters. Now in those days the god Thamus was the king of the whole country of Egypt; and he dwelt in that great city of Upper Egypt which the Hellenes call Egyptian Thebes, and the god himself is called by them Ammon. To him came Theuth and showed his inventions, desiring that the other Egyptians might be allowed to have the benefit of them; he enumerated them, and Thamus enquired about their several uses, and praised some of them and censured others, as he approved or disapproved of them. It would take a long time to repeat all that Thamus said to Theuth in*

praise or blame of the various arts. But when they came to letters, This, said Theuth, will make the Egyptians wiser and give them better memories; it is a specific both for the memory and for the wit. Thamus replied: O most ingenious Theuth, the parent or inventor of an art is not always the best judge of the utility or inutility of his own inventions to the users of them. And in this instance, you who are the father of letters, from a paternal love of your own children have been led to attribute to them a quality which they cannot have; for this discovery of yours will create forgetfulness in the learners' souls, because they will not use their memories; they will trust to the external written characters and not remember of themselves. The specific which you have discovered is an aid not to memory, but to reminiscence, and you give your disciples not truth, but only the semblance of truth; they will be hearers of many things and will have learned nothing; they will appear to be omniscient and will generally know nothing; they will be tiresome company, having the show of wisdom without the reality.

Phaedrus dismisses this tale of Egypt, saying that Socrates can easily invent tales of any country. Socrates says that, according to tradition, the first prophecies were the words of an oak. In those days, men were not as wise as the young of today, and in their simplicity they were content to listen to an oak or even to a stone, so long as it spoke the truth. Why, then, can Phaedrus not simply consider whether a man speaks the truth, rather than who he is and where he is from? Phaedrus accepts this rebuke and confesses that there is truth in Socrates' tale of Egypt.

Socrates next compares writing to a painting which, although having the likeness of life, cannot answer any question that is put to it. Writing is passed around indiscriminately, both to those who can understand it and to those who cannot. If it comes to be abused, maltreated, or simply misunderstood, its parent cannot come to its defence, nor can it defend itself. In contrast, the living word knows when to speak and when to keep silence, and is always able to defend itself. Thus, only the living word can adequately teach the truth.

> ...*it is much nobler to be serious about these matters, and (prefer) the art of dialectic. The dialectician chooses a proper soul and plants and sows within it discourse accompanied by knowledge – discourse capable of helping itself as well as the man who planted it, which is not barren but produces a seed from which more discourse grows in the character of others. Such discourse makes the seed forever immortal and renders the man who has it as happy as any human being can be.* [19]

Socrates tells Phaedrus to go to Lysias and to tell him what the Nymphs have been just been telling them: that if a man composes speeches based on knowledge of the truth, and defends them ably when they are put to the test by spoken arguments, then he should be called neither an orator, nor wise (for only the gods are truly wise), but a lover of wisdom.

Before they leave Socrates offers a prayer to the local deities:

> S: *Beloved Pan, and all ye other gods who haunt this place, give me beauty in the inward soul; and may the outward and inward man be at one. May I reckon the wise to be the wealthy, and may I have such a quantity of gold as a temperate man and he only can bear and*

---

19 Translated by Alexander Nehamas and Paul Woodruff.

carry. – *Anything more? The prayer, I think, is
enough for me.*
P: *Ask the same for me, for friends should have
all things in common.*
S: *Let us go.*

CHAPTER 18

Symposium

He whom Love touches not walks in darkness.

Aristodemus was amongst the guests at a drinking party (symposium) held many years ago to celebrate the success of Agathon's first tragedy, and related the famous conversation that then took place to Apollodorus. Apollodorus recently ran into Glaucon (Plato's half-brother) on the road from Phalerum to Athens. Glaucon had heard a garbled version of the conversation and asked Apollodorus whether he had been present at the symposium. Apollodorus replied that he could not possibly have been present at the symposium, since it occurred many years ago, when they were both but children. Besides, he only became Socrates' friend three years ago, before which he simply drifted about aimlessly.

> *There was a time when I was running about the world, fancying myself to be well employed, but I was really a most wretched thing, no better than you are now. I thought that I ought to do anything rather than be a philosopher.*

Whilst they made their way to Athens, Apollodorus related Aristodemus' account of the conversation to Glaucon. This primed Apollodorus to relate it for a second time to an unnamed friend who is a rich trader.

On the day of the symposium, Aristodemus runs into Socrates who, unusually, has just bathed and put on sandals. Socrates explains that he is going to a symposium at Agathon's to celebrate the latter's victory at the Dionysia, and persuades Aristodemus to come along uninvited. En route to Agathon's, Socrates appears preoccupied and keeps falling behind. As a result, Aristodemus arrives at Agathon's before Socrates, and a slave is sent out to search for him. The slave reports back that Socrates is standing on a neighbour's porch, apparently lost in thought.

Whilst they wait for Socrates, Aristodemus encounters the other guests in the banqueting hall, including Agathon's life-long lover Pausanias, the comedian Aristophanes, a pompous doctor named Eryximachus, and the young if delightful Phaedrus. By the time Socrates joins them, the meal is already half over. Agathon asks Socrates to share his couch so that he may touch him and share the wisdom that he found on the neighbour's porch. Socrates replies that his wisdom is but a shadow in a dream, and that if wisdom could be transmitted by touch, then *he* would be the one to benefit from sitting next to Agathon. Since most of the guests still have a terrible hangover from the previous night's celebrations, they agree to curtail the drinking and engage in conversation. Phaedrus has recently been lamenting that the poets praise all the gods but Love (*Eros*), so Eryximachus suggests that each person, from left to right starting with Phaedrus, make a speech in praise of Love.

Phaedrus says that, according to Hesiod, Acusilaus, and Parmenides, Love is one of the most ancient gods and, as such, brings us the greatest goods: 'For I know not any greater blessing to a young man who is beginning life than a virtuous lover or to the lover than a beloved youth'. Love is better than kindred, rank, money or anything else at imparting the guidance that a young man needs to live a good life, because lovers seek honour in each other's eyes, and nothing shames them more than to be seen committing some inglorious act by their lover. When Homer says that the god breathes courage into the souls of heroes, this is really Love's gift to every lover. Thus Achilles gave his life for Patroclus, even though Patroclus had already been slain by Hector. The gods honour the virtue of love, particularly the return of love on the part of the beloved, since the lover is more god-inspired than the beloved, and therefore more divine. For this reason, the gods sent Achilles, who was the beloved of Patroclus, to the Isles of the Blessed. In conclusion, Love is the most ancient and most mighty of the gods, the most important giver of virtue in life, and of happiness after death.

Pausanias says that it is important not to praise love indiscriminately, since there are in fact two kinds of Love: the love of *Aphrodite Pandemos*, the daughter of Zeus and Dione, and the love of *Aphrodite Urania*, who was born out of the castrated genitals of Uranus. The love of *Aphrodite Pandemos* is a common love that is felt by vulgar men who are attracted more to the body than to the soul and so to less intelligent partners. In contrast, the love of *Aphrodite Urania* is a heavenly love that inspires men to turn to the male youth, who is by nature stronger and more intelligent. A lover inspired by heavenly love does not intend to deceive his beloved, but to be faithful to him and to spend the rest of his life in his company. His beloved should only yield to him once he is convinced that his intentions are just and that his company is ennobling. Together, the lover and the beloved make virtue their central concern, and their affection is genuine because it is based on virtue, and not on rank or money or anything else that is unstable or impermanent. Along with gymnastics and philosophy, the love of male youths is held to be dishonourable 'in countries which are subject to the barbarians,' since tyrants require that their subjects be poor in spirit. In Athens herself, the love-inspired strength of Harmodius and Aristogeiton sufficed to undo Hippias' tyrannical grip over the city. Love forgives 'many strange things' that would be bitterly censured if they were done for any other motive or interest. Thus, a lover's friends would not be angry or ashamed if he were to entreat or supplicate, or lie on a mat at the door, or endure a bitter slavery: 'the actions of a lover have a grace which ennobles them; and custom has decided that they are highly commendable and that there is no loss of character in them...' Thus love is a very honourable thing, but only in so far as it is conducted for the sake of virtue.

Aristophanes has the hiccoughs and yields his turn to Eryximachus who recommends a number of cures for him, amongst which a sneezing cure. Eryximachus offers to extend Pausanias' definition of love. Love is to be found not only in the souls of human beings, but also in animals, plants, heavenly bodies, and all things in the universe. Medicine, athletics, agriculture, and music are all governed by Love, since they all involve the creation of agreement and concord. Thus, Love is the source of all that is good, including order, harmony, temperance, justice, and happiness.

Aristophanes remarks that something as disordered as a sneeze has succeeded in curing something as ordered as his body, but Eryximachus is not impressed by the comedian's jibe. Aristophanes delivers his speech in the form of a myth. A long time ago, there were three kinds of human beings: male, descended from the sun; female, descended from the earth; and androgynous, with both male and female elements, descended from the moon. Each human being was completely round, with four arms and fours legs, two identical faces on opposite sides of a head with four ears, and all else to match. They walked both forwards and backwards and ran by turning cartwheels on their eight limbs, moving in circles like their parents the planets. As they were powerful and unruly and threatening to scale the heavens, Zeus devised to cut them into two 'like a sorb-apple which is halved for pickling,' and even threatened to cut them into two again, so that they might hop on one leg. Apollo then turned their heads to make them face towards

Figure 3: Early human beings, according to the myth of Aristophanes.

their wound, pulled their skin around to cover up the wound, and tied it together at the navel like a purse. He made sure to leave a few wrinkles on what became known as the abdomen so that they might be reminded of their punishment. After that, human beings longed for their other half so much that they searched for it all over and, when they found it, wrapped themselves around it very tightly and did not let go. As a result, they started dying from hunger and self-neglect, and Zeus took pity on them, and moved their genitals to the front so that those who were previously androgynous could procreate, and those who were previously male could obtain satisfaction and move on to higher things. This is the origin of our desire for other human beings; those of us who desire members of the opposite sex were previously androgynous, whereas men who desire men and women who desire women were previously male or female. When we find our other half, we are 'lost in an amazement of love and friendship and intimacy' that cannot be accounted for by a simple desire for sex, but rather by a desire to be whole again, and restored to our original nature. Our greatest wish, if we could have it, would then be for Hephaestus to melt us into one another so that our souls could be at one, and share in a common fate.

Agathon says that each of the previous speakers has spoken of the benefits of Love, but none has spoken of Love himself. He praises Love for being the happiest of all the gods, because he is the most beautiful and the best, and also the youngest and the most delicate, the bravest and the most temperate, and so on. If men are at all like that, it is because love inspires them to be.

> *And at the touch of him every one becomes a poet, even though he had no music in him before; this also is proof that Love is a good poet and accomplished in all the fine arts; for no one can give to another that which he has not himself, or teach that of which he has no knowledge. Who will deny that the creation of the animals is his doing? Are they not all the works of his wisdom, born and begotten of him? And as to the artists, do we not know that he only of them whom love inspires has the light of fame?–he whom love touches not walks in darkness.*

Everyone bursts into applause at the end of Agathon's speech, which is praised for being both beautiful and varied. Socrates, however, says that Agathon reminded him of Gorgias, and asks for Phaedrus' permission to speak the truth about Love, rather than attribute to him 'every species of greatness and glory, whether really belonging to him or not'. By slipping into elenchus mode, Socrates gets Agathon to agree that if love is not of nothing, then it is of something, and if it is of something, then it is of something that is desired, and therefore of something that is not possessed. Socrates next relates a conversation that he once had with a priestess called

Diotima of Mantinea, by whom he was taught the art of love.
Diotima ('honoured by the gods') said that the something
that Love does not possess but desires consists of beautiful
and good things, and particularly of wisdom, which is both
extremely beautiful and extremely good. Love must not be
confused with the object of love, which, in contrast to Love
himself, is perfectly beautiful and perfectly good. If Love does
not possess but desires beautiful and good things, and if all
the gods are beautiful and good, then Love cannot be a god.
Love is in truth the child of Poverty and Resource, always in
need, but always ingenuous. He is not a god, but a great spirit
(*daimon*) who acts as an intermediary between gods and men.
As such, he is neither mortal nor immortal, neither wise nor
ignorant, but a lover of wisdom (*philosophos*). No one who is
wise wants to become wise, just as no one who is ignorant
wants to become wise. 'For herein is the evil of ignorance, that
he who is neither good nor wise is nevertheless satisfied with
himself: he has no desire for that of which he feels no want.'
The aim of loving beautiful and good things is to possess
them, because the possession of beautiful and good things is
happiness (*eudaimonia*), and happiness is an end in itself.
Wild animals enter into a state of love because they seek to
reproduce and thereby to be immortal. Men also seek to be
immortal, and are prepared to take great risks, even to die,
to attain fame and honour. Some men are pregnant in body
and turn to women to beget children who will preserve their
memory, whilst others are pregnant in soul and turn to each
other to beget wisdom and virtue. As their children are more
beautiful and more immortal, men who are pregnant in soul
have more to share with each other, and a stronger bond of
friendship between them. Everyone would rather have their
children than human ones.

> *Who when he thinks of Homer and Hesiod and
> other great poets, would not rather have their
> children than ordinary human ones? Who would*

> *not emulate them in the creation of children such*
> *as theirs, which have preserved their memory and*
> *given them everlasting glory?*

Diotima next told Socrates the proper way to learn to love beauty. A youth should first be taught to love one beautiful body so that he comes to realise that this beautiful body shares beauty with other beautiful bodies, and thus that it is foolish to love just one beautiful body. In loving all beautiful bodies, he learns to appreciate that the beauty of the soul is superior to the beauty of the body, and begins to love those who are beautiful in soul regardless of whether they are also beautiful in body. Once the physical has been transcended, he gradually finds that beautiful practices and customs and the various kinds of knowledge also share in a common beauty. Finally, he is able to experience beauty itself, rather than the various apparitions of beauty. As a result, he exchanges the various apparitions of virtue for virtue itself, thereby gaining immortality and the love of the gods. This is why Love is so important, and why it deserves so much praise.

As the company applauds Socrates, a drunk Alcibiades stumbles in supported by a flute-girl and some revellers. He is wearing a massive garland of ivy, violets, and ribbons with which he crowns Agathon, 'this fairest and wisest of men'. When he catches sight of his lover Socrates, he chides him for sitting next to Agathon, rather than next to 'a joker or lover of jokes, like Aristophanes'. He then picks off some ribbons from Agathon and gives them to Socrates, 'who in conversation is the conqueror of all mankind'. When Alcibiades entreats the company to drink plenty more wine, Eryximachus objects that they cannot simply drink as if they were thirsty, and suggests that Alcibiades also make a speech in praise of Love. Alcibiades refuses on account of his drunkenness and of Socrates' jealousy, and offers instead to make a speech in praise of Socrates.

Alcibiades says that Socrates always makes him admit that he is wasting his time on his political career whilst neglecting his many shortcomings. So he tears himself away from him as from the song of a siren, and then his love of popularity once again gets the better of him. But Socrates himself cares very little whether a person is rich, or famous, or beautiful, or anything else that people admire. He may look like a satyr and pose as ignorant but, like the busts of Silenus, he hides bright and beautiful images of the gods inside him. So impressed was he that he tried several times to seduce him with his famed good looks, but all to no avail. So he turned the tables round and began to pursue him, inviting him to dinner and on one occasion convincing him to stay the night. He then lay beside him and put it to him that, of all the lovers he had ever had, he was the only one worthy of him, and he would be a fool to refuse him any favours if only he could make him into a better man. Socrates then replied,

> *...if you mean to share with me and to exchange beauty for beauty, you will have greatly the advantage of me; you will gain true beauty in return for appearance—like Diomede, gold in exchange for brass.*

CHAPTER 19

Phaedo
('On the Soul')

Tell Evenus this, and bid him be of good cheer;
that I would have him come after me if he be a
wise man, and not tarry...

Phaedo of Elis is with a group of Pythagoreans at Phlius, in
the Peloponnese. Echecrates says that all they know in Phlius
is that Socrates died by taking poison, and that there was
a long interval between his trial and his execution. Phaedo
explains that the Athenian state galley had left on its annual
pilgrimage to Delos on the day before Socrates' trial, and
that no executions were permitted before its return. He then
relates the last hours of Socrates.

Socrates' behaviour in the hour of death was so noble
and fearless that Phaedo did not feel any pity for him. Yet
neither did he feel the unalloyed pleasure that comes from
discussing philosophy. Like all those present, he felt both
pleasure and pain at the same time, 'laughing and weeping by
turns'. Amongst the Athenians there were Apollodorus, Crito
and his son Critobulus, Hermogenes, Epigenes, Aeschines,
Antisthenes, Ctessipus, Menexenus, and some others. 'Plato,
if I am not mistaken, was ill.' Amongst the foreigners there

161

were Simmias and Cebes, both, like Phaedo, Pythagorean philosophers.

When they enter the prison in the morning, they find Socrates with Xanthippe, who is holding their child in her arms. As she is hysterical, he asks that she be taken home. He then sits up on the couch, bends his leg, and rubs it, remarking on the pleasure that he feels at having his chains removed. Pleasure and pain may seem to be opposites, but they are in fact related to one another. 'They are two, and yet they grow together out of one head or stem... when one comes the other follows.' Cebes says that Evenus the poet has been asking why Socrates has suddenly taken to writing poetry. Socrates replies that, throughout his life, he has had dreams telling him to practice and cultivate the arts. Until recently, he had assumed that the dreams were telling him to pursue philosophy, which is the most noble of the arts. However, they might in fact have been telling him to write poetry, and he should not want to die without having lived out his dreams. He began by writing a hymn to Apollo, but then realised that poetry involves not just putting words together, but also telling stories. Being no storyteller himself, he took to putting Aesop's fables into verse.

> *Tell Evenus this, and bid him be of good cheer; that*
> *I would have him come after me if he be a wise*
> *man, and not tarry; and that today I am likely to*
> *be going, for the Athenians say that I must.*

Socrates explains that a philosopher should welcome death, although not take his own life. Man belongs to the gods, and in taking his own life he would incur their wrath. In that case, asks Cebes, why should a philosopher prefer death over giving service to the gods? Socrates replies that death will bring the philosopher to better gods and to better men. The philosopher aims at truth, but his body constantly distracts and deceives him.

> *The body keeps us busy in a thousand ways*
> *because of its need for nurture... It fills us with*
> *wants, desires, fears, all sorts of illusions and*
> *much nonsense, so that, as it is said, in truth and*
> *in fact no thought of any kind ever comes to us*
> *from the body. Only the body and its desires cause*
> *war, civil discord and battles, for all wars are due*
> *to the desire to acquire wealth, and it is the body*
> *and the care of it, to which we are enslaved, which*
> *compel us to acquire wealth, and all this makes*
> *us too busy to practice philosophy. Worst of all, if*
> *we do get some respite from it and turn to some*
> *investigation, everywhere in our investigations the*
> *body is present and makes for confusion and fear,*
> *so that it prevents us from seeing the truth.*[20]

Absolute justice, absolute beauty, or absolute good cannot be apprehended with the eyes or any other bodily organ, but only by pure thought, that is, with the mind or soul. Thus, the philosopher seeks in as far as possible to separate soul from body. As death is the complete separation of soul from body, the philosopher aims at death, and can be said to be almost dead. Only a true philosopher who does not fear death can be said to possess courage and the other virtues. Most men with 'courage' endure death because they are afraid of yet greater evils, just as most men with 'temperance' abstain from one class of pleasures because they are overcome by another class of pleasures.

> *Yet the exchange of one fear or pleasure or pain*
> *for another fear or pleasure or pain, which are*
> *measured like coins, the greater with the less, is*
> *not the exchange of virtue. O my dear Simmias, is*
> *there not one true coin for which all things ought*

---

20 Translated by GMA Grube.

> *to exchange?– and that is wisdom; and only in*
> *exchange for this, and in company with this, is*
> *anything truly bought or sold, whether courage or*
> *temperance or justice.*

Cebes agrees with all this, but points out that most men find it hard to believe that the soul continues to cohere (or exist) after it has left the body, and prefer to believe that it is dispersed like breath or smoke. Socrates brings to mind an ancient doctrine according to which the living are born from the dead. If this doctrine is true, then the soul must continue to cohere after it has left the body. All things come from their opposite; for instance, something that is larger comes from something that is smaller, and something that is weaker comes from something that is stronger. For each pair of opposites, there are two corresponding intermediate processes; for instance, the two corresponding intermediate processes for large and small are increase and decrease. As the opposite of life is death, life and death must come from each other, and the corresponding intermediate processes by which they do so are dying and reviving. If this were not so, everything that partakes of life would soon be dead, and there would be nothing alive left in the world.

Cebes says that Socrates' pet doctrine that 'knowledge is recollection' implies that there was a previous time for learning, and thus that the soul existed somehow before existing in human form. Simmias asks Cebes to remind him of the proofs for this doctrine of recollection. Cebes says that one excellent proof is that, 'if a question is put to a person in the right way, he will give a true answer of himself' (see the *Meno*). Socrates says that another example of recollection is when one sees one thing and is reminded of another; for example, when a lover sees the lyre or the garment of his beloved and forms a picture of his beloved in his mind's eye. Similarly, when one sees equal sticks or equal stones, one is reminded of the idea or Form of Equality. However, 'equal' sticks or 'equal' stones fall short of being perfectly equal, and thus fall short of the Form of Equality. One perceives 'equal' sticks or 'equal' stones through the senses, and it is also through the senses that one becomes aware that they fall short of the Form of Equality. This implies that knowledge of the Forms is anterior to knowledge obtained through sensory perception, and thus that knowledge of the Forms is obtained before (or at) the time of birth. 'Learning' is the process of recovering this knowledge, and it is in this sense that 'knowledge is recollection'. One who has knowledge ought to be able to give a reason for what he knows (see the *Theaetetus*), but most men are unable to give reasons on matters such as justice, beauty, and goodness because they are still in the process of recollecting this knowledge, which they acquired in a previous life but forgot at the moment of birth.

Simmias and Cebes have been persuaded that the soul exists before birth, but not that it continues to exist after death. Socrates says that this has already been proven: if the soul existed before birth (as per the doctrine that knowledge is recollection) and if life comes out of death (as per the argument from opposites), then the soul must continue to exist after death. What is compound is dissoluble and changing, whereas what is un-compounded is indissoluble and unchanging. As the Forms (for example, beauty) are unchanging, they must be un-compounded. In contrast, their particulars (for example, a beautiful horse) are in a constant state of change, and so must be compound. Particulars are perceived with the senses, whereas the Forms can only be perceived with the mind. Similarly, the body is perceived with the senses, whereas the soul can only be perceived with the mind. Thus, the soul appears to belong to the class of things that are un-compounded and unchanging. When the soul and the body are intermingled, the soul uses the body as an instrument of perception but is confused by what she sees, which is always changing and never constant. In contrast, when she returns into herself, she once again passes into the realm of the unchanging, and her state is then that of wisdom. Just as the gods rule over men, so the soul rules over the body. Thus, whereas the body is akin to the mortal, the soul is akin to the divine, which is unchanging, immortal, and eternal.

Different souls do not all suffer the same fate after death. The soul of the philosopher is most detached from the body, and so is able to depart to the realm of the unchanging, 'to the divine and immortal and rational: thither arriving, she lives in bliss and is released from the error and folly of men, their fears and wild passions and all other human ills...' In contrast, the soul that is the servant of the body is weighed down by earthly cares, and wanders the earth as a ghost until her desires are satisfied and she passes into another body. If she was unjust or violent in her previous human life, she may pass into a wolf or a hawk, whereas if she was virtuous but un-philosophical, she may pass into a gentle, social animal such as a bee or an ant, or, indeed, a human being.

Socrates finishes and a prolonged silence falls upon the gathering. Cebes and Simmias begin exchanging whispers, and Socrates asks them whether they have any doubts about his argument. They respond that, whereas they do have some doubts, they are reluctant to share them with him and disturb him in his misfortune. Socrates smiles quietly, remarking that if he cannot even persuade his friends that he welcomes his fate, he is unlikely to persuade anyone else.

> *Will you not allow that I have as much of the spirit of prophecy in me as the swans? For they, when they perceive that they must die, having sung all their life long, do then sing more than ever, rejoicing in the thought that they are about to go away to the god whose ministers they are. But men, because they are themselves afraid of death, slanderously affirm of the swans that they sing a lament at the last, not considering that no bird sings when cold, or hungry, or in pain...*

Simmias says that one might make a similar argument about harmony and the lyre. Harmony in the attuned lyre is invisible, beautiful, and divine, whilst the lyre itself is physical and akin to the mortal. Yet one cannot break the lyre or cut its strings and then argue that the harmony still exists. Cebes says that, whilst it has been sufficiently demonstrated that the soul existed before birth, it has not been sufficiently demonstrated that it continues to exist after death; just as a tailor wears out several cloaks in his lifetime, so the soul may outlive several bodies in its lifetime, yet grow old and die.

Socrates warns his friends that, just as there are misanthropists or haters of men, so there are 'misologists' or haters of ideas. A man is a misanthrope because he has frequently been disappointed by those in whom he trusted, and has come to believe that no one has any good in him. He fails to realise that the very good and the very evil are both rare, and that most men fall between one extreme and the other. Similarly, a man is a misologist because he has frequently been deceived by an argument, and has come to believe that all arguments are inherently unstable. There is no greater evil than to be a misologist and to be unable to discover the truth about anything. Thus, they should avoid becoming misologists and pursue their debate on the immortality of the soul. They should also avoid behaving like the common, vulgar man, who engages in debate with the aim not of discovering the truth, but of having his position accepted.

> *I would ask you to be thinking of the truth and not of Socrates: agree with me, if I seem to you to be speaking the truth; or if not, withstand me might and main, that I may not deceive you as well as myself in my enthusiasm and, like the bee, leave my sting in you before I die.*

Socrates has Simmias and Cebes agree that knowledge is recollection, and thus that the soul must have existed in some other place before existing in the human form. In this case, the soul cannot rightfully be compared to a harmony, since a harmony could not possibly exist prior to the lyre. Second, whereas a lyre may be more or less harmonious than another lyre, a soul cannot be more or less soul than another soul. Third, the goodness or evilness of a soul cannot be compared to the harmony or disharmony of a lyre, since a harmonious lyre has more harmony than a disharmonious lyre, whereas it has been admitted that a soul cannot be any more or less soul than another soul; if the soul is harmony, then no soul is disharmony, and every soul is without vice. Fourth, whereas the soul rules the body and is often at variance with it, a harmony does not rule a lyre and cannot be out of tune with it.

Having thereby responded to Simmias, Socrates responds to Cebes. When Socrates was a young man, he had a passion for the natural sciences, and thought that it was quite splendid to know the causes of everything, why a thing is, and why it is created and destroyed. However, he soon realised that he had no aptitude for this sort of enquiry, since it made him unlearn everything that he thought that he knew, and he found himself no longer knowing the causes of anything. He then came to hear about the teachings of Anaxagoras, according to which mind is the cause of everything, and causes each thing to be such that it is best for it to be. Thus, to learn about the cause of anything, one need only ask how it is best for that thing to be. Although initially taken by this idea, Socrates came to the conclusion that it involved nothing more than providing purely physical explanations for things. For example, Anaxagoras might say that Socrates is sitting here because his body is made up of bones and muscles, rather than because he was sentenced to death and thought it just not to escape.

> *I thought that as I had failed in the contemplation*
> *of true existence, I ought to be careful that I did*
> *not lose the eye of my soul; as people may injure*

*their bodily eye by observing and gazing on
the sun during an eclipse, unless they take the
precaution of only looking at the image reflected
in the water...*

Socrates then formulated a secondary account of causation
which involves not an explanation of things in themselves, but
the formulation of theories about them. The most plausible
theory is then retained, and whatever agrees with the theory
is true, and whatever disagrees with it is false. Socrates and
Cebes concur that the most plausible theory is in fact the
Theory of the Forms according to which there are such things
as the Form of Justice, the Form of Beauty, and so on. On this
account, something is beautiful not because of its colour or
shape, but because it participates in the Form of Beauty. Two
is two because it participates in the Form of Two, not because
it is the addition of one and one (two) or the division of one
(also two). A man is taller than another man because the
one participates in the Form of Tallness whereas the other
participates in the Form of Shortness, not because the one
is taller 'by a head' and the other is shorter 'by a head'. In
this case, not only has the same cause ('by a head') been given
for both tallness and shortness, but the tall man is only tall
on account of a head, which is itself short! Cebes, Simmias,
and the others mark their assent, and Socrates continues.
Opposite Forms, for example, Tall and Short or Hot or Cold,
cannot admit of one another. A thing that participates in a
Form is compelled not only to participate in that Form, but
also to participate in other, intimately connected Forms. For
example, three bundled pencils are compelled not only to
participate in the Form of Threeness, but also in the Form of
Oddness; by participating in the Form of Oddness, they cannot
admit of its opposite, namely, the Form of Evenness. A soul
that is intermingled with a body is invariably accompanied by
life, suggesting that the soul is intimately connected with life,
and thus that it cannot admit of its opposite, namely, death.

Therefore, when the body dies, the soul does not die, but simply withdraws from the body.

After the death of the body, the soul travels to a place of judgement, and then to one of several places. The earth is spherical and upheld in the middle of the heavens by its own equipoise. Our world is merely one of several hollows on the surface of the earth where air and water have gathered, and we are just like 'frogs about a marsh'. Above these hollows lies the true surface of the earth, which contains not air and water, but pure ether. The people living on the true surface of the earth have more acute senses and sharper intellects than we do, and are able to see the heavenly bodies as they truly are. In contrast, we are like the creatures living at the bottom of a sea, thinking that the sea is the sky, and knowing nothing of the purer and fairer world that lies beyond. The hollows on the surface of the earth are connected by great subterranean rivers of water, fire, and mud which flow into and out of Tartarus, a hollow so deep that it pierces right to the other side of the earth. Of these four rivers, Oceanus, Acheron, Pyriphlegethon, and Cocytus, Oceanus is the largest, and surrounds the earth. The souls of those who have been good and virtuous ascend to the surface of the earth, whereas the souls that have been purified by philosophy ascend to places that are still higher and more beautiful. The souls of those who have been neither good nor evil go to the shores of the Acherusian Lake where they are punished and rewarded according to their deeds and returned to the earth. Finally, the souls of those who have been evil go to Tartarus, from where they never return.

Socrates says that it is time for him to take his bath and thereby save the women the trouble of washing his corpse. Crito asks whether he has any instructions for his friends. He replies that they should continue to look after themselves by leading the philosophical life. Crito then asks how he should like to be buried, but he merely smiles at Crito's inability to understand that it is not he but his corpse that is going to be buried. After his bath, he speaks to the children and women of his household, and then returns amongst his friends. As the sun is setting, the gaoler comes in to ask him to drink the hemlock. The gaoler cannot hold back his tears as he describes him as the gentlest, most noble, and best man ever to have graced the prison. Crito tells him that there is still time for him to eat and drink and be with his friends; however, he feels that it would be unfitting to cling on to the dregs of life. So he offers a prayer to the gods and calmly and easily drinks the poison. His friends break into tears as he does so, but he chides and silences them. He walks about to help the poison spread through his body and then lies on his back and waits for it to act. As his body becomes cold and stiff, he uncovers his head and utters his last words, 'Crito, I owe a cock to Asclepius; will you remember to pay the debt?'[21]

> *Such was the end, Echecrates, of our friend, whom*
> *I may truly call the wisest, and justest, and best of*
> *all the men whom I have ever known.*

---

21 A cock was sacrificed by ill people hoping for a cure, and Socrates probably meant that death is a cure for the ills of life.

CHAPTER 20

Republic (Politeia)

[democracy] is a charming form of government,
full of variety and disorder, and dispensing a sort
of equality to equals and unequals alike.

Socrates and Glaucon are returning to Athens from a religious festival in Piraeus when they are waylaid by Polemarchus, Glaucon's brother Adeimantus, Niceratus, and several others. Arriving at the house of Polemarchus, they find his father Cephalus, his brothers Lysias and Euthydemus, Thrasymachus the Chalcedonian, Charmantides the Paeanian, and Cleitophon. Cephalus, who appears very much aged, chides Socrates for not coming more often. Socrates responds that he likes nothing better than to converse with aged men. Can Cephalus tell him what it is like to be old?

Cephalus replies that old men often complain that all the pleasures of life are gone. However, he finds that this release from the passions brings a great sense of calm and freedom. Socrates points out what many people think, namely, that the only reason Cephalus finds old age so easy to bear is that he is rich. Cephalus quotes Thermistocles' reply to the Seriphian when the latter told him that he was famous not because he had any merit, but because he was an Athenian: 'If you had been a native of my country or I of yours, neither of us would have been famous'. Similarly, age cannot be a light burden to the good poor man, but neither can the bad rich man ever be at peace. Socrates remarks that people like Cephalus who have inherited their wealth tend to be indifferent to money, whereas people who have acquired their wealth cannot talk about anything else, for which reason they make for very bad company. Cephalus opines that the greatest benefit of wealth is a clear conscience, since the wealthy man need never deceive or defraud anyone. Socrates asks whether there is then nothing more to justice than this, to speak the truth and to pay one's debts. Yet it would be unjust to return his knife to a madman, whereas it would be just to lie to him about its whereabouts. Cephalus leaves to overlook some sacrifices, and his son Polemarchus takes over the argument. Polemarchus quotes Simonides in saying that justice is the repayment of a debt, that is, the giving to each man that which is due and proper to him. In sum, justice is to do good to one's friends and evil to one's enemies. Socrates points out a number of problems with this definition of justice, not least that it seems counterintuitive for justice to involve doing any evil at all, and that our poor judgement means that we are not always friends with the most virtuous people.

At this point, the sophist Thrasymachus breaks into the conversation 'like a wild animal'. He proclaims that justice is nothing other than the interest of the stronger, and thus that it is for subjects to do that which is commanded to them by their rulers. Socrates responds that the goal of every art or rule is the interest of the subjects and not that of the artist or ruler. For example, the physician, in so far as he is a physician, aims not at his own interest but at that of his patient. Thrasymachus disagrees with Socrates: the unjust is stronger, for which reason his subjects do whatever is in his interest. The just is always a loser in comparison to the unjust, whether in private contracts, in dealings with the State, or in the exercise of public office. The highest form of injustice is tyranny, wherein the tyrant himself is happiest, and those

173

who refuse to do injustice are most miserable. If men censure injustice, it is not because they shrink from committing it, but because they fear of becoming its victims. Socrates insists that the goal of every art or rule is the interest of the subjects, for which reason no one is willing to rule without remuneration. Remuneration for ruling comes in one of three forms: money, honour, or a penalty for refusing. As good men care nothing for avarice or ambition, they are only willing to rule if there is a penalty for refusing, and the worst part of this penalty is that they should be ruled by bad men.

> *For there is reason to think that if a city were composed entirely of good men, then to avoid office would be as much an object of contention as to obtain office is at present; then we should have plain proof that the true ruler is not meant by nature to regard his own interest, but that of his subjects; and every one who knew this would choose rather to receive a benefit from another than to have the trouble of conferring one. So far am I from agreeing with Thrasymachus that justice is in the interest of the stronger. This latter question need not be further discussed at present; but when Thrasymachus says that the life of the unjust is more advantageous than that of the just, his new statement appears to me to be of a far more serious character.*

Thrasymachus confirms that he deems the life of the unjust to be the more advantageous, classing injustice with wisdom and virtue, and justice with their opposites. Socrates says that the wise and good do not desire to gain more than their like, but only to gain more than their unlike and opposite. For example, a musician who adjusts his lyre desires to exceed not the musician, but only the non-musician. In contrast, the ignorant and bad desire to gain more than both their like and their unlike. Similarly, the just desire to gain no more than the just, whereas the unjust desire to gain more than both the just and the unjust. Thus, the just are like the wise and good, and the unjust are like the ignorant and bad. Justice creates harmony and friendship, whereas injustice creates hatred and fighting. For this reason, the just are better able to take concerted action than the unjust, and so are stronger than the unjust. In fact, if the bad are able to achieve anything at all, it is because they still have a remnant of justice. Justice is desirable because it is the excellence of the soul, without which a man cannot live well, and without which he cannot be happy. Socrates concludes that he is no better off for all this; his original aim had been to define justice, not to show why justice is desirable.

[Book II] Glaucon says that he has not been persuaded that to be just is always better than to be unjust. All goods can be divided into one of three classes: goods such as harmless pleasures that are desirable in themselves; goods such as gymnastics, the care of the sick, or the various ways of making money that are desirable for what they bring; and goods such as knowledge, sight, or health that are desirable both in themselves and for what they bring. To which of these three classes does justice belong? Socrates replies that justice belongs to the class of goods that are desirable both in themselves and for what they bring. Glaucon points out that most people disagree with Socrates and think that justice belongs to the class of goods that are desirable only for what they bring. They think that to do injustice is good, but that to suffer injustice is evil, and that the evil is greater than the good. Therefore, they agree amongst themselves not to do injustice. If a just man could get hold of the legendary ring of Gyges which makes its bearer invisible, he would most surely behave unjustly. This demonstrates that the just man is just because he is weak and fears retribution, and not because justice is desirable in itself. The truly just man who cares only for justice and not for the appearance of justice will be thought unjust and will suffer every kind of evil until the day that he understands that he should only seem, but not be, just. In contrast, the unjust man who is resourceful enough to seem just will be thought just and will always get the better of everyone and everything. Adeimantus adds that, whereas people do praise justice, they praise it for what it brings rather than for itself. Realising this, the superior man devotes himself not to justice itself, but only to the appearance of justice. Adeimantus says that he does not truly believe this argument, but is pressing it so as to provoke Socrates to take its other side and demonstrate that justice is desirable in itself.

Socrates says that there are two kinds of justice, that of the individual and that of the State, and proposes to begin his enquiry into the nature of justice with the justice of the State, which is larger and thus easier to locate. 'And if we imagine the State in process of creation, we shall see the justice and injustice of the State in process of creation also.' A State arises out of our necessities for food, shelter, clothing, and such like, and its aim and purpose is to meet these necessities. Different people are naturally suited to different roles and specialisation results in better quality and greater quantity. Thus, each person should perform the role that he is naturally suited to, and perform it to the exclusion of all others. Socrates paints an idyllic picture of this 'healthy' State in which all our basic necessities are met. However, Glaucon points out that people desire more than just basic necessities, for instance, they desire to lie on sofas, to dine off tables, and to have sauces and sweets. Socrates says that such a 'luxurious' State calls upon greater resources than the State can provide, and so leads to warring. To fight wars, the State requires a specialised class of warriors or 'guardians'. If guardians are to be effective, they need to have a large number of physical and spiritual qualities. However, nature cannot be relied upon to provide them with these qualities, and must therefore be supplemented with education. As the education of guardians is the most important aspect of the State, Socrates goes through it in great detail. The education of guardians should have two divisions, gymnastic for the body, and music for the soul. Music includes literature, which may be either true or false, as in the case of children's stories which are the first type of literature that a future guardian would come across.

> *You know also that the beginning is the most important part of any work, especially in the case of a young and tender thing; for that is the time at which the character is being formed and the desired impression is more readily taken.*

Thus, the first thing to do would be to establish a censorship of the writers of fiction. This censorship would apply not only to children's stories but also to 'greater' works of fiction such as those of Homer and Hesiod which misrepresent gods and heroes, or do not represent them as they should be represented. God must always to be represented as he truly is, that is, as good, and as the author of good only.

[Book III] As future guardians must not fear death, stories about heroes should not present them as fearing death or lamenting the death of others, and should not present Hades as a horrible place. Nor should heroes be presented as being overcome by laughter, since a fit of laughter which is indulged to excess almost invariably produces a violent reaction. In all cases, heroes should be presented as honest, pious, temperate, and such like. Socrates says that, whereas he has pronounced himself on stories about the gods and about heroes, he cannot as yet pronounce himself on stories about men because these often portray evil men as happy and injustice as profitable, which are precisely the sorts of claims that his exercise is aiming to disprove. Having considered the content of stories, Socrates considers their style, and compares the dramatic form to the lyric form. He then considers other forms of art such as melody and song, painting, sculpture, and architecture, in each case censuring that which may hinder the education of future

177

guardians. He notes that, as a result of all this censorship, the luxurious State is looking increasingly like the healthy State. Finally, Socrates discusses the subject of love, which is the last of the topics under music, 'for what should be the end of music if not the love of beauty?' Whereas true love, which is the love of beauty and order, is temperate and harmonious, the love of the body, which is lust, is intemperate and disharmonious. For this reason, the lover and the beloved are to be forbidden from displaying any form of affection that goes beyond that which may exist between a father and son.

Socrates next considers gymnastic, training in which should also begin in early years. Gymnastic should not consist in ordinary athletics, but in a military gymnastic that is more suited to action on the battlefield. It is often supposed that the two arts of music and gymnastic are designed one for the training of the soul and the other for the training of the body. However, both are chiefly designed for the improvement of the soul. If the mind devotes itself exclusively to gymnastic, it develops a temper of hardness and ferocity, whereas if it devotes itself exclusively to music, it develops a temper of softness and effeminacy. Thus, the future guardian must practice both music and gymnastic, and in such proportions as to be courageous but not hard and gentle but not soft. In the midst of discussing gymnastic, Socrates discusses the role of physicians, who should only be trained to treat those with a single, curable ailment. Those with a chronic illness should be left to die naturally.

Having discussed the class of producers and the class of guardians, Socrates goes on to discuss the third and last class of citizen in his ideal State, the class of rulers. Rulers should be chosen from amongst the guardians after close observation and rigorous testing of their loyalty to the State. Guardians who are chosen as rulers should receive further education; guardians who are not chosen as rulers should no longer be known as 'guardians' but as 'auxiliaries,' whose role it is to implement the will of the rulers. Socrates says that all the citizens should be told a useful lie so as to promote allegiance to the State and enforce its three-tiered social order. According to this 'myth of the metals,' every citizen is born out of the earth of the State and every other citizen is his brother or sister. Yet God has framed them differently, mixing different metals into their soul: gold for the rulers, silver for the auxiliaries, and brass or iron for the husbandmen and craftsmen. Children are usually made of the same metal as their parents, but if this is not the case the child must either descend or ascend in the social order. If ever a child made of brass or iron was to become a guardian, the State would be destroyed. As guardians are made of divine gold and silver, they should have nothing to do with the earthly sorts which have been 'the source of many unholy deeds'. Guardians should not have any private property; they should live together in housing provided by the state, and receive from the citizens no more than their daily sustenance.

[Book IV] Adeimantus objects that people would be miserable if they could not own property and enjoy luxuries; they would be no better off than mercenaries, quartered in the city and perpetually mounting guard. Socrates adds that they would not be able to take a journey of pleasure or keep a mistress, 'which is thought to be happiness'. His aim in founding the ideal State was not the disproportionate happiness of any one class, but the greatest happiness of the whole, since it is in this kind of State that justice is most likely to be found. Nonetheless, it remains possible that guardians would be the happiest of men in spite, or because, of their deprivations. Socrates says that the arts and crafts are equally liable to degenerate under the influence of wealth as they are under the influence of poverty: 'the one is the parent of luxury and indolence, and the other of meanness and viciousness, and both of discontent'. However, there would be no money in the ideal State, and so neither wealth nor poverty. Adeimantus asks how a state with no money would go to war, especially against an enemy who was rich and powerful. Socrates replies that an army of however many rich men would be no match for an army of however few trained warriors. Thus, the ideal State would not need to be particularly large, and should certainly not be so large as to be ungovernable.

Education is all important since well educated men will easily grasp the general principles of the ideal State and apply them to its every aspect, for example, to the possession of women and to the procreation of children, which will follow the general principle that friends have all things in common. The Ideal State 'moves with accumulating force like a wheel' as good education implants good constitutions which improve more and more with time. Good education is so important that the curricula for music and gymnastic should be preserved in their original form, and no innovation should be made: '...when modes of music change, of the State always change with them'.

Having set forth the general principles of the ideal or virtuous State, Socrates is ready to define the virtues of wisdom, courage, temperance, and justice by identifying them within the virtuous State. Wisdom is to be found in the guardians, who are the fount of wisdom in the State. As long as they rule, the State can be said to be wise. Courage is to be found in the auxiliaries who protect the city and its interests by means of their courage, which Socrates defines as 'the knowledge of what is and what is not to be feared'. 'Courage,' says Socrates, 'is a kind of salvation.' In contrast to wisdom and courage, temperance and justice are found in all classes of citizen. Temperance is like a harmony which 'runs through all the notes of the scale,' and which can be defined as 'agreement of the naturally superior and inferior, as to the right rule of either, both in states and individuals'. Finally, justice is 'doing one's own business,' that is, doing what one is best suited to do, and thus what is best for the State as a whole. This principle of specialisation is the only virtue left in the State once the other virtues of wisdom, courage, and temperance have been abstracted, and it is also their ultimate cause and condition.

If a State can be just, then individuals can also be just, and Socrates proposes to verify his definition of justice by identifying justice in the individual. The just man, he says, is 'he in whom the several qualities of his nature do their own work'. Just as Society is divided into three classes of citizen, so the soul is divided into three qualities or parts. In the just man, the rational part rules over the passionate part which is its subject and ally, and both these parts rule over the appetitive or concupiscent part. The rational part lusts after truth, the passionate part lusts after honour, and the appetitive part lusts after food, drink, sex, and money. The rational part corresponds to the class of guardians, the passionate part to the class of auxiliaries, and the appetitive part to the class of producers. The just man who is ruled by the rational part of the soul is more likely to be virtuous, that is, less likely to dishonour his father and mother, fail in his religious duties, and so on. The just man 'sets in order his own inner life, and is his own master and his own law, and at peace with himself...' Justice and injustice are to the soul what health and disease are to the body; virtue is the health and beauty and well-being of the soul, whereas vice is its disease and weakness. Now that Socrates has defined individual justice and injustice, it remains for him to determine which is the more profitable. All that he says here is that, if justice is the health of the soul, and if health is desirable in itself, then justice also is desirable in itself. Plato revisits this question in Book IX.

> *The argument seems to have reached a height from which, as from some tower of speculation, a man may look down and see that virtue is one, but that the forms of vice are innumerable; there being four special ones which are deserving of note... there appear to be as many forms of the soul as there are distinct forms of the State... There are five of the State, and five of the soul...*

The first or virtuous form is that of monarchy or aristocracy, in which rule is exercised by one distinguished man or by many.

[Book V] Socrates begins to enumerate the four vicious forms. However, Polemarchus and Adeimantus interrupt him and ask him to explicate his point about women and children, whom he said should be held in common. He replies,

> *Are dogs divided into hes and shes, or do they both*
> *share equally in hunting and in keeping watch*
> *and in the other duties of dogs? Or do we entrust*
> *to the males the entire and exclusive care of the*
> *flocks, while we leave the females at home, under*
> *the idea that the bearing and suckling of their*
> *puppies is labour enough for them?*

If women are to have the same duties as men, they must receive the same education, namely, music and gymnastic and also the art of war which they must practise like the men. Although men and women do have different natures, women ought to have the same pursuits as men because, men, their natures divide into the appetitive, spirited, and rational classes. The wives of guardians should be held in common, as should their children, and no parent should know his child, nor the child his parent. Thus, everyone would be considered family, and loyalty would no longer be divided between family and State, but would be to State only. The best of either sex should be united with one another as often, and the worst with one another as seldom, as possible. Copulation should only take place during certain festivals, and any children born from copulation outside these festivals should be killed. Weddings should take place to sanction copulation but should only be maintained for the duration of copulation. To prevent incest, guardians should consider every child born between seven and ten months after their copulation as their own, and these children should in turn consider that group of guardians as father and mother, and one another as brother and sister.

Despite the community of families and the community of property, Socrates insists that the lives of guardians would be more blessed than that of Olympic winners, since guardians will be free from quarrels and 'little meannesses' such as,

> ...*the flattery of the rich by the poor, and all the pains and pangs which men experience in bringing up a family, and in finding money to buy necessaries for their household, borrowing and then repudiating, getting how they can, and giving the money into the hands of women and slaves to keep – the many evils of so many kinds which people suffer in this way are mean enough and obvious enough, and not worth speaking of.*

> ...*if any of our guardians shall try to be happy in such a manner that he will cease to be a guardian, and is not content with this safe and harmonious life, which in our judgement, is of all lives the best, but infatuated by some youthful conceit of happiness which gets up into his head shall seek to appropriate the whole State to himself, then he will have to learn how wisely Hesiod spoke, when he said, 'half is more than the whole'.*

Socrates next discusses the guardians' behaviour at war. A guardian who behaved in a cowardly fashion should be demoted to the appetitive class. Children training to become guardians should attend the battlefield to learn from their elders and inspire them with bravery; they should attend on horseback, so that they might escape in case of defeat. Defeated enemies should be treated with respect. If they are Greek, they should not be enslaved and their lands should not be destroyed. If they are barbarian, anything goes.

Socrates at last returns to the question of whether such an ideal State is possible. Word expresses more than fact, and all one can hope for is a State that resembles rather than coincides with the ideal State. Even such a State could not exist 'until all philosophers are kings, or the kings and princes of this world have the spirit and power of philosophy, and political greatness and wisdom meet in one'. True philosophers are lovers of truth, and not mere 'lovers of sounds and sights' who have a sense of beautiful things but no sense of absolute Beauty, and a sense of just things but no sense of absolute Justice. The universe is divided into that which is completely, that which is in no way, and that which both is and is not. That which is completely is the object of knowledge, that which is in no way is the object of ignorance, and that which both is and is not is the object of opinion. Only the Forms are completely, and only true philosophers can have a sense of the Forms. Thus, only true philosophers can have knowledge.

[Book VI] From this, it appears that the State should be entrusted only to true philosophers. The true philosopher is a spectator of all time and existence. As such, he does not think much of human life and does not fear death. For this reason, he cannot be cowardly or otherwise mean, but is instead just and gentle and otherwise virtuous. Adeimantus objects that most philosophers are 'strange monsters, not to say utter rogues,' and even the best of them are made useless to the world by their study. Socrates agrees with Adeimantus, but explains that, if philosophers are strange monsters, this is because people with the qualities of a true philosopher tend to be waylaid by their ambitious and covetous friends and relatives. The gap that is left behind is filled by undeserving charlatans with maimed and disfigured souls. 'Are they not exactly like a bald little tinker who has just got out of durance and come into a fortune; he takes a bath and puts on a new coat, and is decked out as a bridegroom going to marry his master's daughter, who is left poor and desolate?' A small number of people with the qualities of a true philosopher are not diverted from philosophy, perhaps because they are in exile or in poor health, or because they have come to despise the arts, or because they hold society in contempt. If even they are useless to the world, this is not their own fault, but the fault of the people who will not let themselves be guided by them. These people are like mutinous sailors who each want to be chosen as captain or navigator, and look upon the true navigators as good-for-nothings and star-gazers. Socrates next discusses the education of the philosopher-king in the ideal State. The philosopher-king is to be picked from the class of the guardians and must have reached the highest knowledge of all, namely, the knowledge of the Good, by which all other things are made useful.

You are further aware that most people affirm pleasure to be the good, but the finer sort of wits say it is knowledge... And you are aware too that the latter cannot explain what they mean by knowledge, but are obliged after all to say knowledge of the good?

The metaphor of the sun
1. Just as it is by the light of the sun that the visible is made apparent to the eye, so it is by the light of truth and being – in contrast to the twilight of becoming and perishing – that the nature of reality is made apprehensible to the soul. 2. Just as light and sight may be said to be like the sun, and yet not to be the sun, so science and truth may be said to be like the Good, and yet not to be the Good; it is by the sun that there is light and sight, and it is by the Good that there is science and truth. 3. Just as the sun is the author of nourishment and generation, so the Good is the author of being and essence. Thus, the Good is beyond being, and the cause of all existence.

The metaphor of the line
A line is cut into two unequal parts, and each of them is divided again in the same proportion. The two main divisions correspond to the intelligible world and to the visible world. One section in the visible division consists of images, that is, shadows and reflections, and is accessed through imagination.

185

The other, higher section in the visible division consists of sensible particulars and is accessed through belief. One section in the intelligible division consists of Forms and is accessed through thought, but via sensible particulars and hypotheses, as when geometers use a picture of a triangle to help reason about triangularity, or make appeal to axioms to prove theorems. The other, higher section in the intelligible division also consists of Forms but is accessed by understanding, a purely abstract science which requires neither sensible particulars nor hypotheses, but only an unhypothetical first principle, namely, the Form of the Good. The purpose of education is to move the philosopher through the various sections of the line until he reaches the Form of the Good.

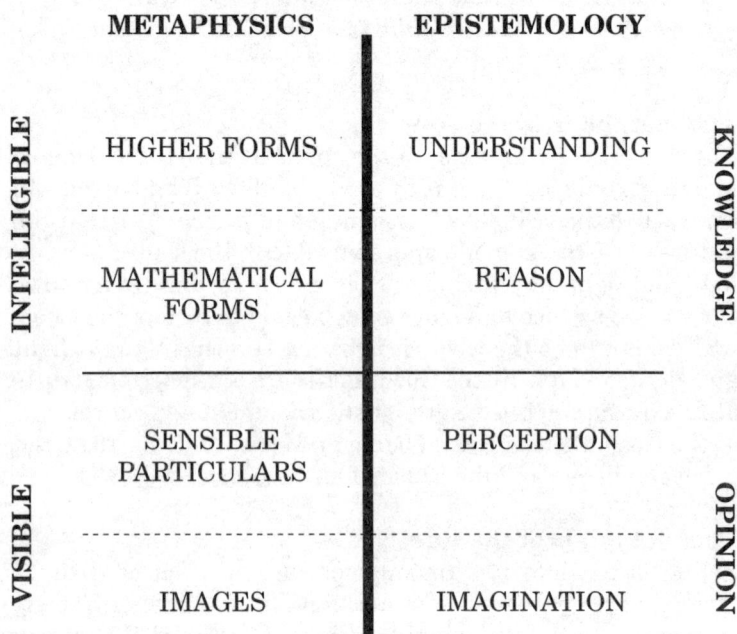

	METAPHYSICS	EPISTEMOLOGY	
INTELLIGIBLE	HIGHER FORMS	UNDERSTANDING	**KNOWLEDGE**
	MATHEMATICAL FORMS	REASON	
VISIBLE	SENSIBLE PARTICULARS	PERCEPTION	**OPINION**
	IMAGES	IMAGINATION	

Figure 4: Plato's line

[Book VII]

The metaphor or allegory of the cave

Human beings have spent all their lives in an underground cave or den which has a mouth open towards the light. They have their legs and their necks chained so that they cannot move, and can see only in front of them, towards the back of the cave. Above and behind them a fire is blazing, and between them and the fire there is a raised way along which there is a low wall. Men pass along the wall carrying all sorts of statues, and the fire throws the shadows of these statues onto the back of the cave. All the prisoners ever see are the shadows, and so they suppose that they are the objects in themselves.

If a prisoner is unshackled and turned towards the light, he suffers sharp pains, but in time he begins to see the statues themselves and thereby moves from the cognitive stage of

Figure 5: Plato's cave

imagination to that of belief. The prisoner is then dragged out of the cave, where the light is so bright that he can only look at the shadows, and then at the reflections, and then finally at the objects themselves: not statues this time, but real objects. In time, he looks up at the sun, and understands that the sun is the cause of everything that he sees around him, of light, of vision, and of the objects of vision. In so doing, he passes from the cognitive stage of thought to that of understanding.

The purpose of education is to drag the prisoner as far out of the cave as possible; not to instil knowledge into his soul, but to turn his whole soul towards the sun, which is the Form of the Good. Once out of the cave, the prisoner is reluctant to descend back into the cave and get involved in human affairs. When he does, his vision is no longer accustomed to the dark, and he appears ridiculous to his fellow men. However, he must be made to descend back into the cave and partake of human labours and honours, whether they are worth having or not. This is because the State aims not at the happiness of a single person or single class, but at the happiness of all its citizens. In any case, the prisoner has a duty to give service to the State, since it is by the State that he was educated to see the light of the sun.

> *The State in which the rulers are most reluctant to govern is always the best and most quietly governed, and the State in which they are most eager, the worst... You must contrive for your future rulers another and a better life than that of a ruler, and then you may have a well-ordered State; for only in the State which offers this, will they rule who are truly rich, not in silver and gold, but in virtue and wisdom, which are the true blessings of life... And the only life which looks down upon the life of political ambition is that of true philosophy. Do you know of any other?*

Socrates next discusses the education and selection of the philosopher-kings in quite some detail. In addition to the normal curriculum, prospective philosopher-kings should be educated in mathematics and, especially, in dialectics, as it is by abstract reasoning that the soul can be drawn from becoming to being. However, dialectics should not be taught to anyone under the age of 30, and only at the age of 50 should the most distinguished students raise the eye of the soul to the universal light and behold the absolute Good. Socrates ends with the suggestion that the ideal State might be instituted by taking over an already existing State, banishing every citizen above the age of 10, and educating the remaining children according to the principles of the ideal State.

[Book VIII] At the beginning of Book V, Socrates had begun to enumerate the four forms of vice of the State and of the soul so as to contrast them with the monarchy or aristocracy of the ideal, virtuous State. These four forms of vice are, from bad to worse, timocracy, oligarchy, democracy, and tyranny, and represent the various stages of degeneration that the ideal State is bound to go through. States are not made of oak and rock, but of men, and so come to resemble the men that they are made of. Aristocracies are made of just and good men; timocracies of spirited, that is, proud and honour-loving, men; oligarchies of misers and money-makers; democracies of men who are overcome by unnecessary desires; and tyrannies of men who are overcome by unlawful desires. Socrates provides a detailed account of the degeneration from aristocracy to tyranny via timocracy, oligarchy, and democracy. Democracy in particular arises from the revolt of the poor in an oligarchy. The State is 'full of freedom and frankness' and every citizen is able to live as he pleases. 'These and other kindred characteristics are proper to democracy, which is a charming form of government, full of variety and disorder, and dispensing a sort of equality to equals and unequals alike.' However, citizens are overcome by so many unnecessary desires that they are ever spending and never producing, and are 'void of all accomplishments and fair pursuits and true words'. As a result, the State is ruled by people who are not fit to rule.

[Book IX] Socrates gives a detailed description of the genesis, psychology, and *modus vivendi* of the tyrant so as to demonstrate that this most unjust of men is also the most slavish and the most unhappy. The tyrant is constantly overcome by lawless desires which lead him to commit all manner of heinous act. His soul is full of disorder and regret, and is incapable of doing what it truly desires. The life of the political tyrant is even more wretched than that of the private tyrant, first, because the political tyrant is in a better position to feed his desires, and, second, because he is everywhere surrounded and watched by his enemies, of whom he is the prisoner.

Socrates provides a second proof that the most unjust is the most unhappy, and the most just the most happy. There are three classes of men: lovers of wisdom, lovers of honour, and lovers of gain, and there are three kinds of pleasure, which are their several objects. Each class of man claims that the life which involves the most of what he loves is the best of lives. However, only the lovers of wisdom, that is, the philosophers, are to be believed, since only they have experienced all three kinds of pleasure. Furthermore, only the pleasure of philosophy is a pure, positive pleasure, since the other forms of pleasure merely involve relief from pain. Socrates calculates that the king lives precisely 729 times more pleasantly than the tyrant.

> *What a wonderful calculation! And how enormous*
> *is the distance which separates the just from the*
> *unjust in regard to pleasure and pain!*

[Book X] Socrates moves on to discuss poetry (the arts of imitation), which he says ought to be banned for three reasons. First, poetry is an imitation that is thrice removed from the truth, and that could easily be wrought without knowledge of the truth. 'The poet is like a painter who... will make a likeness of a cobbler though he understands nothing of cobbling; and his picture is good enough for those who know no more than he does, and judge only by colours and figures.' Second, poetry imitates and indulges the histrionics of the inferior, irrational part of the soul at the expense of the poise and equanimity of the rational part, which are difficult to understand and imitate. Third, poetry can lead even the best of us to partake vicariously in intemperate displays of emotion, and even to import these ignoble jests into our lives. For all these reasons poetry ought to be banned from the ideal State. Socrates very much regrets this, as he is greatly charmed in particular by the poetry of Homer.

Socrates next discusses the 'greatest prizes and rewards which await virtue,' in the context of which he offers a proof for the immortality of the soul. Anything that is destroyed is necessarily done so not by good but by evil. However, evil, that is, injustice and the other vices, does not seem to dissolve or destroy the soul of evil men. Therefore, the soul cannot be destroyed and is immortal, and the greatest prizes and rewards which await justice and virtue are to be found not in this life but in the next. Socrates concludes the *Republic* with an eschatological myth, the Myth of Er. Er was slain in battle but came back to life twelve days later to tell of what he saw when he was dead. His soul went on a journey with a great company to a meadow with four openings, two into the heavens and two into the earth. Judges sat in this meadow and ordered the good souls into the heavens and the bad ones into the earth. Meanwhile, clean and bright souls floated down from the other opening in the heavens, and dusty and worn out souls rose up from the other opening in the earth. Each soul had returned from a thousand year journey, but whereas the clean souls spoke merrily of that which they had experienced in the heavens, the dusty souls wept at that which they had endured in the underground. Souls that had committed heinous crimes,

191

such as those of tyrants or murderers, were not permitted to rise up to the meadow, and were condemned to an eternity in the underground. After seven days in the meadow the souls travelled for five more days to the spindle of Necessity, a shaft of intensely bright light that extends into the heavens and holds together the universe. There the souls were asked to come forth one by one and to choose their next life from a scattered jigsaw of human and animal lives. Not having known the terrors of the underworld, the first soul hastily chose the life of a powerful dictator, only to discover that he was fated, amongst other evils, to devour his own children. His previous life had been virtuous out of habit rather than out of philosophy, and so his judgement was very poor. In contrast, the souls that had known the terrors of the underworld often chose a better, more virtuous life, but on no other basis than experience. Thus, many of the souls exchanged a good destiny for an evil or an evil for a good. The soul of wily Odysseus, which was the last to come forth, sought out the life of a private man with no cares. This he found lying about, neglected by everybody else. After this, the souls travelled through the scorching Plain of Oblivion and encamped by the River of Forgetfulness. Each soul was required to drink from the river's water so as to forget all things, but the souls which had not been saved by wisdom drank more than was necessary. In the night as they slept, the souls shot up like stars to be reborn into their chosen lives. As they did so, Er opened his eyes to find himself lying on his funeral pyre.

CHAPTER 21

Parmenides

You cannot conceive the many without the one.

The Parmenides is narrated by Cephalus of Clazomenae in Ionia. Cephalus and some fellow Clazomenaeans encounter Adeimantus and Glaucon in the Agora at Athens and ask to meet their half-brother Antiphon. Their hope is that Antiphon might relate to them a conversation between a youthful Socrates and Parmenides and Zeno, which was once related to him by Zeno's friend Pythodorus. Since that time, Antiphon has given up philosophy for horses. The party make their way to Antiphon's house, where they find him in the act of giving a bridle to a smith to be fitted.

Antiphon is initially reluctant to relate the famous conversation, but later relents. He says that Parmenides and Zeno came to Athens at the great Panathenaea, when the former was about sixty-five years old, 'very white with age, but well favoured,' and the latter about forty, and 'tall and fair to look upon'. They lodged with Pythodorus, where Socrates, then a very young man, came to see them along with several others. Zeno recited his treatise, and had very nearly finished when Pythodorus walked in accompanied by Parmenides and Aristoteles. When Zeno had finished reciting his treatise, Socrates asked for the first thesis of the first argument to be repeated.

Does Zeno maintain that, if being is many, then it must be both like and unlike, and that this is impossible because the like cannot be unlike, nor the unlike like? Zeno replies that this is precisely his meaning. If the unlike cannot be like, nor the like unlike, then being cannot be many. Socrates asks whether the sole purpose of everything that Zeno has said is to disprove the being of the many. When Zeno admits that it is, Socrates says that Zeno is like Parmenides' second self, and merely puts what Parmenides says in another way: Parmenides says that The All is one, Zeno that there is not many. 'And so you deceive the world into believing that you are saying different things when really you are saying much the same.' Zeno responds that his arguments are meant to protect those of Parmenides against ridicule. They are addressed to the partisans of the many, 'whose attack I return with interest by retorting upon them that their hypothesis of the being of many, if carried out, appears to be still more ridiculous than the hypothesis of the being of one'.

Socrates next asks Zeno whether he also thinks that there is an idea of likeness in itself, and another idea of unlikeness which is the opposite of likeness, in which the many participate. Things which participate in likeness become in that degree like, and those that participate in unlikeness become to that degree unlike, and those that participate in both become both like and unlike in the degree to which they participate in either. May not all things participate in both, and thus be both like and unlike? If a person could prove the absolute like to become unlike or vice versa, that would be a wonder, but there is nothing extraordinary in showing that things which participate in likeness and unlikeness become both like and unlike in the degree to which they participate in either. Nor is there anything extraordinary in showing that things which participate in one and many are both one and many. However, if it could be shown that the absolute one was many, or that the absolute many was one, then that would be truly amazing.

Parmenides says that he admires Socrates' bent of mind, and asks him whether this was his own distinction between ideas in themselves and the things which partake of them. – Tell me, do you think that there is an idea of likeness apart from the likeness which we possess, and of the one and many, and of the just and the beautiful and the good? – Yes. – What about human beings, or fire, or water? – I'm not sure. – What about hair, mud, dirt, or anything else which is vile and paltry? – Certainly not, visible things are such as they appear to us, although I sometimes get disturbed, and begin to think that there is nothing without an idea; but then again, when I have taken up this position, I run away, because I am afraid that I may fall into a bottomless pit of nonsense.

Yes, Socrates... that is because you are still young; the time will come, if I am not mistaken, when philosophy will have a firmer grasp of you, and then you will not despise even the meanest things; at your age, you are too much disposed to regard opinions of men.

But tell me, is your meaning that things become like by partaking of likeness, great by partaking of greatness, and so on? – Yes, that is my meaning. – Then each individual partakes either of the whole of the idea or of a part of the idea? – Yes, there cannot be any other mode of participation. – Then do you think that the whole idea is one, and yet, being one, is in each one of the many? – Why not? – Because one and the same thing will exist as a whole at the same time in many separate individuals, and will therefore be in a state of separation from itself. – Nay, but the idea may be like the day which is one and the same in many places at once, and yet continuous with itself. – You mean to say, that if I were to spread out a sail and cover a number of men, there would be one whole including many? – I think so. – And would you say that the whole sail covers each man, or a part of it only, and different parts different men? – The latter. – Then, Socrates, the ideas themselves will be divisible, and things which participate in them will have a part of them only and not the whole idea existing in each of them? – That seems to follow. – Then would you like to say that the one idea is really divisible and yet remains one? – Certainly not. – Suppose that you divide absolute greatness, and that of the many great things, each one is great in virtue of a portion of greatness less than absolute greatness – is that conceivable? – No. – Or will each equal thing, if possessing some small portion of equality less than absolute equality, be equal to some other thing by virtue of that portion only? – Impossible. – Then in what way, Socrates, will all things participate in the ideas, if they are unable to participate in them either as parts or wholes? – That is a question which is not easily answered.

Parmenides says that Socrates conceived of ideas such as, for example, greatness when he looked at a number of great objects and saw one and the same idea or nature in all of them. – And if you go on and allow your mind in like manner to embrace in one view the idea of greatness and of great things which are not the idea, and to compare them, will not another greatness arise, which will appear to be the source of all these? – It would seem so. – Then another idea of greatness now comes into view over and above absolute greatness and the individuals which partake of it; and then another, over and above these... and so on *ad infinitum*. – But may not the ideas be thoughts only, and have no proper existence except in our minds? For in that case each idea may still be one, and not experience this infinite multiplication. – Yet the thought must be of something which is the same in all and is the idea? – From that there is no escape. – Then you must either say that everything is made of thoughts, and that all things think; or that they are thoughts but have no thought. – Neither. The ideas are patterns fixed in nature, and other things partake of them by becoming like them. – If the individual is like the idea, must not the idea also be like the individual, in so far as the individual is a resemblance of the idea? – Impossible. – And when two things are alike, must they not partake of the same idea? – They must. – And will that not be the idea itself? – Certainly. – Then the idea cannot be like the individual, or the individual like the idea. – Quite true. – Thus the theory that other things participate in the ideas by resemblance has to be given up, and some other mode of participation devised. – It would seem so.

The greatest difficulty is yet to come: an opponent of the ideas will argue that the ideas are not within the range of human knowledge, and thus that their existence can hardly be disproved. At the same time, a proponent of the ideas will not affirm that the ideas are subjective. Therefore, any relation in the ideas is a relation that concerns the ideas only, and any relation in the objects after which the ideas are named is a relation between the objects only, and has nothing to do with the ideas themselves. – How do you mean? – For example, the idea of a slave in the abstract is relative to the idea of a master in the abstract, yet this correspondence of ideas has nothing to do with the particular relation of my slave to me or of your slave to you. Similarly, absolute knowledge corresponds to absolute truth and being, and particular knowledge corresponds to particular truth and being. – Clearly. – Whilst there is a subjective knowledge which is of the subjective truth, the ideas themselves are not subjective, and therefore not within our ken. – They are not. – And there is worse to come. If absolute knowledge is the most exact knowledge, then it pertains to God. However, this implies that God cannot have knowledge of the sphere of human things. – Yet, surely, to deprive God of knowledge is monstrous. – These are some of the difficulties with ideas. There will always be a suspicion, either that they do not exist, or that they are beyond human knowledge. – I agree with you.

And yet, Socrates, said Parmenides, if a man, fixing
his attention on these and the like difficulties, does

> *away with ideas of things and will not admit that*
> *every individual thing has its own determinate*
> *idea which is always one and the same, he will*
> *have nothing on which his mind can rest; and so*
> *he will utterly destroy the power of reasoning, as*
> *you seem to me to have particularly noted.*

I think that your difficulties arise out of your attempting to define abstractions before you have had sufficient training. Your enthusiasm is noble and divine, but I fear that unless you discipline yourself by dialectic, truth will elude your grasp. – What is this discipline? – That which you heard Zeno practising; at the same time, I give you credit for saying to him that you did not care to examine the perplexity in reference to visible things, but to objects of thought only. – There appears to me to be no difficulty in showing that visible things are like and unlike and may experience anything. – Quite true, but you should go further and consider the consequences which follow from a given hypothesis, and also the consequences which follow from the denial of that hypothesis. For example, you should consider the consequences which follow from the assumption of the existence of the many, and also from the denial of the existence of the many: and similarly of likeness and unlikeness, motion and rest, generation and corruption, and even being and not being. In each case, you should look at consequences to the things supposed and to other things, both in themselves and in relation to one another. – What you are suggesting seems to be a tremendous business. Can you give me an example?

> *I cannot refuse, said Parmenides; and yet I feel*
> *rather like Ibycus, who, when in his old age,*
> *against his will, he fell in love, compared himself*
> *to an old racehorse, who was about to run in a*
> *chariot race, shaking with fear at the course he*
> *knew so well...*

Note: The remainder of the dialogue is taken up by Parmenides' display, in which a young Aristoteles (later one of the Thirty Tyrants) takes the place of Socrates as Parmenides' interlocutor. This second half of the dialogue consists of an unrelenting series of arguments which are difficult to characterise, let alone interpret. Only the first part has been included here, so as to give the reader a flavour of the arguments.

One is not many, and therefore has no parts, and therefore cannot be a whole, since a whole is that of which no part is wanting. Thus, the one cannot have a beginning, middle, nor end, and must therefore be unlimited. Being unlimited, the one is formless, and being formless, it is not in any place. In particular, it cannot be in another which would encircle and touch it at many points, nor in itself, because that which is self-contained is also contained, and therefore not one but two. Given this, is the one capable of either motion or rest? Motion is either change of substance, or motion on an axis, or from one place to another. Neither is possible for the one, unless it is to change into something that is not the one, or unless it is to have parts or place. Yet more impossible than existence in place is coming into being in place, since that which has no parts can never be at one and the same time neither wholly within nor wholly without anything. And more impossible still is the coming into being either as a whole or parts of that which is neither a whole nor parts. Thus, the one is immoveable. But neither (as has been said) can the one be contained in anything, and if not in anything then not in the same, whether itself or some other. Thus, the one is capable of neither motion nor rest.

Neither is one the same with itself or any other, or other than itself or any other. For if other than itself, then other than one, and therefore not one; if the same with other, then other, and other than one. Neither can one whilst remaining one be other than other; for other, and not one, is the other than other. But if not other by virtue of being one, not by virtue of itself; and if not by virtue of itself, not itself other, and if not itself other, not other than anything. Parmenides proceeds in similar style to consider whether the one can be the same with itself, whether it can be like or unlike itself or other, whether it can be equal or unequal to itself or other, and whether it can be older or younger or of the same age than itself. He reaches the conclusion that the one is outside of time, and neither is, has been, nor will be, and neither becomes, has become, nor will become. As there are no other modes of being than these, the one is not at all, and is not the one. As that which is not cannot admit of any attribute or relative, the one cannot admit of either name or word or idea or science or perception or opinion. Thus, the one is neither named, nor uttered, nor known, nor perceived, nor imagined. But can all this be true about the one? 'I think not.' And so Parmenides starts all over again.

CHAPTER 22

Theaetetus

*...for wonder is the feeling of a philosopher, and
philosophy begins in wonder.*

This dialogue was probably written in memory of Theaetetus,
an eminent mathematician and long-time friend of Plato. The
dialogue treats of the nature of knowledge and is widely regarded
as the founding treatise of epistemology. The dialogue opens on
Terpsion and Euclides, both Socratics from Megara. Terpsion
runs into Euclides, who has just met with a badly wounded
Theaetetus. Euclides tells Tersion that Theatetus has caught
dysentery and is likely to die. Euclides recalls that a very young
Theaetetus had once met with an elderly Socrates, who had
been struck by his natural ability. Socrates had related their
conversation to Euclides, who had written it down for posterity.
Terpsion is keen to hear this conversation, so Euclides asks a
slave boy to read it out to them.

Socrates asks Theodorus which of the Athenian youths are
showing signs of turning out well. The mathematician heaps
praise on Theaetetus, whom he describes as snub-nosed and
globe-eyed and similar in appearance to Socrates. Theodorus
hails Theaetetus and calls him to their side, whereupon
Socrates offers to examine him. Socrates says that to learn is
to become wiser about that which one is learning. What makes

men wise is wisdom, which is the same thing as knowledge, since the things which men know about are also those which they are wise about. *But what exactly is this thing called knowledge?* Theaetetus replies that subjects such as geometry, arithmetic, astronomy, and music are knowledge, as are crafts such as cobbling and carpentry. Socrates points out that he asked what knowledge is, not what one might have knowledge of, nor how many branches of knowledge there are. Theaetetus agrees with Socrates that, unless they know what knowledge is, they cannot know what 'knowledge of something' is, and contrasts his ease in defining mathematical terms with his difficulty in defining knowledge.

Theaetetus admits that he has thought about this problem many times before and suffers from his lack of an adequate solution. Socrates says, 'These are the pangs of labour, my dear Theaetetus; you have something within you which you are bringing forth'. Socrates compares himself to a midwife, who can establish whether a woman is pregnant, induce labour, calm its pain, and bring about the delivery of a healthy child. He differs from a midwife only in that he works with men rather than with women, and with the soul rather than with the body. Just like the midwife is past bearing age, so he is barren – not of children, but of wisdom. All he can do is to bring forth wisdom in others, and the triumph of his art is 'in thoroughly examining whether the thought which the mind of the young man brings forth is a false idol or a noble and true birth'. Sometimes the young man takes all the credit for himself, leaves him sooner than he should, and once again begins to set more value upon phantoms than upon the truth. In such cases the young man loses whatever he gave birth to and miscarries whatever remains in him. Then one day he realises that he is an ignorant fool and falls upon his knees, begging to return. Socrates warns that, should Theaetetus give birth to a phantom or false idol, he will tear it away from him and expose it.

*And if I abstract and expose your first-born, because
I discover upon inspection that the conception
which you have formed is a vain shadow, do not
quarrel with me on that account, as the manner
of women is when their first children are taken
from them. For I have actually known some who
were ready to bite me when I deprived them of a
darling folly.*

So, now, can Theaetetus tell him, what is knowledge? Theaetetus offers that one who knows something is one who perceives
what he knows, that is, that knowledge is nothing other than
perception. Socrates says that this was in fact the opinion of
Protagoras, who said that 'man is the measure of all things,
of the existence of things that are, and of the non-existence
of things that are not'. However, if a wind is blowing and one
man feels cold and another feels warm, this does not mean
that the wind is both warm and cold. Therefore, Protagoras
must have put out this saying as a riddle for common people,
whilst teaching a secret doctrine to his pupils, namely, that
nothing can truly be called either warm or cold, great or
small, or heavy or light, since 'out of motion and change and
admixture all things are becoming relatively to one another,
which 'becoming' is by us incorrectly called being, but is really
becoming, for nothing ever is, but all things are becoming'.
Heraclitus, Empedocles, and everyone except Parmenides
agree with Protagoras that all things are in flux and motion,
and there are many ways of proving that flux and motion
are the source of being and becoming. For example, physical
exertion is good for the body and study and learning are good
for the soul, whereas rest and idleness only lead to wasting
and to forgetting.

Applying Protagoras' doctrine to sense perception, a given
colour comes into being through the interaction of the eye
and the object of perception, such that the colour is neither in
the object of perception nor in the eye, but in something that

has come into being between them, and which is private to the percipient. This explains why colour does not appear the same to one person as it does to other animals and to other human beings. Indeed, it does not even appear the same to that person from one moment to the next, since everything including the person is in a constant state of flux and motion. At the same time, nothing can truly become different unless it actually changes. For example, six dice may be more by half than four, and fewer by half than twelve, but in either case there are still six dice.

> *T: Yes, Socrates, and I am amazed when I think*
> *of [these contradictions]; by the Gods I am!*
> *And I want to know what on earth they mean;*
> *and there are times when my head quite*
> *swims with the contemplation of them.*
> *S: I see, my dear Theaetetus, that Theodorus had*
> *a true insight into your nature when he said*
> *that you were a philosopher, for wonder is*
> *the feeling of a philosopher, and philosophy*
> *begins in wonder.*

Socrates next helps Theaetetus to unearth the hidden 'truth' of a certain school, which holds that there is nothing but motion, and out of this motion is generated both sense perception and the object of sense perception 'which are ever breaking forth and coming to the birth at the same moment'. For example, when the eye and an object meet together and give birth to the sensation of the colour white, the sight flowing from the eye and the whiteness flowing from the object combine in producing the colour white, such that the eye is no longer sight but a seeing eye and the object is no longer whiteness but a white object. Thus, there is no one self-existent thing, but everything is becoming and in relation. If this is true and 'everything is which appears,' how might one account for phenomena such as dreams, madness, and illusions of the senses, which give rise to false perceptions? For example, who is to say that we are not asleep and our thoughts but a dream? Perhaps it ought to be stipulated that whenever one says that a thing is or becomes, he must say, as in the above example, that it is or becomes *in relation to something else*, and never that it is or becomes absolutely. This enables Theaetetus to conclude that knowledge is perception, that he has knowledge of whatever he perceives, and that whatever he perceives is true to him. Socrates says,

> *Then this is the child, however he may turn out,*
> *which you and I have with difficulty brought into*
> *the world. And now that he is born, we must run*
> *round the hearth with him, and see whether he is*
> *worth rearing, or is only a wind-egg and a sham.*

Theodorus asks Socrates to confirm that Theatetus is correct, but Socrates says that he is not 'a bag full of theories' and knows only just enough to extract theories from others. He does, however, offer a series of objections to the idea that knowledge is perception. For example, (1) if knowledge is perception, why should a pig or a 'dog-faced baboon' not also be the measure of all things? (2) Granted that man is the measure of all things, why should Protagoras be any more correct than anyone else? (3) Anyone who has learned x and preserved it in his memory can be said to know x, even though he no longer perceives it. (4) Whereas one easily applies adverbs such as 'sharp' and 'dull' or 'clear' and 'unclear' to the perception of x, he does not apply these adverbs to the knowledge of x, suggesting that the perception of x and the knowledge of x are not one and the same thing.

Socrates regrets that Protagoras is no longer alive to argue for himself. Posing as Protagoras, he argues that one must attend to the meaning of terms as they are commonly used in argument: for example, a man who has learned x and preserved it in his memory can be said to know x because there is a sense in which he perceives it. Furthermore, since there are no such things as false beliefs, one cannot be said to have true beliefs or false beliefs, but only good beliefs or bad beliefs. In other words, whilst all beliefs are true, not are all beliefs are beneficial, and the goal of education is to replace true but harmful beliefs with true but beneficial beliefs. Socrates switches roles and argues against his 'Protagoras' that, if all beliefs all true, then the common belief that 'not all beliefs are true' must also be true, which is a contradiction. Furthermore, by arguing that the truth is relative whereas the beneficial or the good is absolute, 'Protagoras' has admitted that his theory cannot be general in its application. Socrates then embarks on a long digression in which he compares the orator to the philosopher, and portrays the philosopher as a high- but absent-minded star-gazer. The apparent purpose of this digression is to contrast a life consecrated to what appears just to one consecrated to what is beneficial.

> *I mean to say, that those who have been trained*
> *in philosophy and liberal pursuits are as unlike*
> *those who from their youth upwards have been*
> *knocking about in the courts and such places, as a*
> *freeman is in breeding unlike a slave.*

Socrates further argues that the doctrine that 'man is the measure of all things' cannot be extended to judgements about the future, since it seems ludicrous to assume that things simply happen as one expects them to do so. In any case, if Heraclitus' doctrine of flux and motion is true, then everything is constantly changing and no truth statement can be made about anything. Socrates' final argument is offered neither against Protagoras ('man is the measure of all things') nor against Heraclitus ('all things are in flux and motion'), but directly against Theaetetus ('knowledge is perception'): knowledge cannot equate with perception because the universal notions that we apply to objects perceived by the sense organs, for example, being and not-being, likeness and unlikeness, or odd and even, are not themselves perceived by the sense organs.

> *T: Indeed, Socrates, I cannot answer; my only*
> *notion is, that these [universal notions], unlike*
> *objects of sense, have no separate organ,*
> *but that the mind, by a power of her own,*
> *contemplates the universals in all things.*
> *S: You are a beauty, Theaetetus, and not ugly, as*
> *Theodorus was saying; for he who utters the*
> *beautiful is himself beautiful and good. And*
> *besides being beautiful, you have done me*
> *a kindness in releasing me from a very long*
> *discussion, if you are clear that the soul views*
> *some things by herself and others through the*
> *bodily organs. For that was my opinion, and I*
> *wanted you to agree with me.*

Socrates next says that knowledge consists not in sense perception, but in reasoning about sense perception. Taking his cue from Socrates, Theaetetus offers that knowledge is belief; however, since not all beliefs are knowledge, knowledge is to be equated only with *true* belief. What then, asks Socrates, is the nature of *false* belief? If all things are either known or unknown, then what one knows, one cannot but know, and what one does not know, one cannot know. It follows that one can neither suppose that what he knows is what he does not know, nor that what he does not know is what he knows, and thus that one cannot have a false belief. Perhaps one can have a false belief in thinking of something that is not. However, if one who perceives something of necessity perceives something that exists, it stands to reason that one who thinks of something of necessity thinks of something that is. If this is true, then one cannot think of something that is not, and therefore cannot have a false belief.

The metaphor of the wax tablet

To solve this problem of false belief, Socrates asks Theaetetus to suppose that his memory is like a block of wax on which there are impressions of those things which he remembers and, therefore, knows. 1. If he knows both Theaetetus and Theodorus but perceives neither, he cannot possibly form a false belief that the one is the other. 2. If he knows either Theaetetus or Theodorus and perceives neither, he cannot possibly form a false belief that he whom he knows is he whom he does not know. 3. If he knows neither Theaetetus nor Theodorus and perceives neither, he cannot possibly form any false belief about them at all. The only way he can form a false belief about them is by matching a perception of one or the other to an incorrect impression on the block of wax. In other words, a false belief can be formed not when there is a mismatch between two objects of perception, nor when there is a mismatch between two objects of thought, but when there is a mismatch between one object of each type. Unfortunately, there are certain false beliefs, such as false beliefs about arithmetic, which cannot be explained in this way.

The metaphor of the aviary

To explain such beliefs, Socrates compares the memory to an aviary with all kinds of birds, each representing a separate piece of knowledge. There are two phases of hunting the birds: one in which they are entered into the aviary, and one in which they are caught and held in the hand. A false belief occurs when, in this second phase of hunting, the wrong bird is caught and held in the hand. For example, if one thinks that 5 and 7 make 11, this is because he made a mistake and caught 11 instead of 12. Unfortunately, this is an infinitely regressing solution: if there is a problem about confusing two things, the problem cannot be resolved simply by postulating that it is really a problem about confusing another, corresponding two things.

Socrates next offers a direct argument against the proposition that knowledge is true belief. Since an orator can bring one into a state of true belief without bringing him into a state of knowledge, knowledge and true belief cannot be the same thing. Theaetetus recalls a man who held this position and argued that knowledge is true belief *with an account*. Socrates tells Theaetetus of a dream in which everything is either a primary element or a complex of such. Whereas it is possible to offer an account of complexes in terms of their primary elements, no account can be given of primary elements themselves. Thus, if knowledge is true belief with an account, knowledge can only be of complexes, but not of primary elements which can only ever be perceived, but never known. If the dream is correct, a complex such as the first syllable of 'SOCRATES' either is no more than its elements 'S' and 'O,' or is something over and above these elements. In the first case, one cannot know the syllable without also knowing its elements 'S' and 'O,' such that there can be no knowledge of complexes unless there is also knowledge of elements. In the second case, one cannot know the syllable without also knowing something above and beyond its elements 'S' and 'O,' such that the syllable's elements 'S' and 'O' no longer define and form part of the syllable. In this case, the syllable is in itself an element and, since there can be no knowledge of elements, neither can there be knowledge of the syllable. Finally, whereas the dream suggested that there can be no knowledge of primary elements, our common experience suggests that it is in fact more basic and more important to learn elements such as letters and notes than to learn complexes such as words and tunes.

Having refuted his dream, Socrates offers three explanations of what might be understood by 'an account'. (1) An account consists of vocalising one's thoughts, in which case anyone who vocalises a correct judgement will turn out to have knowledge. (2) An account of x consists in a statement of the elements of x, in which case anyone or anything that could string out the letters in 'Theaetetus' in their correct order could be said to have knowledge of 'Theaetetus'. (3) An account of *x* consists in marking out *x* from all other things, for example, marking out the sun from all other things by saying that it is the brightest of the bodies in the sky. However, if knowledge of the sun requires us to mark out the sun from all other things, true belief about the sun also requires this, if it is not to be true belief about something else. On the other hand, if knowledge of the sun requires us not merely to form a true belief about the sun but to *know* it, then the definition of knowledge is true belief + knowledge, which is circular. Socrates concludes that knowledge is neither perception, nor true belief, nor true belief with an account.

> S: *And are you still in labour and travail, my*
> *dear friend, or have you brought all that you*
> *have to say about knowledge to the birth?*
> T: *I am sure, Socrates, that you have elicited from*
> *me a good deal more than ever was in me.*
> S: *And does not my art show that you have*
> *brought forth wind, and that the offspring*
> *of your brain are not worth bringing up? ...*
> *But if, Theaetetus, you should ever conceive*
> *afresh, you will be all the better for the present*
> *investigation, and if not, you will be soberer*
> *and humbler and gentler to other men, and*
> *will be too modest to fancy that you know*
> *what you do not know.*

CHAPTER 23

Sophist

*And the wish of all of us, who are your friends,
is and always will be to bring you as near to the
truth as we can without the sad reality.*

The *Sophist* and *Statesman* form part of a trilogy the third
element of which, *Philosopher*, was never written. In the
Sophist, Theodorus and Theaetetus introduce Socrates to a
stranger from Elea, who is a disciple of Parmenides and Zeno,
and a 'true philosopher'. Socrates says that true philosophers
are divine persons who appear in various forms and go
unrecognised by the ignorance of men. Sometimes they appear
as sophists, sometimes as statesmen, 'and then, again, to
many they seem to be no better than madmen'. To whom are
the terms 'philosopher,' 'statesman,' and 'sophist' applied to in
Italy? The stranger replies that it is no mean task to define
precisely the nature of the three. Socrates asks him whether
he would prefer to do so in the form of a long oration or by
the method of question and answer. The stranger chooses the
latter, and chooses Theaetetus as his interlocutor. He begins
by enquiring into the nature of the first of the three kinds of
philosopher, that is, the sophist.

In order to best define the sophist, the stranger proposes
to define some 'lesser example which will be a pattern of the

greater,' and chooses to define the angler, who is a familiar and yet not very interesting or important person. The angler appears to be a man of art, and of arts there are two kinds, (1) the productive or creative arts which bring into existence things that did not exist before, for example, agriculture, the tending of mortal creatures, the art of constructing or moulding vessels, and the art of imitation, and (2) the acquisitive arts which conquer by word or deed things which exist already, for example, learning, trading, fighting, and hunting. The art of the angler appears to be one of the acquisitive arts. The acquisitive arts may be further divided into exchange, which is voluntarily, and acquisition, which occurs by force of word or deed, and may be termed 'conquest'. Conquest may be further divided into conquest by open force, that is, fighting, and conquest by secret force, that is, hunting. Hunting may be further divided into the hunting of lifeless prey, that is, diving, and the hunting of living prey, that is, animal hunting. Animal hunting may be further divided into land-animal hunting and water-animal hunting, and water-animal hunting may be further divided into fowling and fishing. Fishing may be further divided into fishing by enclosures such as nets and baskets and fishing by a blow, which may be termed 'striking'. Striking is done either by night with spears or by day with barbed spears or barbed hooks. Barbed spears are impelled from above, whereas barbed hooks are jerked into the head and lips of the fish, which is then drawn from below upwards. This, finally, is the art of the angler.

The stranger proposes to discover the art of the sophist by using the same method. Like the angler, the sophist is an artist, and the resemblance does not end there. They are both hunters of animals, the former of water animals and the latter of land animals. The angler goes to the sea and to the rivers, whereas the sophist goes to the rich meadowlands where generous youth abide. Hunting of land animals may be divided into hunting of wild land animals and hunting of tame land animals. Man is a tame land animal who may be hunted either by force, for example by pirates or tyrants, or by persuasion, for example, by lawyers or orators. Persuasion may be divided into public persuasion and private persuasion, and private persuasion may be divided into bringing gifts or receiving hire. Those who practice private persuasion by bringing gifts are termed 'lover,' and those who practice private persuasion by receiving hire are termed 'sophist'. Sophists may please or flatter in return for their maintenance, or may profess to teach virtue in exchange for a round sum.

Sophists are many-sided creatures, and may yet be traced in another line of descent. The acquisitive art has not only a branch of hunting but also a branch of exchange, with exchange being either giving or selling, with the seller being either a manufacturer or a merchant, with the merchant being either a retailer or an exporter, and with the exporter exporting either food for the body or food for the soul. Trading in food for the soul can be divided into the art of display and the art of selling learning, with learning being either a learning of the arts or a learning of virtue. The seller of learning of the arts is termed 'art-seller,' and the seller of learning of virtue is termed 'sophist'.

The sophist may be traced in yet other lines of descent. Instead of exporting his wares to another country, the sophist may stay at home and retail goods which he not only merchandises, but also manufactures. Or he may be descended from the acquisitive art in the combative line, which divides into the pugnacious, the controversial, and the disputatious arts. The disputatious arts include an eristic section, which has a division of disputes in private for gain about the general principles of right and wrong. This too may be termed the art of the sophist.

The processes of division themselves may be divided into that which separates like from like and that which separates the better from the worse. This latter is termed 'purification,' which is either of animate bodies or of inanimate bodies. Internal purifications of animate bodies are medicine and gymnastic and external purifications of animate bodies are 'the not very dignified art of the bath-man'. Purifications of inanimate bodies are fulling and furbishing and other such humble processes with ludicrous names. Not that dialectic despises humble processes or ludicrous names, without which it would not be able to find a general term with which to distinguish purifications of the soul from those of the body. Dialectic only ever has one concern – truth.

Purification is the taking away of evil, of which there are two kinds in the soul, vice, which answers to disease or discord in the body, and ignorance, which answers to deformity in the body. Thus, the unintelligent soul may be regarded as deformed and devoid of symmetry. In the case of the body, medicine cures disease and gymnastic cures deformity. In the case of the soul, chastisement cures vice and instruction cures ignorance. Ignorance may be divided into simple ignorance and ignorance having the conceit of knowledge, which may be termed 'stupidity'. Education can correspondingly be divided into the time-honoured moral training of our forefathers, which gives much trouble and does little good, and another which proceeds upon the notion that all ignorance is involuntary, and convicts a man out of his own mouth by pointing to him his inconsistencies and contradictions.

> *They cross-examine a man's words, when he thinks that he is saying something and is really saying nothing, and easily convict him of inconsistencies in his opinions; these they then collect by the dialectical process, and placing them side by side, show that they contradict one another about the same things, in relation to the same things, and in the same respect. He, seeing this, is angry with himself, and grows gentle towards others, and thus is entirely delivered from great prejudices and harsh notions, in a way which is most amusing to the hearer, and produces the most lasting good*

> *effect on the person who is the subject of the*
> *operation... he who has not been refuted, though*
> *he be the Great King himself, is in an awful state*
> *of impurity; he is uninstructed and deformed*
> *in those things in which he who would be truly*
> *blessed ought to be fairest and purest...*

The sophist might be thought to be the minster of this art, although the former may be compared to the wolf, which is the fiercest of animals, and the latter to the dog, which is the gentlest. If the sophist can be defined by so many different names and kinds of knowledge, this is because his art is so poorly understood. However, his most prominent characteristic is that he is a disputer; he disputes and teaches others to dispute about all things. Whilst it is impossible to know and understand all things, the sophist makes others believe that he does. The painter professes to make all things, and young children who see his imitations from a distance are liable to take them for realities; similarly, the sophist professes to know all things, and young men who hear his words from a distance from the truth are liable to be deceived by them. However, as they grow older they learn by sad experience to see and feel the truth of things, and all their dreamy speculations are overturned by the facts of life. 'And the wish of all of us, who are your friends, is and always will be to bring you as near to the truth as we can without the sad reality.'

The art of imitation may be divided into the art of making likenesses and the art of making appearances. Like the sophist, the sculptor and painter make use of illusions, and, like the sophist, their imitations are not likenesses but appearances. But how can anything be appearance only? The existence of appearance only, that is, of falsehood, implies the existence of non-being, which the great Parmenides spent all his life denying. 'Never,' he said, 'will you show that not-being is,' and his words literally bore witness to themselves. Not-being cannot be attributed to any being and, because all numbers are, cannot be attributed any number either. If not-being cannot be attributed any number either singular or plural, then it cannot be predicated or expressed or even thought about. And if it cannot be thought about, then it cannot be refuted, and the sophist will not be got out of his hole.

It is impossible to speak of falsehood, false opinion, and imitation without falling into a contradiction, unless it can be demonstrated that there is some sense in which non-being is. 'And therefore I must venture to lay hands on my father's argument; for if I am to be over-scrupulous, I shall have to give the matter up.' Parmenides and the other philosophers used to talk in a light and easy strain, each in the form of their own mythus or story. Thus, one spoke of three principles warring and at peace again, marrying and begetting children; another spoke of two principles, dry and moist or hot and cold, which also form relationships. The Eleatics said that all things are one, and the Ionian and Sicilian muses spoke of a one and many which are held together by enmity and friendship, ever parting, ever meeting. Not all insisted upon perpetual strife, and some spoke of alternation only. None, however, had any regard for whether they were understood or not.

Let us begin, then, with an examination of being. Would the dualistic philosophers say that being is a third element besides hot and cold, or would they rather identify it with one or both of them? Would the philosophers of the one consider that being and the one are two names for the same thing? In that case, how could they justify there being two names when there is nothing but the one? Being is conceived as a whole, as Parmenides sings, and a whole has parts. However, that which has parts is not one, since unity is indivisible and does not admit of parts. So either being is one because its parts are one, or being is not a whole. In the former case, one has parts, and in the latter, there is still plurality, since there is both being and a whole that is apart from being. If being is not a whole, then it lacks something of the nature of being, and becomes not-being. Since that which has number is a whole of that number, being could not have number, and since nothing comes into being except as a whole, being could not have come into being. 'And there will be innumerable other points...'

What about the other philosophers, the materialists who define being and body as one and will hear of nothing but body ('terrible fellows they are'), and their opponents who believe that being consists in ideas, and break up body into the most minute fractions until they are lost in generation and flux? The materialists would admit to the existence of a body having a soul which may be just by the possession of justice, wise by the possession of wisdom, and so on. They would argue that the soul, though invisible, has a kind of body, but with regards to justice, wisdom, and the like, they would not venture either to deny their existence, or to maintain that they are corporeal. If both the corporeal and the incorporeal exist, what is the nature which they have in common, and which is attributed to being? The materialists would not be able to answer this question, but, if they were, they might say that 'being is the power of doing or suffering, that is, of being affected or being affected by another'. In contrast to the materialists, the friends of ideas distinguish essence (being) from generation (becoming), and hold that the soul participates in the former, which is immutable, and the body in the latter, which is variable. They would deny the truth of this most recent definition of being, and argue that doing and suffering applies not to being but only to becoming. Our response is that the soul knows, and being is known; knowing and being known are active and passive and akin to doing and suffering. That which is known is affected by knowledge, and therefore is in motion, and being surely cannot be devoid of motion and soul, for there can be no thought without soul, or soul without motion. Yet neither can thought be devoid of some principle of rest or stability, and so the philosopher must include both the moveable and the immoveable in his idea of being. However, motion and rest are contradictions, and if one asserts that they both exist, he does not mean to say that motion is rest or rest motion, but that there is some third thing which is being and which neither rests nor moves. But how can there be such a thing? This is a second difficulty about being, and one that is at least as great as that about not-being.

> *Then let us acknowledge the difficulty; and as being and not-being are involved in the same perplexity, there is hope that when the one appears more or less distinctly, the other will equally appear; and if we are able to see neither there may still be a chance of steering our way in between them, without any great discredit.*

Let us now ask what it means to predicate many names to the same thing, for example, 'good,' 'tall,' 'fat,' 'tanned,' to man. Nothing is easier than to argue that the one cannot be many, or the many one, denying that man is good and instead insisting that man is man and good is good. Let us ask those who make this argument together with our previous opponents whether (1) being and rest and motion and all other things are incommunicable with one another, or (2) they are all communicable with one another, or (3) some are communicable and others are not. In the first instance, rest and motion would not be able to participate in being, and so would not be, and all theories would be swept away. In the second instance, motion would rest, and rest would move, either of which is impossible. So only the third instance remains. In the alphabet and musical scale, some letters and notes combine or do not combine with some others, and the laws by which they combine and do not combine are known to the grammarian and musician.

> *And as classes are admitted by us in like manner to be some of them capable and others incapable of intermixture, must not he who would rightly show what kinds will unite and what will not, proceed*

by the help of science in the path of argument? And will he not ask if the connecting links are universal, and so capable of intermixture with all things; and again, in divisions, whether there are not other universal classes, which make them possible? – To be sure he will require science, and, if I am not mistaken, the very greatest of all sciences. – How are we to call it? By Zeus, have we not lighted unwittingly upon our free and noble science, and in looking for the sophist have we not entertained the philosopher unawares?

The division according to classes, which neither makes the same other, nor makes other the same, is the business of the true dialectician and philosopher, and only he is able to see clearly one form pervading a scattered multitude, and many different forms contained under one higher form, and one form knit together into a single whole and pervading many such wholes, and many forms existing only in separation and isolation. Like the sophist, the philosopher is not easily discovered. Whereas the former hides in non-being, the latter is dark from excess of light.

Let us now return to the pursuit of the sophist. Given that some things are communicable and others are not, it is prudent to examine the principal classes which are capable of admixture, with the aim of discovering a sense in which non-being might be. The highest classes are being, rest, and motion. Of the three, rest and motion exclude each other, but are both included in being. Each of the three is other than the remaining two, but the same with itself. What is the meaning of 'other' and 'same'? Sameness cannot be either rest or motion, because it is predicated both of rest and motion. Nor can sameness be being, because being is attributed to both rest and motion, whereas sameness is not. For these reasons, sameness is a fourth class. Other cannot be identified with being because other is relative and so cannot have the absoluteness of being.

For this reason, other is a fifth class which pervades all other classes, which are other than the other classes. There are then five classes: (1) being, (2) motion, which is not (3) rest, and because participating both in the same and other, is and is not (4) the same with itself, and is and is not (5) other than the other. And motion is not being, but partakes of being, and therefore is and is not in the most literal sense. Thus, it has been discovered that not-being is the principle of the other which pervades all other classes, including being. 'Being' is one thing, and 'not-being' includes and is all other things; it is not the opposite of being, but a kind of being, namely, that of the other. It follows that the not-beautiful is not any less real than the beautiful, the not-great any less real than the great, and so on. Although the sophist may no longer deny the existence of not-being, he may yet deny that non-being can enter into the sphere of thought and discourse. For this reason, it is necessary to examine speech, opinion, and imagination.

With regards to speech, let us ask of words what has been asked of ideas and of the letters of the alphabet: to what extent can they be connected with one another? Some words describe actions and some describe agents, but no combination of words can be formed without one of each. In both 'Theaetetus sits' and 'Theaetetus flies,' Theaetetus is the subject, but the former says of him that which is true, whereas the latter says of him that which is other than true, that is, false, and false discourse. If speech can be both true and false, so can thought and opinion and imagination. For thought is but silent speech, opinion is but silent affirmation or denial, and imagination is but the presentation of opinion in some form of sense. And therein has false opinion been discovered, and the sophist exposed.

CHAPTER 24

Statesman (Politicus)

*...every man seems to know all things in a
dreamy sort of way, and then again to wake up
and know nothing.*

Theodorus asks the stranger to proceed with either the
statesman or the philosopher. The stranger chooses the
statesman and asks to give Theaetetus a rest and have
the young Socrates (not Socrates, but a namesake) as his
interlocutor. The statesman is a man of art and science,
and the arts and sciences may be divided into practical and
theoretical. Before proceeding any further, let us ask whether
the king, statesman, master, and householder do not practise
the same science. Anyone who is in a private station but able
to advise the ruler of a country can be said to have the science
of the ruler. A large household may be compared to a small
state, and so the master and householder do not differ from
the king or statesman as far as government is concerned.
Thus, the king, statesman, master, and householder practice
the same science, namely, the royal or political or economical
science. A king achieves far more with his mind than with
his hands, for which reason the royal science is more akin
to theoretical science than to practical science. Theoretical
science may be further divided into a science of judging and

a science of ruling and superintending, and the royal science is clearly more like the latter. The king is a wholesale dealer in command, and is to be differentiated from inferior officers who merely retail his commands to others. Unlike these inferior officers, the king is in the class of supreme rulers who practice the 'ruling-for-self' science. All rulers command for the sake of producing some object; objects may be divided into living and lifeless, and rulers into rulers of living objects and rulers of lifeless objects. The king is a ruler of living objects, and has the task of rearing living animals. The rearing of living animals may be further divided into the rearing of the individual and the rearing of flocks or herds. The king is not a groom, but a herdsman, and rears herds. The stranger asks the young Socrates to divide the art of the herdsman, which he does into the art of rearing beasts and the art of rearing men. The stranger chides the young Socrates for being in too much of a hurry to get to man, and compares his division to one of the human race into Hellenes and Barbarians, rather than into male and female. The young Socrates' division is the sort of division an intelligent crane would make, putting cranes into a class by themselves for their special glory, and jumbling together all others, including man, in the class of beasts. An error of this kind can only be avoided by a more regular division, and 'the safer way is to cut through the middle'. In this case, we forgot to divide the whole class of animals into gregarious and non-gregarious, having forgotten the previous division into tame and wild.

Let us begin again at the rearing of herds. The rearing of herds may be divided into the rearing of land- and water-herds, and land-herds may be divided into walking and flying. 'And where shall we look for the political animal? Might not an idiot, so to speak, know that he is a pedestrian?' Tame, walking, herding animals may be divided into the horned and the hornless, and the hornless may be divided into animals having and not having cloven feet, and mixing and not mixing the breed. The king clearly has care of walking, herding animals which do not have cloven feet and do not mix the breed. There are only two species left, man and pig (!), and man is the only one that is a biped. A quicker route to man would have been to divide land animals into bipeds and quadrupeds, and then bipeds into winged and wingless.[22]

Let us go back to the beginning, join the links, and define the art of the statesman. Theoretical science was divided into a science of judging and a science of ruling and superintending, and the science of ruling and superintending had a part which was a science of wholesale command. The science of wholesale command was divided into the ruling of lifeless objects and the ruling of living objects, that is, of living animals. The ruling of animals was divided into the tending of the individual and the tending of flocks or herds. The rearing of herds was divided into the rearing of land- and water-herds, and land-herds were divided into walking and flying. Walking herds were divided into horned and hornless, and the hornless were divided into animals having and not having cloven feet, and mixing and not mixing the breed. Walking, herding animals which do not have cloven feet and do not mix the breed were divided into bipeds and quadrupeds, and at last man was arrived at and the royal or political science was found. And yet the political shepherd has not been clearly distinguished from his rivals, for instance, merchants, husbandmen, and physicians, who will dispute his right to rear the herd. 'Then let us make a new beginning, and travel by a different road... there is a famous tale, of which a good portion may with advantage be interwoven, and then we may resume our series of divisions, and proceed in the old path until we arrive at the desired summit.'

In the quarrel of Atreus and Thyestes, God reversed the motion of the sun and the stars as a testimony to the right of Atreus. There is a time when God directs the revolutions of the world, and a time when he lets go and the world revolves in the opposite direction. There are thus two cycles of the world, one

---

22 Kangaroos were not known to the Ancients.

in which the world is governed by God and receives life and immortality, and another in which the world is let go and has a reverse movement. Changes in the cycle of the world result in great destruction of men and animals, and at the beginning of the last cycle there were only very few men and animals remaining. These had the course of their lives reversed, at first returning to youth and beauty, and then vanishing away; the dead returned to life, and rose up from the earth. Such was the age of Cronos, in which animals and men were born not from procreation but from the earth, and of which our ancestors have preserved the memory in their traditions. God ruled the world, and other inferior deities ruled parts of it in his name. God shepherded man, just as today man shepherds the inferior animals. There were no private possessions or families, no strife or war. The climate was mild, the earth bore food in abundance, and man dwelt naked in the open air with the animals, whose language he shared. 'Such was the life of man in the days of Cronos, Socrates; the character of our present life which is said to be under Zeus, you know from your own experience.' If the earthborn men employed these advantages with a view to philosophising, or merely to telling stories, then there can be no question that they were far happier than the men of today. One day God let go of the helm and made himself a spectator. Fate and innate desire reversed the motion of the world, and a mighty earthquake wrought a new destruction on animals. Man emerged as ruler amongst the animals, and followed the instructions of God, at first precisely, but afterwards with less exactness. Discord and destruction set in, and the danger of universal ruin reared its head. God feared so much that the world would be dissolved into chaos and infinity that he returned to the helm and restored order. The cycle of life and generation was reversed, and infants grew into young men, and young men into greybeards, before all dying and sinking into the earth. Animals and men no longer rose from the earth, but required to be self-created and self-nourished. Man was left helpless and defenceless, alone amongst wild beasts, without arts or knowledge, and without food. Then Prometheus brought him fire, Hephaestus and Athena taught him the arts, and other gods gave him seeds and crops. With the help of these god-given gifts, man ordered the course of his life for himself and became his own master, ever living and growing, and ever changing.

The myth points at two errors in our account of the king. The first and greater error was to choose a god for our king, and the second and lesser error was to fail to define the nature of the king's functions. The form of the divine shepherd is higher than that of a king, and the kings of today very much resemble their subjects in education and breeding. Earlier, we spoke of a class of supreme rulers who practice the ruling-for-self science over living animals, not individually but collectively in flocks or herds, which we called the art of rearing a herd. Our error lay there somewhere, for we never included or mentioned the king or statesman. The statesman does not 'rear' his herd, but 'cares for,' 'manages,' or 'tends' it, all terms which do not imply feeding or any other special duty. Having remodelled the name, we may divide as before, first dividing the divine from the human shepherd or manager, and then dividing the latter into the management of willing and unwilling subjects, that is, royalty or tyranny, which are utterly distinct. The manager of willing subjects is the true king.

And yet the figure of the king is not yet perfected. 'What is the imperfection which still remains?' 'The higher ideas, my dear friend, can hardly be set forth except through the medium of examples; every man seems to know all things in a dreamy sort of way, and then again to wake up and know nothing.' Like the child who is learning his letters, the soul recognises some of the first elements of things, but then no longer when they are translated into the difficult language of facts. Let us take as an example of an example something small, say, the weaving of wool. All possessions are either creative or preventive; those that are the preventive sort

are either antidotes or defences; defences are either arms
or screens; screens are either veils or shields against heat
and cold; shields against heat and cold are either shelters
and coverings; coverings are either blankets or garments;
garments are either in one piece or of many parts; garments
of many parts are either stitched or fastened; garments that
are fastened are either made of plant fibres or made of hair;
garments that are fastened that are made of hair are either
cemented with water and earth or fastened with their own
material. These latter are called clothes, and are made by the
art of weaving. Despite having drawn several distinctions, we
still have not distinguished the art of weaving from kindred
arts. Prior to weaving, the material requires carding, and so
the art of carding is also involved in the making of clothes.
Then there are the arts which make the weaver's tools, and so
on. Arts can be either causal and principal, or co-operative and
subordinate. To the causal class belong the arts of working the
wool such as carding and spinning and washing and mending.
There are two great categories of working the wool, namely,
composition and division. Carding is of the latter sort. But
our main concern is with the art of working the wool which
composes, twisting and interlacing the threads. This, finally,
is the art of weaving.

Why go through this long and tedious process of division
instead of saying at once that weaving is the art of twisting
and interlacing threads? To answer this question we need to
consider the whole nature of length and shortness, excess and
defect. The difference between good and evil is the difference
between a mean or measure and excess or defect. All things
must be compared, not only with one another, but also with
a mean or ideal standard, without which there would be no
beauty or art, neither the art of the statesman, nor that of
weaving, nor any other. 'For all these arts are on the watch
against excess and defect, not as unrealities, but as real evils,
which occasion a difficulty in action; and the excellence of
beauty of every work of art is due to this observance of measure.'

To find the art of the statesman, or indeed any art, we need to show that things can be compared to a mean or standard. The art of measurement can be divided into one concerned with relative size and another concerned with a mean or standard. Many accomplished men say that the art of measurement has to do with all things, and though they may be right, they fail to distinguish between classes and confuse the 'more' and the 'too much,' which are in fact very different things. Hence the importance of distinguishing between classes. Another point is this: when a schoolboy is asked to spell a particular word, this is with a view to improve his spelling generally; when we search for the statesman, this is with a view to improving our power of reasoning generally.

> *Still less would any rational man seek to analyse the notion of weaving for its own sake. But people seem to forget that some things have sensible images, which are readily known, and can be easily pointed out when any one desires to answer an enquirer without any trouble or argument; whereas the greatest and highest truths have no outward image of themselves visible to man, which he who wishes to satisfy the soul of the enquirer can adapt to the eye of sense, and therefore we ought to train ourselves to give and accept a rational account of them; for immaterial things, which are the noblest and greatest, are shown only in thought and ideas, and in no other way, and all that we are now saying is said for the sake of them.*

Let us return to our search for the statesman, and apply to it the example of weaving. The royal art has been separated from that of other shepherds and herdsmen, but not from the causal and co-operative arts which exist in states. These do not admit of division, and since they cannot be bisected they must be carved out like a victim into members or limbs. There are the arts of making or furnishing (1) instruments, (2) vessels, (3) vehicles, (4) defences, (5) ornaments, (6) gold, silver, wood, and bark, and (7) food and care for the body. These seven classes of co-operative arts include almost every description of property, but neither has anything to do with the royal art. There remains only the class of slaves and ministers amongst whom the true rivals to the king are to be found. They are neither the slave, nor the hireling, nor the trader or merchant, nor government officials such as heralds and scribes who are only servants of the king, nor diviners and priests who, although swollen with pride and prerogative, are also only servants of the king.

The next contender is the politician, 'the chief of sophists and most accomplished of wizards, who must at any cost be separated from the true king or statesman'. The true forms of government are three, monarchy, oligarchy, and democracy. These expand into six according to the criteria of voluntary and involuntary, poverty and riches, and law and absence of law. Monarchy divides into royalty and tyranny, oligarchy divides into aristocracy and plutocracy, and democracy may be with or without law. Government is a science, and the many cannot attain to science. In any Greek city, there are perhaps no more than fifty good draught-players, and certainly not as many kings. A true government must therefore be a government of one, two, or the few.

> *And these, whether they rule with the will, or against the will of their subjects, with written laws or without written laws, and whether they are poor or rich, and whatever be the nature of their rule, must be supposed, according to our present view, to rule on some scientific principle; just as the physician, whether he cures us against our will or with our will, and whatever be his mode of treatment – incision, burning, or the infliction of some other pain – whether he practises out of a*

> *book or not out of a book, and whether he be rich or*
> *poor, whether he purges or reduces in some other*
> *way, or even fattens his patients, is a physician*
> *all the same, so long as he exercises authority over*
> *them according to rules of art, if he only does them*
> *good and heals and saves them. And this we may*
> *lay down to be the only proper test of the art of*
> *medicine, or of any other art of command.*

The young Socrates objects to the notion of politicians ruling in the absence of law. The stranger explains that the best thing is not for the law to rule, but for the king to rule, because the law is an ignorant tyrant who 'does not perfectly comprehend what is noblest and most just for all and therefore cannot enforce what is best'. 'The differences of man and actions, and the endless irregular movements of human things, do not admit of any universal and simple rule. And no art whatsoever can lay down a rule which will last for all time.' So why are we compelled to make laws at all? The training master has a general rule of diet and exercise which is suited to the constitutions of the majority, and the same is true of the legislator, who cannot 'sit at every man's side all through his life'. As only very few people are able to attain to the science of government, the true political principle is to assert the inviolability of the law, which, though not ideal, is second best, and best for the imperfect condition of man. If the multitudes decided to regulate the arts and sciences and to indict any 'cloudy prating sophist' who sought to enquire into the truth of one or other of the arts, 'all the arts would utterly perish, and could never be recovered... And human life, which is bad enough already, would then become utterly unendurable.' However, things would be even worse if the multitudes appointed as guardian of the law someone who was both ignorant and interested, and who perverted the law. If a guardian or some other person tried to improve the law, he would be acting in the spirit of the law-giver. However, law-givers are few and far between, and in their absence the next best thing is to obey the law and preserve customs and traditions.

Given this, which of the six forms of government other than true government is the least bad? The government of one is the best and the worst, the government of few is less good and less bad, and the government of the many is the least good and the least bad. That is to say, democracy is the worst of all lawful governments, and the best of all lawless ones, 'in every respect weak and unable to do any great good or any great evil'. However, the rulers of all these states, unless they have knowledge, are merely maintainers of idols, and themselves idols, no better than imitators and sophists.

Enough of politicians; there still remain some other and better elements that need to be separated off from the royal science, namely, the arts of the general, the judge, and the orator. There are inferior sciences such as law and persuasion and others, and a superior science which determines whether law or persuasion is to be learnt or not. Clearly, the science which determines whether law or persuasion is to be learnt or not is higher than that of law or persuasion, just as the science which makes the laws is higher than that which only administers them. This higher science is none other than the political science of the king or statesman.

The state may be compared to a web. Virtue is of many parts, of which courage and temperance, which are antagonistic to each other. Yet courage and temperance pervade all nature and include under them the whole class of the good and beautiful. The good and beautiful may be divided into that which is described in terms expressive of motion or energy, and that which is described in terms expressive of rest or quietness. However, excess in the former is termed 'violence' or 'madness,' and excess in the latter is termed 'sluggishness' or 'cowardliness'. These opposite characters cannot be reconciled, and their antagonism in the State results in the most hateful of all disorders. Orderly people seek peace and imperceptibly pass into the condition of slaves, whereas the courageous seek war and are soon destroyed by their enemies. The true art of government consists in testing human natures in childish play, discarding those that are evil and lacking in courage and temperance and the other virtues, and entrusting those that remain to proper educators. Once educated, the statesman blends the citizens together, weaving the warp of courage with the woof of temperance. First, the eternal element of the soul is bound with a divine cord, and then the animal nature is bound with human cords. The eternal element of the soul consists of the honourable, the just, and the good, which only the statesman can implant in the properly educated. He then implants the lesser human bonds such as those of union for the sake of offspring. Most people marry for wealth or power, or receive with open arms those who are like themselves, the courageous marrying the courageous and the temperate the temperate. Over the course of several generations, the former tend to madness and the latter to feebleness and ineffectuality. The temperate are careful and just but lacking in power of action, whereas the courageous are all the opposite. Thus, no state can prosper in which either of these natures is lacking, and the best of all states is that which the true political science weaves by blending the two natures into a single texture.

CHAPTER 25

Philebus

*...he who never looks for number in anything,
will not himself be looked for in the number
of famous men.*

Protarchus, the son of Callias, takes over from his teacher
or elder friend Philebus in the argument that Socrates and
Philebus have been having. For Philebus, pleasure is the
greatest human good, whereas for Socrates it is wisdom or
mind. Socrates proposes to enquire into the nature of pleasure,
which he says takes the most varied and even unlike of forms.
For example, the fool takes pleasure in his foolish fancies and
hopes, whereas the wise man takes pleasure in his wisdom.
Protarchus says that, although pleasure may spring from
opposite sources, pleasure is always pleasure in so far as it is
pleasure. Socrates says that colours too are always colours in
so far as they are colours, and yet black is opposed to white;
figures too are always figures in so far as they as they are
figures, and yet there is great variety amongst figures. If
Protarchus is to maintain that all pleasures are good, he must
identify the common property that makes them so. To do this,
he needs to come to an understanding of the principle of the one
and the many, according to which one thing may be many and
many one. Socrates does not mean the one in terms of sensible

objects such as those that they have just been discussing, but of abstract unities such as 'man,' 'ox,' 'beauty,' or 'the good'. Do these abstract unities exist? Is an abstract unity divided and dispersed amongst different sensible objects, or does it exist in its entirety in each object? How is either possible?

The knowledge of how to proceed by regular steps from one to many, and from many to one, makes the difference between eristic, the mere art of disputation, and dialectic. One must begin by looking for one idea or class in everything and, having found it, proceed to look for two, if there are two, or for three or some other number, dividing each of these units until at last the unity with which he began is seen not only to be one and many, but also a definite number. Thus, it is not by knowing either that the sounds of speech are one or that the sounds of speech are infinite that one is made a grammarian, but by knowing the precise number and nature of the sounds: '...he who never looks for number in anything, will not himself be looked for in the number of famous men'. Socrates accordingly considers the number and nature of the kinds of pleasure and wisdom. At this point, he has a dreamy recollection that the greatest good must be both perfect and sufficient, and thus that it is neither pleasure nor wisdom. Neither the life of pure pleasure nor the life of pure wisdom is perfect and sufficient when compared with the union between the two. Nonetheless, the element by which this mixed life is good is far more akin to mind than to pleasure.

Socrates proposes to divide all existing things into three classes according to whether they are finite, infinite, or a union of the two. Whereas the class of the finite is denoted in terms of number and quantity, the class of the infinite cannot be reduced to measure by number and quantity, and is denoted in comparative terms of more or less such as 'greater' and 'lesser' or 'hotter' and 'colder'. In the third or mixed class, the finite gives law and order to the infinite, which gives rise to generation. In this class are included health, strength, the seasons, harmony, beauty, and the like. As cause is not the same as effect, and as every effect requires a cause, there must be a fourth class, which is the cause of the union of finite and infinite, that is, the cause of generation. Life clearly belongs to the third or mixed class and pleasure to the infinite class. However, wisdom or mind is more difficult to place. The elements of earth, air, fire, water exist in our body as they exist in the cosmos, but they are less pure and less fair in our body than in the cosmos, from where they come into our body. As for the body, so for the soul: the elements of the finite, the infinite, the union of the two, and the cause of this union exist in our soul. As the first three exist in the cosmos, the fourth or cause must also exist in the cosmos. This fourth or cause is nothing other than wisdom or mind, which is thus the ruler of the universe.

The natural seat of pleasure and pain is the mixed class. The dissolution of the harmony in animals results in pain, and its restoration results in pleasure. For instance, hunger is dissolution and pain, whereas eating is replenishment and pleasure. A second class of pleasures and pains are hopes and fears, which are produced by expectation, and are of the mind only. As the pleasures and pains in this second class are unalloyed, one might clearly see from them whether pleasure is itself desirable, or whether this desirableness is not rather the attribute of something else: '...whether pleasure and pain, like heat and cold, and other things of the same kind, are not sometimes to be desired and sometimes not to be desired, as being not in themselves good, but only sometimes and in some instances admitting of the nature of good'. Since pains and pleasures result from the dissolution and restoration of harmony, may there not be a neutral state without neither dissolution nor restoration? If so, there is a third state over and above those of pleasure and pain in which a man who chooses the life of wisdom may live. As the gods cannot be supposed to feel either joy or sorrow, this life may be the most divine of lives.

The second class of pleasures and pains involves memory, which is the preservation of consciousness. In many cases, a painful want in our body may be balanced by a pleasant hope of replenishment in our mind. This pleasant hope of replenishment is based on the memory of pleasure which is the opposite of our actual bodily state, and is thus not in the body but in the mind: 'And the argument, having proved that memory attracts us towards the objects of desire, proves also that the impulses and the desires and the moving principle in every living being have their origin in the soul [mind]'. In that case, may not pleasures, like opinions, be either true or false? Both pleasures and opinions are true in the sense that they are real. However, there are some pleasures that are associated with right opinion and knowledge, and others that are associated with falsehood and ignorance. Opinion is based on mental words and images that result from perception and memory. These mental words and images may be correct or mistaken, and may be of the past, present, or future, including future pleasures and pains. These 'hopes' are propositions which are sometimes true and sometimes false, such that there may be pleasure about things which were not, are not, and will not be, which is pleasure still, albeit false pleasure. The bad commonly delight in false, that is, bad, pleasures; the good in true, that is, good, pleasures. And the same can be said for pain, fear, anger, and the like. Socrates demonstrates the existence of false pleasures by another argument. If body's pain and mind's pleasure, which both belong to the infinite class, can occur simultaneously and coalesce into one, then one is liable to be deceived by their distance and relation, in which case pleasures and pain are not false based on false opinion, but false in themselves.

In passing from pleasure to pain and pain to pleasure, one experiences a third, neutral state which may appear pleasurable or painful but is in fact neither. Some natural philosophers do not admit of this third state, and affirm that pleasure is nothing but the absence of pain. They say that the nature of anything is best grasped through its greatest instances, and thus that the nature of pleasure is best grasped through the most intense pleasures. The most intense (although not the most frequent or persistent) pleasures are those of the body and not of the mind, of disease and not of health, of the intemperate and not of the temperate. An example is itching or scratching, in which pleasure and pain are mixed, and pleasure consists in the relief of pain. Pleasures of the mind may also be mixed with pain, as in anger or envy or love, or the mixed feelings of the spectator of tragedy or of the greater drama of life.

Then there are the unmixed pleasures, of which the aforementioned natural philosophers deny the existence. These pure and unmixed pleasures arise (1) from the beauty of form, colour, sound, smell, and (2) from the acquisition of knowledge. Unmixed pleasures have measure, whereas all other pleasures belong to the infinite class, and are thus liable to every species of excess. Just as the purity of white paint consists in the quality of the white colour and not in the quantity of white paint, a small amount of pure pleasure is always more pleasant and more true than a great amount of pleasure of another kind. It has been argued that pleasure is always a generation, and has no true being. If this argument is correct, and if generation is always for the sake of essence, then pleasure must always be for the sake of essence. That for the sake of which something else is done is in the class of the good, whereas that which is done for the sake of something else is in some other class. Thus, pleasure is in some other class than the class of the good.

Having considered pleasure, Socrates next considers wisdom or mind. There are two kinds of knowledge, the one creative or productive, and the other educational and philosophical. The creative or productive arts have an element of number and measure in them, and can be further divided into two classes according to whether they are less exact, as in music, or more exact, as in carpentering.

> *I mean to say, that if arithmetic, mensuration, and weighing be taken away from any art, that which remains will not be much... The test will be only*

> *conjecture, and the better use of the senses which*
> *is given by experience and practice, in addition to*
> *a certain power of guessing, which is commonly*
> *called art, and is perfected by attention and pains.*

Arithmetic itself can be divided into two classes according to whether it is used in the concrete, as in building and binding, or in the abstract, as in philosophy. Borrowing the analogy of pleasure, the use of philosophical arithmetic is purer than that of popular arithmetic. Those arts that are animated by the philosophical impulse far surpass all others in purity, accuracy, and truth, and first among them is dialectic which is 'the science which has to do with all that knowledge of which we are now speaking'.

> *...for I am sure that all men who have a grain of*
> *intelligence will admit that the knowledge which*
> *has to do with being and reality, and sameness*
> *and unchangeableness, is by far the truest of all.*

Protarchus says that he has often heard Gorgias maintain that the art of persuasion, which is rhetoric, is by far the best of them all. Socrates replies that he is not claiming that dialectic is the greatest or best or most useful of arts, but that it has the greatest amount of truth – not even Gorgias would quarrel with that. Wisdom and mind are concerned not with things which are becoming, but with things which are eternal and unchangeable and unmixed, and should thus be honoured more than pleasure.

Having considered the kinds of pleasure and wisdom, Socrates is in a position to mix them. However, he first recapitulates the question at issue. Philebus said that pleasure is the good and that it is has one nature. Socrates on the other hand denied this and further maintained that it has not one but two natures, that mind partakes more than pleasure of the good, and that the two together are more eligible than either alone.

'And now reason intimates to us, as at our first beginning, that we should seek the good, not in the unmixed life but in the mixed.' There are pure and impure pleasures and pure and impure sciences. Both the pure *and* the impure sciences should be admitted into the mixture, since without the impure sciences none of us would ever find our way home. Music too should be included, 'if human life is to be a life at all'. With regard to the pleasures, the pure pleasures should certainly be admitted into the mixture, followed by those pleasures which, although impure, are necessary. These include the pleasures which accompany health and temperance and the other virtues, but not those which accompany folly and vice, and which are the ruin of the arts and sciences. The final ingredient in the mixture should be truth, without which nothing can truly be created or subsist.

This mixture, which is the good, has three chief elements: beauty, symmetry, and truth. These three elements taken together are the single cause of the mixture, and that by which the mixture is the good. Given this, any man can decide which of pleasure or mind is more akin to the good. Mind is certainly more akin to truth than to pleasure: '...pleasures, like children, have not the least particle of reason in them; whereas mind is either the same as truth, or the most like truth, and the truest'. And Mind is also more akin to symmetry and to beauty than pleasure: 'No one, Socrates, either awake or dreaming, ever saw or imagined mind or wisdom to be in aught unseemly, at any time, past, present, or future'. Not pleasure, then, ranks first in the scale of good, but measure and harmony. Second comes the symmetrical and beautiful and perfect and sufficient. Third, mind and wisdom. Fourth, sciences and arts and true opinions. And fifth, pure or painless pleasures. Socrates concludes that,

> *Though they must both resign in favour of another,*
> *mind is ten thousand times nearer and more akin*
> *to the nature of the conqueror than pleasure.*

CHAPTER 26

Timaeus

As being is to becoming, so is truth to belief.

At the beginning of the *Timaeus*, Socrates runs through a speech that he gave on the previous day. The speech is about the institutions of the ideal state, which are, or closely resemble, those of the *Republic*. Socrates asks to see this ideal state set in motion with an account of how it might engage in a conflict with its neighbours. In response to Socrates, Hermocrates asks Critias to relate a tale that he heard from his grandfather, who heard it from his father, who heard it from Solon, who heard it from an Egyptian priest in Saïs on the Nile Delta. According to this Egyptian priest, Athens was first founded nine thousand years ago, at which time she was the fairest, best-governed, and most god-like of all cities. The citizens of this Ancient Athens accomplished many great deeds, but their greatest deed of all was to fend off an unprovoked invasion by Atlantis, an island empire that lay beyond the pillars of Heracles, and that was larger than all Libya and Asia put together. Following Athens' victory over the Atlanteans, the earth was ravaged by earthquakes and floods, and in a single day and night of misfortune Athens fell to the ground and Atlantis sank into the sea. Critias says that an account of the antediluvian Athens might shed light on the workings of the ideal state. He asks Timaeus, a philosopher and statesman from Locris in Italy, to deliver the first part of this account, from the origin of the universe to the creation of man.

Timaeus calls upon God and begins. What always is and never becomes is apprehended by intelligence and reason, and what never is and always becomes is conceived by opinion with the help of sensation. The world is visible and tangible and hence sensible; if it is sensible, then it always becomes, and if it always becomes then it is created and must have a cause or Creator. The world is the most fair of creations, and must therefore have been created according to an eternal archetype which, being eternal, cannot have been created. What is said of the eternal archetype can be said with certainty, whereas what is said of the world, which is merely an ever changing copy of the eternal archetype, can be said only with probability. 'As being is to becoming, so is truth to belief.' Thus, any account of the origin of the universe cannot attain to truth and certainty, but only to belief and probability.

God is good and, being free from jealousy, desired for all things to be like him. Hence, he created order out of the disorder of the sensible world, and made the sensible world into a living creature by putting intelligence in soul and soul in body. The created world is complete because it is a copy of the eternal archetype and so includes within itself all the species of living things. As the created world is complete, there is nothing left over with which a second or other world might be created. For this reason, the created world must be unique. The sensible world, being sensible, is visible and tangible, – visible and therefore made of fire, – tangible and therefore solid and made of earth. Fire and earth must be united with a third element which is their mean. Whereas a surface calls for one mean, a solid body such as the earth calls for two means. Thus, God introduced air and water to bond fire and earth, and he arranged all four elements proportionally: as fire is to air, air is to water; as air is to water, water is to earth.

As the sphere is the most beautiful and perfect of forms and comprehends and averages all other forms, God created the world in the form of a sphere. And as circular motion is the most uniform and most intellectual of all movements, he set the sphere into motion by making it rotate within itself. The world soul he created from a harmonically proportioned mixture of both divisible and indivisible Sameness, Difference, and Being, which he then shaped into two intersecting circles of Sameness and Difference. He then placed the world soul into the middle of his creation and diffused it in every direction. Seeking to make his creation as eternal as possible, he conceived of time as the moving image of eternity and brought it into being by creating the heavenly bodies: the sun, the moon, and the five other stars. Being perfect, self-sufficient, and intelligent, God's creation is in itself a god.

God next created the animals according to the four species that exist in the eternal archetype: heavenly gods, birds, fishes, and land animals. He then asked the heavenly gods to make mortal men out of human souls, which he manufactured from the inferior residue of the world soul, and to whom he showed the nature of the universe. Once a human soul is implanted into a human body, it is overwhelmed by sense experience and affections, which it can only conquer with appropriate nurture and education. However, the human body is designed to help it in this task; for example, the eyes are designed to see the heavenly bodies and their motion, which gives the knowledge of number and time, the power of enquiry, and, the greatest blessing of all, philosophy.

Timaeus points out that, whereas he has only been speaking of the works of Mind, creation is made up of both the works of Mind and the works of Necessity. He originally distinguished between two kinds of being, what always is and what always becomes. However, there is also a third kind of being called the receptacle of all becoming, the formless, invisible, and universal material or space from which all things are made up or instantiated. The four elements of fire, air, water, and earth are made up of particles which are geometrical solids. Every geometrical solid is bounded by surfaces, every surface is divisible into triangles, and every triangle is divisible into right triangles which are either isosceles or scalene. Thus, every particle is made up of isosceles and scalene triangles. Whereas there is only one kind of isosceles right triangle (given by 45°/45°/90°), there are infinitely many kinds of scalene right triangles. However, the most excellent scalene right triangle is the one where the square of the longest side is triple the shortest side (given by 30°/60°/90°). The surfaces of a particle are either an equilateral triangle or a square; those that are an equilateral triangle are made up of 6 scalene right triangles whereas those that are a square are made up of 4 isosceles right triangles.

– Particles of fire are tetrahedrons with 4 equilateral triangle surfaces and 24 scalene right triangles.

– Particles of air are octahedrons with 8 equilateral triangle surfaces and 48 scalene right triangles.

– Particles of water are icosahedrons with 12 equilateral triangle surfaces and 120 scalene right triangles.

– Particles of earth are cubes with 6 square surfaces and 24 isosceles right triangles.

Transmutation of the elements can occur, but only amongst fire, air, and water, whose particles are made up of scalene right triangles. There is also a fifth element called quintessence. Particles of quintessence are dodecahedrons, and God used them as a model for the twelve-fold division of the zodiac.

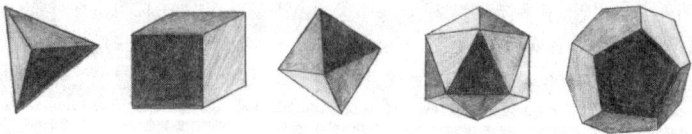

Figure 6: The five Platonic solids.

The particles of each of the four elements have properties that are determined by their constitution and that in turn determine how the particles act and react with one another. These actions and reactions perpetuate a state of non-uniformity which is a necessary condition for motion and thus for the actions and reactions themselves. Each of the four elements exists in a number of varieties, and each of these varieties has distinct sensible properties. However, an account of these sensible properties first requires an account of sensation itself, including an account of pleasure and pain. In contrast to the parts of the body that are not easily moved such as the bones or the hair, the parts of the body that are easily moved such as the eyes and the ears readily transmit the motion of particles to the mind. Ordinary sensations cause neither pleasure nor pain, which are caused by, respectively, sudden replenishments and sudden disturbances of the body. Other affections include rashness and fear, which are foolish counsellors; anger, which is hard to appease; and hope, which is easily led astray. To these affections the heavenly gods mingled irrational sense and all-daring love, and thereby created man.

Having described the physiology and psychology of perception, Timaeus describes the compartmentalisation of the soul, the formation and functions of the various bodily parts, and the diseases of the body and soul and the provisions for their treatment. He ends with a brief account of the generation of woman and non-human animals.

CHAPTER 27

Critias

They despised everything but virtue, caring little
for their present state of life, and thinking lightly
of the possession of gold and other property,
which seemed only a burden to them...

The *Critias* was designed to be the second part of a trilogy,
preceded by the *Timaeus* and succeeded by the *Hermocrates*.
Unfortunately, the latter was never written and the *Critias*
was left unfinished, literally breaking off in mid-sentence.
Scholars sometimes combine the *Critias* with the *Timaeus* as
the *Timaeus-Critias*.

Timaeus has at last come to the end of his account of the
origin of the universe and the creation of man. He offers a prayer
to God asking for just retribution if he has unintentionally said
anything wrong; just retribution in this case would consist in
being set right and given knowledge, which is the best of all
medicines. Critias asks for forbearance for what he is about to
say, adding that it is far easier to speak well of the gods than
to speak well of men. People are easily satisfied when an artist
tries to imitate nature, but they are quick to find fault when
a man tries to paint the human form, with which they are all
too familiar. Socrates grants Critias his request, and extends
his indulgence to both Timaeus and Hermocrates. However,

he warns Critias that he will need a great deal of indulgence if he is to outperform Timaeus. Hermocrates exhorts Critias to invoke Apollo and the Muses and to attack the argument like a man.

Critias says that, in ancient times, the Earth was divided amongst the gods by allotment. Hephaestus and Athena, who are brother and sister and united in their love of philosophy and art, obtained the land of Attica, which was then particularly suited to the cultivation of virtue and wisdom. They populated Attica with a brave race of children of the soil and taught them the art of good government. Whilst some of their names are still remembered, their actions have been lost to time, as there have since been many floods (including the deluge of Deucalion), and those who survived these floods were mountain-dwellers who knew nothing of the art of writing. There were various classes of citizens, including artisans, husbandmen, and a superior class of twenty thousand warriors. These warriors dwelt apart on the summit of the Acropolis, and were educated, and had all things, in common. The areas which are now the islands of Greece were high hills covered in good soil, but this soil was washed away by the floods, leaving whatever remained looking like the bones of a dead body. Before that Attica was the most fertile land in the world, abounding in rich plains and pastures that were irrigated by underground springs. Its people were endowed with intelligence and the love of beauty, for which reasons they lived in moderation, pursued virtue, and excelled in their work.

Whereas Hephaestus and Athena had obtained Attica, Poseidon had obtained the island of Atlantis. Poseidon fell in love with the mortal Cleito who dwelt together with her parents Evenor and Leucippe in a low mountain near a fertile plain in the centre of the island. To secure his love, the god enclosed the mountain with rings of various sizes, two of land and three of sea. Here Cleito bore him five pairs of male twins. The eldest sibling, Atlas, was made king of the centre island, and the other nine siblings were made kings of other parts of the island. As their relations were regulated by the injunctions of Poseidon, the ten kingdoms remained at peace. Critias describes in great detail the fabulous riches of Atlantis amongst which fruit trees and forests, herds of elephants, and minerals including the legendary precious metal orichalcum. With these fabulous riches, the Atlanteans built temples and palaces, harbours and docks, bridges and canals, aqueducts and baths, and a very large standing army with ten thousand chariots and twelve hundred ships.

> *For many generations, as long as the divine nature lasted in them, [the Atlanteans] were obedient to the laws, and well-affectioned towards the god, whose seed they were; for they possessed true and in every way great spirits, uniting gentleness with wisdom in the various chances of life, and in their intercourse with one another. They despised everything but virtue, caring little for their present state of life, and thinking lightly of the possession of gold or other property, which seemed only a burden to them; neither were they intoxicated by luxury; nor did wealth deprive them of their self-control; but they were sober, and saw clearly that all these goods are increased by virtue and friendship with one another, whereas by too great regard and respect for them, they are lost and friendship with them.*

However, the virtue of the Atlanteans began to weaken,

> *...when the divine portion began to fade away, and became diluted too often and too much with the mortal admixture, and the human nature got the upper hand, they then, being unable to bear their fortune, behaved unseemly, and to him who had an eye to see grew visibly debased, for they*

*were losing the fairest of their precious gifts; but
to those who had no eye to see the true happiness,
they appeared glorious and blessed at the very time
when they were full of avarice and unrighteous
power. Zeus, the god of gods, who rules according to
law, and is able to see into such things, perceiving
that an honourable race was in a woeful plight,
and wanting to inflict punishment on them, that
they might be chastened and improve, collected all
the gods into their most holy habitation, which,
being placed in the centre of the world, beholds
all created things. And when he had called them
together, he spake as follows –* [The dialogue ends,
literally in mid-sentence.]

*Here, first of all men for pure justice famed,
And moral virtue, Aristocles lies;
And if there e'er has lived one truly wise,
This man was wiser still; too great for envy.*

Plato's epitaph, according to Diogenes

247

Index of Metaphors

Index of Myths

Index of Principal Themes

	Beauty	Courage	Death/afterlife	Dialectic/elenchus	Education	Friendship	God/the gods	Happiness	Justice/law	Knowledge	Language	Love	Madness
Meno				✓	✓		✓		✓	✓			
Crito		✓	✓				✓		✓				
Apology		✓	✓	✓	✓		✓		✓	✓			
Euthyphro				✓			✓		✓				
Clitophon				✓	✓	✓			✓				
Gorgias			✓	✓	✓		✓	✓	✓	✓			
Protagoras		✓		✓	✓		✓		✓	✓	✓		✓
L. Hippias									✓				
G. Hippias	✓			✓					✓	✓			
Lysis	✓					✓	✓			✓		✓	
Charmides				✓					✓	✓			
Laches		✓		✓	✓					✓			
Alcibiades				✓	✓	✓		✓	✓			✓	

	Beauty	Courage	Death/afterlife	Dialectic/elenchus	Education	Friendship	God/the gods	Happiness	Justice/law	Knowledge	Language	Love	Madness
Critias							✓						
Timaeus							✓						
Philebus	✓			✓									
Statesman				✓					✓				✓
Sophist				✓	✓								
Theaetetus				✓						✓			✓
Parmenides										✓			
Republic		✓		✓	✓		✓	✓	✓	✓		✓	
Phaedo			✓		✓		✓						
Symposium	✓		✓	✓		✓	✓	✓				✓	
Phaedrus	✓			✓	✓	✓	✓	✓	✓	✓		✓	✓
Ion					✓		✓						
Cratylus				✓							✓		
Euthydemus					✓			✓			✓		

	Money	Philosophy/philosophers	Piety	Pleasure	Poetry	Politics	Self-knowledge	Rhetoric/sophistry	The soul	Temperance	The Theory of the Forms	Virtue	Wisdom
Meno								✓	✓		✓	✓	✓
Crito	✓	✓				✓							
Apology	✓	✓				✓		✓				✓	✓
Euthyphro			✓										
Clitophon								✓				✓	
Gorgias		✓		✓		✓		✓	✓	✓		✓	
Protagoras			✓	✓	✓	✓		✓	✓			✓	✓
L. Hippias								✓				✓	
G. Hippias	✓							✓					
Lysis													✓
Charmides						✓	✓		✓	✓			✓
Laches									✓			✓	✓
Alcibiades						✓	✓		✓			✓	✓

	Money	Philosophy/philosophers	Piety	Pleasure	Poetry	Politics	Self-knowledge	Rhetoric/sophistry	The soul	Temperance	The Theory of the Forms	Virtue	Wisdom
Critias						✓							
Timaeus		✓							✓				
Philebus				✓				✓					✓
Statesman						✓					✓	✓	
Sophist		✓						✓					
Theaetetus		✓											✓
Parmenides		✓									✓		
Republic	✓	✓			✓	✓			✓	✓	✓	✓	✓
Phaedo		✓		✓					✓		✓	✓	
Symposium		✓			✓						✓	✓	✓
Phaedrus		✓		✓				✓	✓		✓		
Ion					✓								
Cratylus		✓											✓
Euthydemus		✓					✓	✓				✓	✓

Index of Characters

Ajax, Greek Hero of the Trojan War
Cratylus
Alcibiades, Athenian general and statesman, lover of Socrates
Alcibiades, **Protagoras**, *Gorgias, Euthydemus,* **Symposium**
Anaxagoras, pre-socratic philosopher, tutor of Pericles
Greater Hippias, Gorgias, Apology, Cratylus, Phaedrus, Phaedo
Antiphon, half-brother of Plato
Parmenides
Antisthenes, philosopher and follower of Socrates
Phaedo
Anytus, prosecutor of Socrates, Meno's host in Athens
***Apology*, Meno**
Aphrodite Pandemos, goddess of physical love, daughter of Zeus and Dione
Symposium
Aphrodite Urania, goddess of true love, born out of the castrated genitals of Uranus
Phaedrus, Symposium
Apollo, god of light, truth, and the arts
Phaedrus, Phaedo, Critias
Apollodorus, follower of Socrates
Apology*, Symposium, *Phaedo
Archelaus, tyrant of Macedonia
Gorgias
Archilochus, archaic Greek poet
Ion
Aristides, one of the ten commanders under Miltiades at the Battle of Marathon, father of Lysimachus
Laches, Gorgias, Meno
Aristides, grandson of Aristides, son of Lysimachus
Laches, *Theaetetus*
Aristodemus, follower of Socrates
Symposium
Aristogeiton, lover of Harmodius, co-assassin of Hipparkhos
Symposium
Aristophanes, comic playwright
Apology, **Symposium**
Aristoteles, later became a member of the Thirty Tyrants
Parmenides
Asclepius, god of medicine and healing
Ion, Phaedo
Astyanax, son of Hector
Cratylus

Athena, goddess of wisdom, war, and strategy
    Statesman, Critias
Atlas, son of Cleito, king of the centre island in Atlantis
    Critias
Atreus, mythological king of Mycenae, brother of Thyestes, father
of Agamemnon and Menelaus
    Statesman
Boreas, the northern wind
    Phaedrus
Callias, rich Athenian who is host to Protagoras
    Protagoras, **Apology**, *Cratylus, Theaetetus*
Callicles, host to and student of Gorgias
    Gorgias
Cebes, Pythagorean philosopher, follower of Socrates
    Phaedo, *Crito*
Cephalus, elderly arms manufacturer, father of Polemarchus,
Euthydemus, and Lysias
    Republic, *Phaedrus*
Cephalus of Clazomenae, narrator of the Parmenides
    Parmenides
Chaerephon, friend and follower of Socrates
    Charmides, **Gorgias**, *Apology*
Charmantides, mute auditor in the Republic
    Republic
Charmides, uncle of Plato, later one of the Thirty Tyrants
    Charmides, ***Protagoras***, *Symposium*
Chiron, centaur, teacher of Achilles
    Lesser Hippias
Cleinias, father of Alcibiades
    Alcibiades, Protagoras, Gorgias
Cleinias, brother of Alcibiades
    Alcibiades, Protagoras
Cleinias, grandson of Alcibiades, beloved of Ctessipus
    Euthydemus
Cleito, mythological Atlantean, daughter of Evenor and Leucippe
    Critias
Cleophantus, son of Thermistocles
    Meno
Clitophon, oligarchic political leader
    Clitophon, **Republic**
The Corybantes, male crested dancers who worshiped the
Phrygian goddess Cybele with drumming and dancing
    Euthydemus, Ion

Er, warrior who died in battle but came back to life to tell of what he saw when he was dead
  Republic
Eryximachus, a pompous physician
  ***Protagoras**, Phaedrus,* **Symposium**
Eros, god of sexual love and beauty
  Phaedrus, Symposium
Euclides, Socratic philosopher from Megara
  ***Phaedo**,* **Theaetetus**
Eudicos, host to Hippias in Athens
  Greater Hippias, **Lesser Hippias**
Euthydemus, sophist, brother of Dionysodorus
  Euthydemus
Euthyphro, son of Cephalus, brother of Polemarchus
  Republic
Euthyphro, an orthodox and dogmatically religious man
  Euthyphro, *Cratylus*
Evenor, mythological Atlantean, father of Cleito
  Critias
Evenus, sophist or philosopher and poet
  Apology, Phaedrus, Phaedo
Glaucon, brother of Plato
  Symposium, **Republic**, **Parmenides**
Gorgias, sophist and pre-socratic philosopher
  Greater Hippias, **Gorgias**, *Apology, Meno, Symposium, Philebus*
Hades, god of the underworld
  Cratylus
Harmodius, lover of Aristogeiton, symbol of Athenian democracy
  Symposium
Hector, son of king Priam of Troy, leader of the Trojans, arch-nemesis of Achilles
  Cratylus, Symposium
Hephaestus, god of craftsmen and artisans, blacksmith of the gods
  Symposium, Statesman, Critias
Heracles, mythological hero, son of Zeus
  Greater Hippias
Heraclitus, pre-socratic philosopher
  Cratylus, Theaetetus
Hermocrates, a general of Syracuse during the Athenians' Sicilian Expedition
  Timaeus, **Critias**
Hermogenes, impecunious brother of Callias
  Cratylus, ***Phaedo***

Meletus, prosecutor of Socrates
    Euthyphro, **Apology**, Theaetetus
Menexenus, friend of Lysis
    Lysis, *Phaedo*
Meno, aristocrat from Thessaly, mercenary general, follower of Gorgias
    Meno
Metrodorus, pre-socratic philosopher, friend of Anaxagoras, interpreter of Homer
    Ion
Miccus, old friend and admirer of Socrates, wrestling teacher
    Lysis
Midas, king of Pessinus in Phrygia
    Phaedrus
The Minotaur, mythological figure with the head of a bull and the body of a man, inhabited the Cretan Labyrinth, killed by Theseus
    Crito
Musaeus, mythological seer and priest, pupil or son of Orpheus
    Protagoras, Apology
The Muses, spirits who inspire the creation of literature and the arts, they include Calliope (epic poetry), Clio (history), Erato (lyric poetry), Euterpe (music), Melpomene (tragedy), Polyhymnia (choral poetry), Terpsichore (dance), Thalia (comedy), and Urania (astronomy)
    Ion, Phaedrus, Critias
Neoptolemus, Greek hero of the Trojan War, son of Achilles
    Greater Hippias
Nestor, Greek hero of the Trojan War, elderly king of Pylos
    Greater Hippias
Niceratus, father of Nicias
    Laches, *Republic*
Nicias, eminent Athenian general and statesman
    Laches, Gorgias
The Nymphs, female spirits associated with a particular location or landform or with a particular god
    Phaedrus
Odysseus, Greek hero of the Trojan War, king of Ithaca
    Lesser Hippias, Apology, Republic
Orithyia, daughter of King Erechtheus of Athens, raped by Boreas (the north wind)
    Phaedrus
Orpheus, mythological 'father of songs'
    Protagoras, Apology

Pan, pastoral god of shepherds and flocks, companion of the
nymphs, resembles a faun
Phaedrus
Paralus, son of Pericles
Alcibiades, **Protagoras**, *Meno*
Parmenides, pre-socratic philosopher
Parmenides, *Symposium*, *Theaetetus, Sophist*
Patroclus, Greek hero of the Trojan War, lover of Achilles, slayed
by Hector
Symposium
Pausanias, lifelong lover of Agathon
Protagoras, **Symposium**
Pericles, prominent and influential statesman, orator, and general
during the Golden Age
Alcibiades, Protagoras, Gorgias, Meno, Phaedrus, Symposium
Phaedo, philosopher, follower of Socrates
Phaedo
Phaedrus, friend of Socrates
Protagoras, **Phaedrus**, **Symposium**
Phidias, Athenian sculptor, painter, and architect of great renown
Greater Hippias, Protagoras, Meno
Philebus, teacher of Protarchus
Philebus
Pindar, lyric poet
Gorgias
Plato
Apology, *Phaedo*
Polemarchus, wealthy metic, philosopher, son of Cephalus, brother
of Lysias and Euthydemus, executed by the Thirty Tyrants
Phaedrus, **Republic**
Polus, teacher of rhetoric from Acragas in Sicily, follower of Gorgias
Gorgias, *Phaedrus*
Poseidon, god of the sea and of earthquakes
Critias
Prodicus, pedantic sophist and pre-socratic philosopher
Laches, Charmides, Greater Hippias, **Protagoras***, Apology,*
Meno, Euthydemus, Cratylus, Phaedrus, Symposium, Theaetetus
Prometheus, one of the Titans, a champion of humankind amongst
the gods, brother of Atlas, Epimetheus, and Menoetius
Protagoras, Statesman
Protagoras, pre-socratic philosopher
Greater Hippias, **Protagoras***, Meno, Euthydemus, Cratylus,*
Phaedrus, Theaetetus

Protarchus, son of Callias
    Philebus
The Pythian priestess, priestess at the Temple of Apollo at Delphi
    Apology
Pythodorus, friend of Zeno
    Alcibiades, *Parmenides*
Simmias, Pythagorean philosopher, follower of Socrates
    Crito, *Phaedrus*, **Phaedo**
Simonides, lyric poet of the 6th and 5th century BC
    Protagoras, Republic
Sisyphus, king who attempted to trick the gods, and who was
punished by being cursed to roll a boulder up a hill, only to watch it
roll back down again, *ad aeternitatem*
    Apology, *Gorgias*
The slave boy, one of Meno's slaves
    Meno
Socrates
    All
Solon, archon appointed in 594 BC who broadened political
participation in Athens
    Timaeus
Stephanus, son of Thucydides
    Meno
Stesimbrotus, a biographer of the 5th century BC who also wrote
on Homer
    Ion
The stranger from Elea
    Sophist, Statesman
Terpsion, Socratic philosopher from Megara
    Theactctus, *Phaedo*
Thamus/Ammon, king of the gods in Egyptian mythology
    Phaedrus
Theaetetus, eminent mathematician and long-time friend of Plato
    Theaetetus, Sophist, Statesman
Theodorus, mathematician admired by Plato, tutor of Theaetetus
    Theaetetus, Sophist, *Statesman*
Theognis, poet of the 6th century BC
    Meno
Thermistocles, Athenian politician and general, increased the
naval power of Athens
    Gorgias, Meno, Republic
Theseus, legendary founder and king of Athens
    Crito

Theuth, Egyptian god
  Phaedrus
Thetis, sea-goddess, mother of Achilles
  Lesser Hippias
Thirty Tyrants, pro-Spartan oligarchy installed in Athens after
her defeat in the Peloponnesian War in 404 BC
  Apology
Thrasymachus, sophist
  Clitophon, *Phaedrus*, **Republic**
Thucydides, father of Melesias, leader of the Athenian
conservative faction
  Laches, Meno
Thyestes, brother of Atreus
  Statesman
Timaeus, a philosopher and statesman from Locris in Italy
  Timaeus, Critias
Tiresias, mythological blind prophet of Thebes
  Meno
Uranus, sky-god, son and husband of Gaia
  Symposium
Xanthippe, wife of Socrates
  Phaedo
Xanthippus, son of Pericles
  Alcibiades, **Protagoras**, *Meno*
Xanthos/Skamandros, a river god who fought with Hephaestus
  Cratylus
Zeno, philosopher, follower of Parmenides, renowned for his
paradoxes
  Alcibiades, **Parmenides**, *Phaedrus*, *Sophist*
Zeus, king of the gods
  Symposium, Statesman, Critias

By the same author

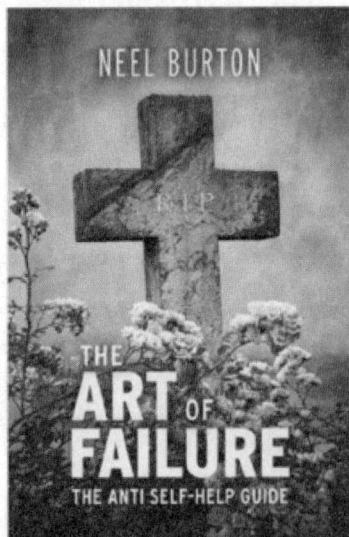

The Art of Failure, The Anti Self-Help Guide
ISBN 978-0-9560353-3-2
Published March 2010

Book description

We spend most of our time and energy chasing success, such that we have little left over for thinking and feeling, being and relating. As a result, we fail in the deepest possible way. We fail as human beings.

The Art of Failure explores what it means to be successful, and how, if at all, true success can be achieved.

By the same author

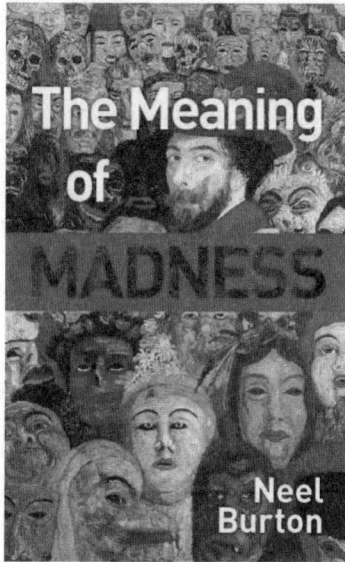

The Meaning of Madness
ISBN 978-0-9560353-0-1
Published November 2008

Book description

Winner of the BMA Young Authors' Award

This book proposes to open up the debate on mental disorders, to get people interested and talking, and to get them thinking. For example, what is schizophrenia? Why is it so common? Why does it affect human beings and not animals? What might this tell us about our mind and body, language and creativity, music and religion? What are the boundaries between mental disorder and 'normality'? Is there a relationship between mental disorder and genius? These are some of the difficult but important questions that this book confronts, with the overarching aim of exploring what mental disorders can teach us about human nature and the human condition.

Book reviews

"A riveting read for anyone looking for a window into the world of mental disorder..."

– Professor Robert Howard, Dean, Royal College of Psychiatrists

"Most books on mental disorder are either polemical or over-technical. This remarkable book by contrast provides a highly readable and at the same time authoritative account that, by combining literary, philosophical and scientific sources, shows the deep connections between 'madness' and some of our most important attributes as human beings."

– Professor Bill Fulford, University of Oxford

"The specific purpose of this young author is to try and demystify the stigma of mental illness. He succeeds brilliantly, not only in explaining different types of mental illness in relatively simple terms, but also in the breadth of understanding he brings to aspects of life outside the mental straightjacket."

– British Medical Association.

"This book is a delight... there is no circumlocution or obliqueness, and the surgical efficiency with which the subjects are addressed makes for maximum comprehension... a really accessible and thorough approach to a complex and often impenetrable subject."

– British Neuroscience Association

"Burton somehow avoids oversimplification. This is all the more remarkable, since his scope is fairly all-embracing, switching smoothly from side-effects of lithium to the nature of existential anxiety, to the quest for meaning in life... His writing is frequently almost poetic, yet he is capable of being crisply definitive... Ultimately, this is a work of contradictions – an undemanding read that could challenge your view of the world."

– Medical Journalists' Association

"This book is packed with striking insights... [Burton's] passion and enthusiasm for the subject never slips."

– Remedy Magazine